W🌐RLDWIDE IDENTITY

W●RLDW▮DE IDENT▮TY

inspired design from forty countries

Robert L. Peters

GLOUCESTER MASSACHUSETTS

ROCKPORT PUBLISHERS

Published in Partnership

icograda
IDA

International Council
of Graphic Design Associations
A Partner of the International
Design Alliance

Works included in this book are listed by country, sorted alphabetically by two-letter country code. Statistics and information appearing in the country profiles is drawn from various sources, including United Nations agencies, Icograda, and international publications, as well as data sourced through Encarta, Encyclopedia Britannica, NationMaster.com, and Wikipedia.org. Statistics were the latest available when this book was written and have been rounded to aid comparisons between countries. GDP per capita refers to gross domestic product as measured on a per person basis, converted to $USD. Area is expressed in metric values: 1000 km^2 = 385.64 square miles.

First published in the United States of America by
Rockport Publishers, Inc., a member of
Quayside Publishing Group
33 Commercial Street
Gloucester, Massachusetts 01930-5089
T +1 978 282 9590
F +1 978 283 2742
www.rockpub.com

Library of Congress Cataloging-in-Publication Data
Peters, Robert L. (Robert Lloyd)
    Worldwide identity : inspired design from forty countries / Robert L. Peters.
        p.   cm.
    ISBN 1-59253-187-3 (hardcover)
    1. Corporate image. 2. Industrial design coordination.
    3. Institutional advertising. 4. Symbolism in advertising. I. Title.
    HD59.2.P475 2005
    659.2'85—dc22   2005010739
                                                                   CIP

ISBN 1-59253-187-3

10 9 8 7 6 5 4 3 2 1

Book and cover design: Circle

Printed in China

Heartfelt thanks to the designers worldwide who submitted their identity works; to Icograda and its 2003–2005 board for their advice; to my helpful team at Circle— Carol MacKay for coordination, Susan McWatt FitzGerald for design, Celina Blandford for the cover, Kevin Guenther for production, and Adrian Shum for writing assistance and research. My thanks also go to Rockport and its publishing team for the confidence, support, editing, and direction provided.

inspired design from forty countries

contents

Preface

Identity Matters

We live in uncertain times of political, social, and economic instability. Information overload, overwhelming change, a threatened ecology, and staggering social imbalance threaten our individual sense of identity and wellbeing. Around the globe, wealth, health, knowledge, and technological progress are not shared equally—the awareness of these gaps, along with discernment of the underlying global inequities that cause them, have never been more apparent—through the democratization of communication tools and the laity's access to new media.

Massive data-storage capabilities now outstrip human ability to access information and distill knowledge. Vertical specialization, in ever-narrower terms of reference, is a phenomenon affecting all professions—graphic design not excepted. At the same time, real-time connectivity with others around the planet has become a reality thanks to technological advances such as the Internet, interactive media, and increased ease of travel.

*Logos have become the closest thing
we have to an international language.*

—Naomi Klein, *No Logo*

*Every single entity, every organism,
every part, everything in nature,
owes its characteristics and identity
to its relationship with other things,
and so we are embedded in this
network of relationships.*

—Fritjof Capra

Culture vs. Monoculture

Identity lies at the very core of culture, and it is the key to our understanding of self. Culture encompasses language, traditions, beliefs, morals, laws, social behavior, and the art of a community. Understanding culture is imperative in avoiding identity crisis and rootlessness—and it's a prerequisite for the effective shaping of identities and communication. Yet, everywhere in our shrinking world, we can witness increased homogenization, erosion of indigenous culture, the emergence of nonplaces (uniform airports, generic shopping malls), and the advancement of what some theorists are calling "serial monotony." Are globalization, free trade agreements, digital technology, the Internet, and increased mobility to blame? Ironically, all have contributed to both the loss of individual and collective identity, and at the same time, have literally "brought the world to our doorstep" along with myriad opportunities this presents for designers around the globe.

Aware of the advancing threat of monoculture, can the world's identity designers help conserve and revive those things that make human culture distinct and unique? Can we mine the historical depth of individuality and breadth of multiculturalism to bring new gems of identity to light? Is there still time to avoid losing our sense of who we are, where we've come from, where we belong, and why these distinctions are so important?

Corporatism and Branding

More than half of the world's top one hundred economies are now corporations (not nations, as one might think). Ninety-nine of the top one hundred companies are headquartered in industrialized nations—of the 63,000 transnational corporations now operating worldwide, more than three quarters are based in North America, Europe, and Japan. The majority of these highly successful corporations enjoy identities developed by talented designers—nevertheless, there is a growing debate within the worldwide design community about the dual (and sometimes conflicting) role that design plays, both in creating wealth and in serving society through the building of culture.

In 2000, Naomi Klein described the brand backlash against unbridled consumerism in her widely read book, *No Logo*: "The corporate hunger to homogenize our communities and monopolize public expression is creating a wave of public resistance..." she wrote, documenting the reclaiming of public spaces and the revolt against corporate power. Many empathized with Klein's attack on "the brand bullies," and with Joel Balkan's depiction (in his recent book *The Corporation*) of corporations as "soulless leviathans—uncaring, impersonal, and immoral," that are "using branding to create unique and attractive personalities for themselves." It's hard to dismiss the almost daily reports of small-town wars against "big-box retailers" (Wal-Mart, et al), culture jamming, brand busting, and the growth of "hacktivism" and "digilantes," as an ever more informed populace joins the fight of "citizenship vs. consumerism." Not a new topic, really—Victor Papanek predicted the "Coca-colonization" and "Disneyfication" of the entire planet a full generation ago.

Over-branded Planet?

So, are we headed for total brand saturation? Will we even know if and when we've become overwhelmed? Human beings around the world are subject to ever more invasive and coercive advertising—adverts in schools, hospitals, doctor's offices, movie theaters, airport lounges, scenic lookouts, washrooms, elevators, on the Internet, on cell phones, on fruit, on public garbage cans, on bus wraps, and in email spam. In Canada (where I am writing this), the average citizen experiences more than 16,000 "brand encounters" in the average day (!), according to statistics from a leading management consultancy (based on my own observations, I would guess this to also be an average in other so-called "developed" nations). Think about it—if you sleep an average of eight hours per day, you and I are each subjected to one thousand brand impressions per hour!

"Brands have run out of juice" read the opening lines of advertising giant's Saatchi & Saatchi website on "Lovemarks—The future beyond brands." As goes the firm's hype, "Lovemarks transcend brands. (They) reach your heart as well as your mind, creating an intimate, emotional connection that you just can't live without. Ever." According to Saatchi & Saatchi's Worldwide CEO, "At the core of every Lovemark is Respect.... A Lovemark's high Respect is infused with these three intangible, yet very real, ingredients: Mystery, Sensuality, and Intimacy. Put simply, Lovemarks inspire 'Loyalty Beyond Reason.'" Critic Rick Poynor (and many others) doesn't buy the Lovemarks rhetoric, however—in a scathing *Eye* article, he writes: "Lovemarks is by turns wince-makingly sentimental, infuriatingly self-satisfied, and intolerably patronizing.... It's not enough that business enjoys unwarranted levels of power and influence and bestows vast rewards upon the lucky few, while deluging the rest of us with idiotic propaganda. It now seeks to present itself as some kind of well meaning global savior, even as it tries to annex just about every worthwhile aspect of life—mystery, sensuality, intimacy, love—for commercial purposes."

Identity and Intellectual Capital

According to the World Intellectual Property Organization (WIPO): "The transformation of creativity and innovation into assets of economic, social, and cultural value is the raison d'être of the intellectual property system." WIPO defines one of its main concerns as "the use of the full potential of the intellectual property system as a tool to create value and enhance economic growth. It considers creativity and inventiveness— the raw material of intellectual property—to be the only natural resource that all countries possess, regardless of their geography, climate, or geological makeup." Hard to argue with—the ability and desire to innovate and solve problems are indeed inherent in all peoples—a great equalizer, when on a level playing field.

Decoration is disguise.

—Le Corbusier (1887–1965)

As opposed to (relatively recent) Western cultures, in most (ancient) Eastern cultures, copying is a time-honored tradition—and arguably, a more sustainable and less wasteful practice than what is seen as the Western luxury of continuous reinvention and individual claim staking—especially when limited resources and the viability of large populations are at stake. In the plastic arts, the primary method for learning has always been replicating the work of revered masters, both as a rote exercise and as a respectful homage. This tradition of copying coincides with an alternative approach I heard expressed recently: can you imagine if only the bad ideas (and faulty identities) were protected, and all the best ideas were shared freely?

Challenges and Opportunities

Corporate identity has been defined as the domain of modernism—and many credit the modern movement and its distilled focus on formal minimalism with creating the common denominators and requisite conditions for globalization. Postmodernists might argue that modernism's leitmotif of "less is more" brought the world a poverty of diversity, a narrowing of visual language, and a doctrine of diminished vernacular (in part through its imposition of Eurocentrism). In today's world of ideas, everything goes. Even as globalism removes old barriers, we can observe the creation of new tribes—intimate, understandable groups with their own identifying characteristics.

Information, ideas, and communication are the new currency in today's virtual world. In this age of ideas, graphic designers play an increasingly vital role in creating economic success, shaping communities, and forming culture. Clearly, designers have real power—we also bear considerable responsibility for how things are consumed, how people are depicted, how media are deployed, and ultimately, what form the future will take. The practice of past decades to homogenize, monopolize, and dominate markets is being questioned and re-examined; can design become more holistic, inclusive, sensitive, eclectic, empowering, and sustainable? Are we working with respect to diverse cultures and their vibrant differences? Can we still make useful contributions to humankind's collective visual vocabulary?

Graphic design ignites passion, identifies, informs, clarifies, inspires, and communicates in our interconnected, interdependent, real-time world. Never has there been a greater need for designers to dig deep, to exercise whole-brain thinking skills, to understand patterns of interconnectivity, to join peer networks, to collaborate with other experts, and to leverage the multiperspective advantages of teamwork. How best to proceed, and to succeed? Start by trusting your feelings. Be honest, and work with integrity. Practice good stewardship. Respect the Earth, avoid green-washing, shun banality (e.g., monoculture), and embrace the vernacular voice. Help break down divisive barriers, raise the bar for civilization—and above all, further the characteristics that matter in making us truly human beings.

—RLP

*Beware that
all in this world
is only signs,
and signs of signs.*

—Marcel Schwab

Introduction

Worldwide Identity

As was stated in this book's call for entries, "graphic designers worldwide have given shape to the identities of corporations, organizations, locations, events, products, and services." Designers living or working in any of the forty-four countries in which the International Council of Graphic Design Associations (Icograda) had members in September 2004 were invited to participate in showcasing their originality, cultural diversity, and quality of identity and brand design. Works appear in this book because they were submitted and were deemed to be of merit. This is not a comprehensive collection, nor is it an exclusive selection—it is a diverse sampling from forty of those fourty-four countries, providing a glimpse of the best practice in the field of designed identity. For every notable inclusion in this book, one could likely find a handful of omissons—keen observers will find both surprising contrasts, as well as some surprising similarities between identities from different countries—they will also find some highly idiosyncratic solutions that are successful precisely because they do break all the rules.

*You only get one chance to
make a first impression.*

*Men on frontiers,
whether of time or space,
abandon their previous identities.
Neighborhood gives identity.
Frontiers snatch it away.*

—Marshall McLuhan (1911–1980)

Corporate Persona

The most effective identities tend to be highly visual, graphically striking, intellectually or emotionally engaging, and memorable—though they may take myriad forms. Some, such as Coca-Cola's dynamic ribbon device, Michelin's pneumatic-bodied Bibendum, and Shell's shell, have been with us for more than a century—today, they are recognized in every corner of the world. Some are loaded with symbolism, such as Apple's metaphoric nibbled fruit, and others are engaging because they act as a blank canvas for the viewer's imagination. Others are context dependent—BMW's advancing split-radiator grille is familiar in rear-view mirrors, the three stripes of Adidas are established on sports pitches, and Pizza Hut's characteristic red roof calls out to the hungry throughout the consumer world. Still others, such as Milka Chocolate's distinctive lilac color, and Harley-Davidson's trademarked motorcycle engine sound, are dependent on technological advances in media.

Without question, the culture of the viewer and the context of the encounter both play a strong role in the cognitive decoding and understanding of identities—the blue beret of U.N. peacekeepers (and its meaning) may be instantly recognizable in Sarajevo or the Golan Heights, yet could easily be mistaken as a fashion statement on a London high street. Depending upon the eye of the beholder, beauty and function can both be found in the simplest of form, as well as in the most ornate of iterations (as one can observe in this book).

Defining Identity

Throughout this book, a variety of terms are used to describe identity and the works submitted. As with any body of work that draws from six continents, finding a common parlance is not an easy task. Understandably, there is considerable debate (healthy disagreement) within the field of semiotics and design practice over a definitive taxonomy for identity—in part because of the vastly varying contexts (developed versus developing world, diverse cultural influences, differing linguistic form), and in part because design's lexicology is still in its developmental adolescence. This said, it is useful to at least attempt some definitions and provide some terms of reference.

Defining identity itself is less problematic than attempting to sort out the varied vocabulary design practitioners use to describe their trade. Identity comes in many different shapes and forms, but always carries with it the double function of signifying differentiation, as well as relationship. Regardless of language or semantic nuance, the former indicates singular character, is about the state of being oneself (and not another), and remaining distinctive under different conditions; the latter centers on kinship, oneness, and likeness. Identification, then, is the act or instance of identifying—both to differentiate and to relate.

Graphic Design

Design is the application of intent. Graphic design is the process by which visual identification, visual communication, and the display of visual information takes form in a planned manner. As the developed world has moved from smokestacks to information-based societies, the role of design has moved rapidly into the forefront of market economies. Beginning with analysis, the design process involves envisioning and creating solutions, and then bringing these solutions to life.

Logo and Logotype

The term "logo" is a short form for "logotype" or "logogram," from the Greek *logos*, meaning word or speech. Chinese ideographic characters or "ideograms" are good examples of logograms—symbols that directly represent ideas or objects. Often, the term logotype is used to describe longer and more easily readable names, while logo refers to shorter names, abbreviations, and acronyms. The interchangeable terms often act as synonyms for graphic trademarks, and they are widely (and inconsistently) used around the world to describe symbols, emblems, monograms, and visual phenomena or other graphic devices used to represent or symbolize a product, service, or entity.

Corporate Identity

The terms "corporate identity" (or, "CI," as it's known in much of the world) and "identity system" evolved during the mid-twentieth century as constructs to control trade dress and the use of trademarks. CI became the discipline through which all visible manifestations were designed as a coherent whole, creating a "corporate persona" and expressing the very raison d'être of an organization. The German word *Erscheinungsbild* provides a particularly apt descriptor for CI, which literally means, "appearance image."

"Corporate culture" refers to the philosophy, values, policies, behavior, and so on, that together, constitute the unique style of a company. "Corporate image," on the other hand, can be seen as the sum impression that the policies, practices, traits, projections, personnel, and operations of a corporation impart to its various publics—employees, stakeholders, customers, vendors, and the general public. Ultimately, corporate identity represents both what a company is, and in relation to others, what it is not. "Identity crisis," on the other hand, can be used to describe an organization's confusion as to its goals and priorities. Unlike branding (which is usually associated with products) corporate identity is about organizational definition and projection.

Brand and Branding

Branding, as in the marking of livestock by means of a burning iron, has been practiced for at least 5,000 years. "Brands" and "branding" are all the buzz today, particularly in North America and the corporate world run by MBA graduates. Brands have been variously defined as "an indelible impression," "a gut feeling or understanding about a product, service, or company," and "a user promise," to list but a few—they typically involve symbolic attributes, and as such, they are also vulnerable to fashion.

Many consultants swear by brands and brand management—others swear at the word, seeing it as the latest term de jour of the marketing world and a "shallow hyper-moniker" that overstates its promise (perhaps to compensate for the surface traits the word brings to mind). A "charismatic brand" has been defined as any product, service, or company for which people believe there is no substitute. The foundation of a brand is a trust relationship, reinforced when positive experience consistently meets or exceeds expectations. Brands can also act as *noms de guerre* or pseudonyms for less recognizable corporate origins, though in most cases brands imply a product-based relationship.

In an increasingly virtual world, "brand equity" can grow to become one of an organization's greatest assets, often providing the best return on investment— Coca-Cola's brand value alone has been pegged at USD $70 billion, representing more than 60 percent of the giant corporation's market capitalization.

Trademarks

Trademarks are traceable throughout recorded history—today's visual language of identification descends from historical precedents such as Egyptian cattle marks from 3000 B.C., two-millennium-old royal monograms, incised ceramic *graffiti* found on antique Greek vases, medieval stonemasons' signs, guild marks, and European printers' marks of the fifteenth century—to name a few. Various definitions exist for trademarks— a common denominator is the proprietary intent of identification, commercial use, and definitive distinction from competitors. Danish designer and author Per Mollerup provides the clearest definition I've found to date, in his richly illustrated *Marks of Excellence*: "The term 'trademark' refers to any letter or combination of letters, pictorial sign, or nongraphic, even nonvisual, sign, or any of combination of these used by an organization or by its members to identify communications, property, and products or to certify products and to distinguish them from those of others."

What's in a Name?

A name designates, and often forms, the cornerstone of an effective identity. The key criterion for a name is appropriateness. Is the name a good fit for the intended purpose, is it distinctive, is it meaningful, is it memorable, is it brief, is it likable, is it protectable, will it have good longevity—and, most recently, is a suitably named domain available for Internet use?

Idem et Idem

Again and again, consistent repetition is the key to perceptual penetration and to an identity achieving the desired share of mind and recognition. With the name as a cornerstone, and with the CI, brand, house style, or signature as the mnemonic building blocks, cohesive application of an identity takes shape as outlined in the "blueprint" of graphic identity standards or guidelines. Typically, these standards address the identity's iteration and applications across the broadest imaginable range of media and audience experiences. The value of consistency cannot be overstated, and it's fair to say that the world's most recognizable identities rely far more on their repeated and cohesive visibility than on brilliance of concept or finessing of the identity's graphic form.

Global Inspiration

Breaking through today's media barrage requires identities and visual communications that are uniquely tailored, memorable, and well-managed; failure to connect with an audience or to stand out just adds to the level of noise. The identities in this book draw on a wide range of sources and a rich repertoire of inspiration—linguistic and visual abbreviations, names, acronyms, indices, icons, signatures, found marks, flags, heraldic images, geometric figures, diagrams, signs, metaphoric motifs, rhetorical devices, mythology, the arts, nature, nonfigurative and pictorial symbols. Some identities reverberate with strictly local harmony, and others relate on a global scale. The aim of this book is to provide an international snapshot of excellence in identity design for clients large and small—the more than 300 identities from forty countries that appear in these pages are the result. My hope is that this body of work will be a stimulating source of inspiration, reflection, and learning.

—RLP

Austria—alpine skiing, cultured evenings of Viennese opera, savoring Mozart Kugeln (chocolates) in Salzburg, The Sound of Music—modern Austria means different things to different people.

Austria

area	83,900 km^2
GDP, per capita	$27,800 USD
official language	German
population	8.2 million

Austria is a prosperous, landlocked country located strategically in central Europe. Its many, easily traversable Alpine passes and valleys have made it a historic crossroad between east, west, north, and south. Austria traces its roots to 1156, when the Duchy of Austria was founded. It gained independence from the German Empire in 1804, and then enjoyed its role at the center of power of the large Austro-Hungarian Empire over the course of the next century. In 1918, after defeat in World War I, the country was reduced to a small republic. Annexed by Germany in 1938, and subsequently occupied by the victorious Allies, Austria emerged in the mid-1950s as a country with "perpetual neutrality," an aspect that became ingrained as part of modern Austria's cultural identity. Today's federal parliamentary democratic republic became a member state of the European Union in 1999.

German-speaking, politically conservative, and predominantly Catholic, Austria shares borders with the Czech Republic, Germany, Hungary, Italy, Liechtenstein, Slovakia, Slovenia, and Switzerland. Its natural resources include oil, coal, lignite, timber, iron ore, copper, zinc, antimony, magnetite, tungsten, graphite, salt, and hydropower. It enjoys a well-developed market economy and a high standard of living.

Statistically (and ironically) Austria has earned the third-highest number of medals in the history of the winter Olympics (its skiers unquestionably set the bar for the world), it experiences more deaths due to falls from cliffs than any other nation (playing in the Alps can be dangerous fun), its citizens have close to the world's highest broadband access, it accepts more asylum seekers per capita than any nation on earth—and yet Austria ranks top in the world for per capita deaths due to obesity and for the greatest per capita number of organ transplants.

= 1 million

design firm   Lichtwitz Büro für visuelle Kommunikation
design team   Kriso Leinfellner, Stefanie Lichtwitz, Harald Niessner,
    Kasimir Reimann, Benedikt Flüeler
project direction   Susanne Tobeiner
house font   Hubert Jocham and URW++

client   **Kunsthaus Graz (Graz Museum of Art)**

K Stands for Art

This new museum of contemporary art in the city of Graz opened in September 2003. Designed by architects Peter Cook and Colin Fournier, the translucent-acrylic-clad "blob" makes a striking statement in its prominent location on the bank of the Mur River. The Viennese design firm Lichtwitz was awarded the corporate identity contract following a two-stage international competition.

Kunsthaus Graz

▲ The museum's logo is illustrated expressively as a hand gesture and on a balloon—it's easy to see how the designers' intelligent and minimalist visual approach lends itself to almost unlimited applications.

▲ The logo's symbol signals an axial *x-y-z* intersection, which also provides visual recall of the initial letter *K*. The logotype's typography introduces the museum's distinctive visual voice.

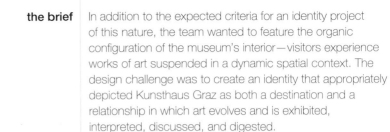

the brief
In addition to the expected criteria for an identity project of this nature, the team wanted to feature the organic configuration of the museum's interior—visitors experience works of art suspended in a dynamic spatial context. The design challenge was to create an identity that appropriately depicted Kunsthaus Graz as both a destination and a relationship in which art evolves and is exhibited, interpreted, discussed, and digested.

the solution
The logo evolved out of an axis, as it might be modeled in three dimensions consisting of x-, y-, and z-coordinates. It represents a spatial relationship and, at the same time, provides interaction and orientation in such a relationship. As a three-dimensional element, the mark depicts an intersection of planes—a change in perspective results in altered geometry—which allows for engaging spatial animation. To enhance the museum's visibility and recognition, the design team developed a distinctive house font and visual palette to further engage the general public. They consciously avoided a defined corporate color, choosing instead to "allow color to be expressed inherently by means of the featured works of art." Adopting a visual voice of "overall reduced, black-and-white, and largely typographic expression" allowed for experimentation with various tactile and surface treatments (for example, qualities such as opaque/transparent, matte/glossy, and so on) for the identity. Beyond the development of the logo, visual palette, and core identity system, Lichwitz also designed the museum's navigation and signage, interiors for the Kunsthaus-Café's Les Vipères, merchandising and promotional materials offered in the museum's gift shop, and the online presence for Kunsthaus Graz. The design of advertising and exhibition catalogs developed by the museum's in-house personnel follows the distinctive and comprehensive visual system set by Lichtwitz.

▲ This art catalog cover incorporates effectively the museum's revenant logo and distinct typographic voice.

▼ The museum's identity was applied effectively to a wide range of promotional materials, such as this messenger bag, molded chocolate bar, and lanyard.

Kunsthaus Graz

Space01, Space02, Camera Austria
Eintrittspreise für alle Ausstellungen

Erwachsene	€ 6,00
in Gruppen ab 7 Personen	€ 4,50
Senioren, Behinderte	
Zivil- und Präsenzdiener	€ 4,50
Studenten, Schüler	€ 2,50
und Lehrlinge	€ 2,50
im Klassenverband	€ 1,50
Familien (2 Erwachsene	€12,00
und 2 Kinder bis 14)	
Führungen	€ 2,50
im Klassenverband	€ 1,50

Dienstag – Sonntag 11:00 / 16:00 Uhr
Donnerstag 11:00 / 16:00 / 18:30 Uhr

Gruppenführungen max. 20 Personen
auf Voranmeldung

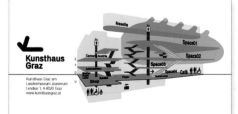

▲ Interior signage and information displays within Kusthaus Graz integrate effectively the monochromatic corporate personality crafted by the designers. The result leaves a distinctive impression on the visitor, without imposing upon the art and the viewer's experience.

◄◄ This promotional flipbook provided an interactive way to show the museum's construction and animate the new identity. As you thumb through the book, the axial logo rotates and exhibits its changeable geometry.

◄ T-shirts identify the museum's interpretive staff and invite dialogue—*Ansprechpartner* means literally "conversation partner."

◄ An entry ticket takes the form of a sticker to be attached to visitors' clothing.

Australia

area	76.9 million km²
GDP, per capita	$29,100 USD
official language	English
population	20 million

The name Australia is from the Latin *australis* (meaning *southern*), dating back to second-century legends of *terra australis incognita* (an unknown southern land). Also known as "the land down under," both monikers bespeak one of Australia's enduring realties—it is a long way away from the rest of the world, at least as measured by Eurocentric cartographers. The Commonwealth of Australia is the borderless, sixth-largest country in the world and the only one to occupy an entire continent—the centerpiece of Australasia/Oceania. Australia is a federal parliamentary democratic state with the British queen as monarch (a referendum to change to a republic was defeated in 1999).

The exact date of Australia's first human habitation is questionable, though 50,000 years ago seems likely, following a period of massive ecological upheaval. The first Australians were the remote ancestors of the current Australian Aborigines, arriving by land bridges and sea from today's Southeast Asia. Later immigrants descended from British penal colonies, as well as nineteeth- and twentieth-century free settlers from around the globe. Australia became a commonwealth of the British Empire in 1901, then took advantage of its natural resources to develop its agricultural and manufacturing industries and made a major contribution to the British effort in World Wars I and II.

Most of Australia is desert or semiarid, and 40 percent of the land is covered by sand dunes. The southeast and southwest corners enjoy a temperate climate and moderately fertile soil, and the country's north has a tropical climate with some rainforests and grasslands. Uniquely famous Australian fauna include koalas, kangaroos, emus, platypuses, wombats, and echidnas.

Australia's creativity, as seen in films, opera, music, painting, theater, dance, crafts, and design, is today achieving worldwide recognition.

= 1 million

the good starts
STUDY FOR REFUGEE YOUTH

design firm   Designland
art director   Katherine Chadwick
designer   Katherine Chadwick

client   **Victorian Foundation for Survivors of Torture**
This "human" mark represents the client's initiative:
a "supportive and educational platform to help aid refugee
youth in their settlement in a new country and culture."
A layering of hands forms a bird in flight, signifying the
coming together of individuals on a journey of liberation,
growth, and discovery."

design firm   Designland
art director   Andrew Budge
designer   Andrew Budge

client   **Designland**
This design firm identity "encapsulates the irreverent attitude
of the studio's principals," according to the designer. A unique
combination of the high-tech (LED light matrices) with the
handcrafted (needlepoint) provides a memorable solution.

design firm   Hemisphere Group
art director   Clayton Smith
designer   Clayton Smith

client   **Western Australian Mobile Marketing (WAMM)**
This pop art–derivative logo provides a fresh, vibrant identity for
WAMM, a partner of Vodafone Australia, which offers its clients
mobile phone advertising opportunities. The goal was to "break
away from the clutter of competitors" in a way that would
translate well in all forms of advertising media.

design firm   Three's a Crowd
art director   Natalie Lippiatt
designers   Beck Storer
    Georgina Lovel

client   **Flying Squirrel**
The name and logo of this online children's fashion store
represent the fun and innocence of youth. Distinctive and
easy to recognize, the squirrel character riding a paper
plane represents "a sense of quirkiness, energy, fun, and
innocence," according to the designers, whereas the script
logotype suggests movement through the air.

design firm | Voice
art directors | Scott Carslake
Anthony Deleo
designers | Scott Carslake
Anthony Deleo
client | **P&A Chartered Accountants**

Good with Numbers

the brief The challenge was to create a distinctive identity to
communicate clearly the services provided by P&A,
which include accounting and financial services.

the solution The designers constructed the logotype by rotating, flipping,
and positioning individual Bodoni numerals to create the
P&A letterforms. To reinforce this distinctive approach, the
identity always employs an overprint technique that creates a
third color. As the designers point out, "If one looks closely,
he or she will be able to identify the individual numerals." The
client was happy with the solution and, as one of the firm's
partners stated with a wink, "We are good with numbers."

▲ Individual numerals from the Bodoni typeface
were combined to create the logotype.

▼ Application of the logotype to a reception
window makes the numeric construct obvious
in an engaging, memorable fashion.

cube3

design firm   Octavo Design
art director   Gary Domoney

client   **Cube³**

Melbourne-based Cube³ specializes in the design, planning, and construction of contemporary residential developments. The challenge for Octavo Design was to generate a name and identity to express the firm's architectural approach and to appeal to a design-savvy audience in a clean, contemporary manner. They used modular letterforms to produce a minimalist yet clever typographic/architectonic solution. The number *3* graphically forms a three-dimensional box, creating an excellent mnemonic device.

design firm   Octavo Design
art director   Gary Domoney

client   **C31 (community television station)**

The design brief called for an identity to reflect the station's "arrival" as a regular free-to-air broadcaster to create a unique position among its rivals. The solution uses thirty-one dots to form an eye and represents the letter *C* alongside the numeral *31*. As explained by art director Gary Domoney, "The dots represent individuals coming together on common ground, and the eye is symbolic of these individuals' shared vision for the future of the visual medium."

D
Davidson Design

design firm   Davidson Design
art director   Grant Davidson
designer   Grant Davidson

client   **Davidson Design**

The self-designed brand signature for an award-winning firm in Melbourne set out to be distinctive, modern, stylish, intelligent, and timeless. The resulting icon combines upper- and lowercase Bodoni *d* characters for a classic appearance. The gunmetal gray treatment gives the design a modern edge.

design firm   Davidson Design
art director   Grant Davidson
designer   Grant Davidson

client   **Lynton Crabb Photography**

Lynton Crabb is "an emerging photographer with a quirky name." The brief called for a visual identity to reflect both the quality of photographer's work and his fun-loving personality. The identity needed to have strong appeal with advertising agencies, which are the client's primary audience. As stated by the designer, the solution "creates a fun icon combining a camera and a crab. A model was created, photographed, and retouched." Definitely quirky and one of a kind, this effective visual pun is engaging and aids recall.

design firm	Voice
art directors	Scott Carslake
	Anthony Deleo
designers	Scott Carslake
	Anthony Deleo

client **Colour Cosmetica**

Colour Cosmetica is all about excellence in hair, makeup, fashion, styling, photography, and beauty therapy. The retail store offers exclusive professional cosmetics and perfumes as well as a complete range of beauty services. Its Colour Academy is a school of fashion, offering nationally accredited courses. The academy also offers styling sessions and off-site education for fashion magazines, advertising, media, and the film/art industry.

▲ The client required a new identity and a typographic solution to apply to multiple products and services. They wanted to be seen as contemporary and unexpected, but they wanted to avoid the industry trend of using light sans serif typefaces. The ensuing signature is unmistakably unique, reflecting the creative services, thinking, and personalities associated with the brand. The identity lends itself readily to signage and a wide range of ancillary applications.

design firm	Jeffrey Creative
art director	Paul Troon
designer	Paul Troon

client **Nu Nu Restaurant**

This restaurant in tropical North Queensland provides a contemporary and fresh dining experience. In keeping with the client's desire for "a clean, open feel," the designer found inspiration in Australia's curvaceous coastline and rippling waters. A blind-embossed logotype provides a tactile texture, whereas the deep orange reflects the region's intense tropical colors.

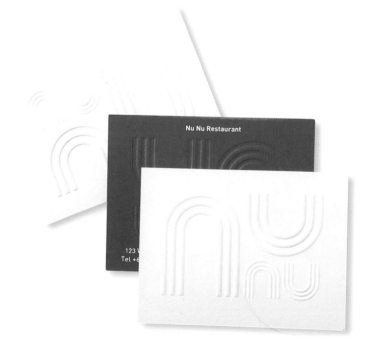

act!vist

design firm   Davidson Design
art director   Grant Davidson
designer   Grant Davidson

client

Barry Robinson, Activist

Activist is an entrepreneurial creative consultancy. The designer explains, "It's a new business model where people of particular skills and experience are hand-picked and brought together for the cause of a brand, product, or service to create some noise, stir things up a little, and give competitors a shake." Regarding the design challenge, he says, "With a name like Activist, this project required the counterbalance of credibility and creativity—here right now, but also here for the long term, passionate, not corporate. If it were to give brands a voice, it needed to have a voice all its own." The solution: "Create a wordmark—where simply by being a design activist and turning the *i* on its head and adding an exclamation mark, the word *act!* is created. Everything else was black and white—in design and in attitude."

glenmar

design firm   Adstract Art P/L
art director   Paul Andrews
designer   Rachel Saliba

client

Glenmar Industries

The symbol design for this global manufacturer of metal castings and forgings needed to reinforce Glenmar Industries' core activity in any language, and it needed to lend itself for use in molds (the design appears as a cast brand in every item Glenmar makes). As the designer explains, "The distinctive lowercase *g* represents a furnace pot, tipped to face the viewer, with the molten metal pouring into the mold below."

Santilli
Group

design firm   Adstract Art P/L
art director   Paul Andrews
designer   Glen Riley

client

Santilli Group

Santilli Group is a commercial property developer, involved in building and construction. The design challenge was to design a unique symbol that depicted innovation. The designer's solution consists of three distinct abstract elements: the interior corner of a room, the external view of a pitched roof, and the outline of a building tower. Together, these elements represent the various aspects of Santilli Group's business. The designer explains, "The blue triangle leads the eye to the brand—set in a clear, bold typeface—whereas the positive upward movement and bold colors suggest that construction rises from the strong Santilli base."

everythingbetween

design firm   3 Deep Design
art director   3 Deep Design
designer   3 Deep Design

client

Everything in Between

The client is a design-driven education program and creative bridge for students, comprising a series of workshops, talks, and collaborations between national and international creative thinkers. The designers explain, "Our office created a logotype and system of parts that looked to communicate the crafted, unique position of the program. The visual identity system had to function in terms of recognition, communication, and identification. The graphic combination of words created a succinct and decorative wordmark that communicated the inherent nature of the program. Everything in Between professional practice and student life, Everything in Between the idea and the execution, Everything in Between the dream and the day."

design firm	Billy Blue Creative
art director	Mick Thorp
designer	Mick Thorp
client	**Tourism New South Wales**

Brand Sydney

the brief   The goal was simple: to create a consumer brand for the city of Sydney.

the solution   As described by designer Mick Thorp, "The core logo conveys the informality, energy, and excitement of Australia's most famous city. The world-famous Sydney icon, the opera house, is also featured." The gestural, hand-rendered calligraphic style is expressive and energetic—the brush-stroked graphic iconography seems to jump from the signature-like base with a positive buoyancy supported by four vibrant, sun-filled colors. The overall effect is visually engaging and, at the same time, casual and confident.

▲ The logo also works exceptionally well in reversed applications, as shown in this presentation graphic display. Stationery and presentation collateral make good use of the color palette while allowing adequate white space for the logo and slogan to deliver a strong message—even when used in a relatively small size.

► This lamppost banner extends the logo's color palette and makes the confident claim, *There's no place in the world like Sydney.*

design firm	There
art directors	Paul Taboure
	Simon Hancock
designer	Jonathan Lu
client	**Artlight Pty Ltd**

Artlight is a boutique lighting shop that wanted to establish itself as a serious player in the lighting industry. Its audience includes designers, developers, and architects. The brief called for a visual identity to reflect Artlight's business while conveying brand values such as experience, progressiveness, and a "premium yet personable" character. The solution is a linear monogram with the letters AL. The logo is simple and linear in form, with a fresh, clean color; the result is distinct and memorable.

design firm	There
designers	Paul Taboure
	Simon Hancock
client	**Sass Clothing**

Sass is a small business-to-business boutique clothing label in Melbourne. The brief was to revitalize and evolve the brand to a position as one of Australia's leading "affordable fashion" brands. In addition, the new identiy had to be feminine, aspirational, and modern. The solution consists of a clean, linear ligature in the form of the word sass, which reflected the freedom and playfulness of a butterfly.

design firm	Jonathan Lu Design
designer	Jonathan Lu
client	**Rocket**

Rocket is a new, national Australian concept food store selling primarily juice and salads. The design brief was to create an identity that would appeal to a wide target audience and would "stand out against the overwhelming number of competitor juice bars." The project included naming, identity, packaging, and store graphics. The solution took the form of a logotype and an accompanying icon, the "Rocket Man." Although the two marks are never shown together, they have an equal share in the identity.

design firm	IN full view
art director	Nadia Mahfoud
designer	Nadia Mahfoud
client	**Filly & Mare**

The client is a high-fashion women's retail store catering to young female adults and older women who can afford and like to keep up with fashion trends. The brief called for an identity to appeal to both the adventurous as well as the more safe, mature fashion lover. The solution consists of a literal, graphic rendition of a filly and mare, combined with an all-cap logotype set in a fairly traditional manner. The combination of relaxed and formal elements strikes a balance that is both corporate and youthful and has proven appealing to both young and older women.

design firm   Adstract Art P/L
art director   Paul Andrews
designer   Emma Nowak

client

Mayall Australia—Grid

Grid is a high-end manufacturer of wool and sheepskin floor rugs. The challenge was to design a distinctive brand that reflected modern floor rug designs. The solution symbolizes wool fibers and conveys the tactile, natural "feel" of the product. The grid pattern reinforces both the name and the products' contemporary style. Swing tickets for the rugs were printed on a milky, translucent soft plastic with rounded corners, enhancing the soft, contemporary fashion look.

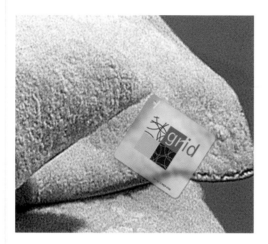 

design firm   Natalie Woolcock Design
art director   Natalie Woolcock
designer   Natalie Woolcock

client

Baarrooka Winery

Baarrooka is a newly established, high-quality boutique winery situated in the Strathbogie Ranges, a two-hour drive from Melbourne. The client requested an identity that could convey the significance of the winery's location, which has a strong Aboriginal cultural background. The name Baarrooka has a literal Aboriginal meaning: "A place where ducks rest on water." The designer focused on spelling out the distinctive name in a strong serif typeface (MrsEaves). Interlinking OOs are integrated with well-recognized Aboriginal dot-painting elements, allowing for a flexible color arrangement. A monochromatic duck feather is used as a playful branding tool and secondary visual element—it is always depicted floating or gently resting, as shown here on the wine labeling, packaging, and collateral materials.

ergo

design firm   Billy Blue Creative
art directors   Mick Thorp
   Justin Smith
designer   Justin Smith

client   **ERGO**

ERGO is a startup procurement company (the name means "therefore," or "the go-between"). The designers were charged with creating an effective name and brand. In response, they developed a logo and supporting visual language that depict partnerships, networks, and integration of suppliers. Clever use of a repeating *O* shape to form the *g* as links in a chain provides a strong mnemonic device that reinforces the name's meaning.

design firm   Mosmondesign
art director   Vlad Mosmondor
designer   Vlad Mosmondor

client   **Dennis Spiluttini/Weston Auto Electrics**

Weston Auto Electrics is a general automotive electrical services provider, specializing in battery repair, accessories exchange, alternators, and starter motors. The logo incorporates the name's initial letters *W* and *A* to "create a powerful spark," as described by designer Vlad Mosmondor. The design is very automotive (think Ferrari red and shiny chrome) and very electric—an appropriate solution in a stylized monogram.

protégé
PROPERTY

design firm   Lumino
art director   Pip McConnel-Oats
designer   Natalie Taylor

client   **Protégé Property**

The client is a newly established property consultancy agent. The brief involved a visual expression of the Protégé philosophy of "unlocking potential" and "creating a distinctive suite of materials that would engender interest and confidence in Protégé's services." The solution entails a symbol that draws its form from the barrels of a lock. As the designer explains, "Protégé's advice can unlock the potential in a property, realizing improved profits and performance." The supporting visual palette balances restrained and vibrant visual colors to "reflect a prudent but innovative firm."

design firms   Linda Fu Design
   Global iCOM
art director   Linda Fu
designer   Linda Fu

client   **Australia-Korea Foundation**

The Australia-Korea Foundation is a joint program between the two nations' governments to build and promote a bilateral relationship through better mutual understanding and cultural exchange at all levels. It targets both Australian and Korean audiences. Called on to create a visual identity "to depict the two countries' harmonious relationship… and to incorporate the image of a kangaroo," the designer faced a very specific brief. Her solution uses a vivid combination of ribbons and the yin-yang element drawn from the Korean national flag to form a kangaroo—the national symbol of Australia. This design creates a distinct and effective logo that represents both cultures.

design firm | IN full view
art director | Nadia Mahfoud
designer | Nadia Mahfoud

client | **Gusto Italiano**

The Good Life

the brief Gusto Italiano began as a wine and water importer, bringing authentic Italian goods to Dutch retailers. Now they are looking to expand their product range. The brief was simple: authenticity was the key. Due to the abundance of Italian-themed restaurants in Amsterdam (which often aren't Italian), the client wished to specifically communicate the authenticity of its products and the added value these brought to those who stocked them.

the solution The designer explains, "After much research, cutting deep through the profusion of Italian clichés, I created a stamplike corporate identity based on the look and feel of Italian vehicle number plates, supporting the idea of transit. The secondary colors used were selected to support the notion of something old being authentic and were inspired by old carbon receipt books, which doubled as the classic gelati colors, creating a genuine Italian atmosphere."

lumino ®

brilliant ideas

design firm Lumino
designer Pip McConnel-Oats

client **Lumino**

Let It Shine

Lumino's office (in Brisbane) and its meticulously produced stationery and print materials incorporate the distinctive identity in a subtle, yet cohesive, manner. Consistency of visual palette provides a real key to the success.

the brief Lumino is a brand design firm that creates powerful brands and brand materials for clients in the professional, retail, property, and service sectors. After obtaining a trademarked brand name, the design challenge was to create an identity that expressed the firm's particular style of design and its values, would excite and impress both clients and peers, and would possess good longevity.

the solution The solution is type-based, using a unique custom-drawn typeface possessing the simplicity, originality, and attention to detail that are the hallmarks of the firm's success. The use of silver, luminous stock and the unique letter *O* are key elements in all Lumino materials.

Bosnia and Herzegovina

area	51,100 km²
GDP, per capita	$1,800 USD
official languages	Bosnian, Croatian, Serbian,
population	4 million

 Bosnia and Herzegovina (B&H) is a mountainous country in the western Balkans. This new republic gained its independence in the Yugoslav wars of the 1990s and, due to the Dayton Accords, is currently a protectorate of the international community, administered by a high representative selected by the European Parliament. B&H is decentralized and divided into two administrative entities: the Federation of Bosnia and Herzegovina (divided into ten cantons), and the Republika Srpska.

Geographically, B&H enjoys scenic mountain vistas, four distinct seasons, rich flora and fauna, and a favorable position close to the Mediterranean. This new nation's capital, Sarajevo, was the former capital of one of the six federal units constituting Yugoslavia—it's known for its pristine beauty, its hosting of the winter Olympics in 1988, and its years of ethnic warfare between Croats, Serbs, and Bosnians broadcast on television screens around the world. (Who can forget Sniper Alley?)

B&H is struggling to emerge from a devastating decade of warfare and turmoil. As Besim Spahic, Ph.D., of the Academy of Fine Arts Sarajevo notes: "Turbulent events, suffering, exodus, and hopelessness can be very good inspiration for all kinds of creation—'hot-blooded' determination is emerging from our creative suffering." This prediction is evidenced by the strong graphic design and advertising work that can be seen in B&H today.

= 1 million

design firm ninAdesign
art director Aleksandra Nina Knežević
designer Aleksandra Nina Knežević

client **Gemini Internet Club**
The client is an Internet café/club. The brief called for an identity that would be original, modern, and relevant to the target group (computer users). The solution uses a distinctively styled logotype that incorporates the images of a mouse and cable to represent the letter *E* in *Gemini*.

design firm ninAdesign
art director Aleksandra Nina Knežević
designer Aleksandra Nina Knežević

client **MARKART**
MARKART is an agency that deals with bookkeeping, taxes, and financial consulting. The desired identity was to be new, modern, and urban in feel with characteristics signaling the firm's function. The design solution uses a clean sans serif typeface set in all caps to signify the confidence and stability of the company, whereas the graphic itself forms an *M* reminiscent of file folders and paperwork that might commonly be seen in conjunction with day-to-day business operations. The effective use of blue color gradations lends an air of sophistication and modernity to the logo.

design firm ninAdesign
art director Aleksandra Nina Knežević
designer Aleksandra Nina Knežević

client **Restaurant Ragusa**
Ragusa is an established Mediterranean restaurant in Sarajevo. Its name, Ragusa, is the ancient name for Dubrovnik, a city on the Croatian coast. The logo employs a traditional typographic approach with distinctive letterforms, calligraphic flourishes, and ornaments to convey a sense of the traditional cuisine served in the restaurant.

design firm ninAdesign
art director Aleksandra Nina Knežević
designer Aleksandra Nina Knežević

client **The Shoes**
The Shoes is a shop that offers both women's and men's footwear. The client requested that its logotype be modern and unique and that it include an illustration of shoes. The designer's solution meets the client's requests with an engaging sense of humor (a woman's leg draped over a man's), distinct fashion flair, a gender-inclusive color palette (pink and blue), and the use of typography that mimics a shoelace.

Belgium

landmass	30,500 km²
GDP, per capita	$29,100 USD
official languages	Dutch, French, German
population	10.2 million

Belgium lies at the crossroads of Europe. Throughout the past 2,000 years, this federal parliamentary democracy and modern-day headquarters of NATO and the United Nations has experienced a constant ebb and flow of different races and cultures. This movement made Belgium one of Europe's true melting pots, with Celtic, Roman, and Germanic cultures made their early imprint, and later in history, the French, Dutch, Spanish, and Austrian cultures exerted their influences.

Belgium gained independence from the Netherlands in 1830 and was occupied by Germany during World Wars I and II. It has prospered in the past half century as a modern, technologically advanced European state and member of the European Union (E.U.) Belgium is territorially divided in the regions of Flanders, Wallonia, and Brussels and on linguistic and cultural issues divided into Dutch, French, and German communities. In recent years, tensions between the Dutch-speaking Flemings of the north and the French-speaking Walloons of the south have resulted in constitutional amendments granting these regions formal recognition and autonomy.

Belgium enjoys an excellent transportation system and is well connected to the rest of Europe via road and rail. French-speaking Brussels, the capital of Belgium, is home to numerous international institutions, including the seat of the E.U. Flemish Antwerp is the second-largest European port and the world's diamond-cutting center. The Belgium economy depends greatly on imports such as food products, machinery, rough diamonds, petroleum and petroleum products, chemicals, clothing and accessories, and textiles. Its main trading partners are Germany, the Netherlands, France, the United Kingdom, Italy, the United States, and Spain. Its main exports are automobiles, food and food products, iron and steel, cut diamonds, textiles, plastics, petroleum products, and nonferrous metals.

= 1 million

design firm   Frank Andries Design
art director   Frank Andries
designer   Frank Andries

client   **N-Allo**

N-Allo is one of Belgium's leading customer contact centers. The designer was asked to develop a logo for the call center, which employs "young, dynamic, and motivated people." The solution is described by the designer as "a talking logo—the text balloon says *N* followed by *Allo*." Crafted with humor and a characteristic wink to add personality, this clean, efficient mark is a highly successful design.

design firm   Frank Andries Design
art director   Frank Andries
designer   Frank Andries

client   **Meys & Zonen**

The client is a national and international moving and storage company. A family business, now run by four sons, the firm has grown to become a midsized company and part of a worldwide network of movers. The logo expresses the designer's view of the firm, which he explains as "small enough to care, big enough to cope." This attitude is typified by at least one member of the family being present at every move, giving confidence to their customers. The logo states simply the corporate name in a clear, bold sans serif font and depicts the presence of the four sons.

design firm   Frank Andries Design
artdirector   Frank Andries
designer   Frank Andries

client   **ECCA**

ECCA, the European Cable Communications Association, is the European trade association of European cable operators and their national associations. The task was to design the logo for the European Cable Modem Standard, EuroModem. The solution uses the forms of the letters *E* and *M* in the shape of identical plug-ins that guarantee an optimal connection. The use of cool colors and geometric shapes appropriately lends a technical feel to the identifier.

design firm   Frank Andries Design
art director   Frank Andries
designer   Frank Andries

client   **Belgian Railways**

The designer was tasked with creating product logos for different types of Belgian Railway Passes: the GoPass for youths under 26; the MultiPass for minigroups; the Golden Railpass for those 60 and older; and B-DagTrips for excursions by train combined with a tourist attraction. A typographic solution matched appropriate fonts and styling with each target group. A common color palette and style vocabulary provide a family look to the four marks, and a link is made between the product logos and the Belgian Railways through the inclusion of the *B* logo of Belgian Railways itself.

design firm   Dorp & Dal
art director Jan Middendorp
designer   Jan Middendorp

client   **FontShop Benelux—Druk**

Druk—The Magazine

Druk is a quarterly magazine used to promote
the typefaces and digital images distributed by
FontShop Benelux. The publication's content
and subject matter is diverse and "always open
to suggestions," according to editor/director Jan
Middendorp. *Druk* concentrates mainly on design
and has included works from such well-known
contributors as KesselsKramer, LUST, UNA
Amsterdam, Opera, Whynot Associates, Rian
Hughes, Jonathan Barnbrook, Akira Kobayashi,
Saki Mafundikwa, Joachim Müller-Lancé, Donald
Beekman, Cosmic Grafica, Typerware, Peter
Bilak, Mariscal, Joost Swarte, Faydherbe/De
Vringer, Skylla, LettError, Barlock, Kontrapunkt,
and many others.

the brief
Jan and his partner Catherine Dal run a two-
person studio out of Ghent, Belgium. Dorp & Dal
(meaning "village and valley") are well known for
their publications and editorial design expertise.
Beginning in 1999, Jan was given a free hand to
shape both the content and look of *Druk*.

the solution
Jan established a consistent approach to the
identity, masthead, and look and feel of *Druk*
by designing a flexible palette of elements that
allowed for constant changeability. Common
denominators of each of the publication's
covers are a black masthead field with yellow
typography expressing the publication title, a
horizontal band containing a defining line, and
the FontShop logo. Cover imagery is handled
in a bold, dynamic fashion that incorporates the
dominant use of yellow and reflects the content
of each issue.

Thirteen issues of *Druk* saw the light of day
between 1999 and 2003, when the title
ceased its publication. Those covers are
shown here.

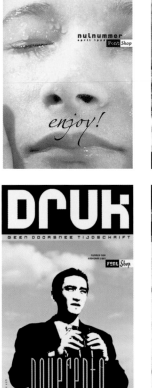

Brazil—remote Amazon, endless beaches, Carnival in Rio, socialite São Paulo, soccer's "Campeo do mundo"… all to the sound of Samba.

Brazil

area	8.5 million km²
GDP, per capita	$7,600 USD
official language	Portuguese
population	182 million

Brazil is the world's fourth largest democracy, fifth largest country, and ninth largest economy. Covering half of South America, it straddles the equator and shares borders with eleven of the continent's thirteen countries.

Brazil—rich in natural resources and a production powerhouse— is one of the largest producers of food, is the world's most biodiverse country, and boasts the world's greatest remaining forests. Highly industrialized, it exports large quantities of lumber, chemicals, cement, iron ore, tin, steel, and manufactured goods. Major Brazilian industries include textiles, shoes, aircraft, motor vehicles and parts, machinery, and equipment, where as the fertile land produces coffee (world's largest exporter), soybeans, wheat, rice, corn, sugar cane, cocoa, citrus fruit, and beef (world's largest cattle herd).

The land itself ranges from sparse to densely populated, with a full 70 percent of Brazilians living along the nearly 5,000 miles (8,000 km) of coast. Infinitely varied landscapes range from flat pampas to Sertao backlands (inland areas) to the annually flooded Pantanal to coastal rainforests to vast Amazonia. A trove of flora and fauna provide a riotous tropical palette of verdant hues: sky blues, shocking pinks and scalding yellows.

A heterogeneous nation of incredible contrasts and cultural diversity, Brazil is at once Third World and First World—from hunter-gatherers to sophisticated urban socialites. Apart from its primary Amerindian, Portuguese, and African roots, today's Brazil has also integrated influences from other past imperial powers—the Spanish, Dutch, French, Italian, German, English, and Japanese. This history results in a richly varied visual vocabulary from which Brazilian designers can draw inspiration.

Design is growing in Brazil, with an estimated 50,000 professional graphic and industrial design practitioners. Brazilian design is colorful and multicultural, and the country's natural resources feature prominently in the visual vocabulary. And Brazilians are certainly style conscious—perhaps from the influence of Portuguese baroque (with its exaggerated attention to detail) and the European architects that shaped the built environment of Brazil's major cities.

= 1 million

imagens da Paz

design firm   Oz Design
art director   Giovanni Vannucchi
designer   Giovanni Vannucchi

client   **Imagens da Paz**
Imagens da Paz (Images of Peace) was created by a group of well-known Brazilian photographers wishing to "create an archive of images that raise values of peace, ethics, and citizenship," to counter the dominant negativity of today's media and to "make pictures available that provoke a positive change in people's consciousness." The designer's concept is expressed clearly through the image: to see things with love.

✚ MINISTÉRIO DA SAÚDE

design firm   Oz Design
art director   Ronald Kapaz
designer   Ronald Kapaz

client   **Ministry of Health, Brazil**
The cross, a universal symbol of health, opens to reflect the tricolor flag of Brazil, reinforcing the designer's idea that "health is about looking inside."

Tamara Grosman

design firm   Oz Design
art director   Ronald Kapaz
designer   Ronald Kapaz

designer   **Tamara Grosman**
This logo for a human resource consultant incorporates the symbol of a balancing doll to express the firm's core competency—restoring balance through human resource coaching.

design firm   Univers Design
art director   Marcelo Aflalo
designer   Marcelo Aflalo

client   **Secretaria de Estado da Cultura— Governo de São Paulo**
The challenge was to create an identity for a state-owned museum (Museus do Estado) and raise awareness for the presence of the state in cultural affairs. The solution is typographic and uses two contrasting elements to demonstrate formal and conceptual diversity—a clean, sans serif *M* is intertwined with expressive ribbonlike strands of a cursive ampersand.

design firm | Claudio Novaes Design
art director | Cladio Novaes
designers | Claudio Novaes
Iran do Espirito Santo

client

Sra. Sopa (Mrs. Soup)

The client specializes in the preparation and sales of cold and hot soups served in thermal cups. The identity is illustrative and playful—Sra. Sopa takes the friendly, beguiling form of a steaming cup alongside her name written in an expressive hand. Red lips, a tanned face, and a sparkling white/aqua eye framed with bold black outlines jump from a sea-blue background to create an engaging and memorable impression. The client's launch strategy was to sell the product from a van parked outside high-traffic nightspots.

design firm | Claudio Novaes Design
art director | Claudio Novaes
designer | Claudio Novaes

client

Zero Filmes | Film Productions

The client is a company specializing in advertising film production. An increasingly competitive market and expansion opportunity led to market repositioning and an updated brand identity for this established player in the Brazilian film industry. The engaging logo comprises bold, amplified typography and a drop-shadowed film canister. Strong in both one- and two-color applications, the identity was easy to apply to various media in a cost-effective and cohesive manner.

design firm Univers Design
art director Marcelo Aflalo
designers Marcelo Aflalo
Claudia Ecard
Carolina Britto
Cristane Novo

client **Arredamento**

Designer Furniture

the brief Arredamento is a well-known producer and nationwide retailer of higher-end, contemporary furnishings with an emphasis on design. The goal was to reposition this established, forty-five-year-old company that had been gradually losing ground to new competition. A clear identity was needed, as was a strategic rethinking of Arredamento's product offering, storefronts, communications, and approach to selling.

the solution The design team at Univers, most of whom have a background in architecture or three-dimensional design, suggested a bold, yet simple and clean, approach to Arredamento's visual identity and its application to communications, store interiors, banners, and signage. The symbol consists of an architectonic monogram in the shape of a chair that incorporates the first few letters of the name, providing good visual recall. The core identity is extended by means of a distinctive color palette and tightly cropped furniture details.

Uma surpresa em cada detalhe.
Nova coleção arredamento

▲ This advertisement shows selective close-up details of Arredamento's new collection. The imagery plays off the negative space in the same manner as the logo, and some of the images incorporate Arredamento's corporate orange to further mimic the logo.

◄ A distinctive pylon sign in the form of a "street totem" features a pattern of chair-shaped cutouts to promote the store's presence to passersby in an engaging yet unobtrusive manner, fulfilling the designers' goal of not adding to "the visual pollution of streetscapes that has reached epidemic proportions." Signs were fabricated of steel and acrylic.

design firm Univers Design
art director Marcelo Aflalo
designers Marcelo Aflalo
Claudia Ecard
Aya Nakai
Carolina Britto

client **Pão de Açúcar**

Picture Perfect

Pão de Açúcar is the biggest food retailer in Brazil, with stores ranging in size from local convenience shops to large supermarkets.

the brief
The initial design brief (in 1996) called for pictograms for one specific store in a residential neighborhood. This job evolved into designs for seventeen subsequent stores and led to the compilation of a complete branding book and pictogram manual. Univers Design has since worked on both interior and exterior architecture for Pão de Açúcar, as well as merchandising design and visual communication.

the solution
The designers wanted to create a visual approach that would communicate well and appeal to a wide audience—those with "sophisticated taste and spending habits" as well as those who are "less visually educated." Pictograms provided an effective approach that could be understood by everyone, and like much of the work done at Univers Design, the icons they developed have "a three-dimensional quality taken from a basic figurative sketch," according to Aflalo. When experienced in situ, this pictographic vocabulary creates a distinctive visual voice as well as provides clear in-store navigation.

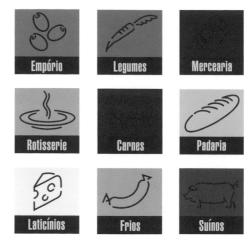

▲ The beauty of pictographic signs is that even young children can "read" the messages they convey. In a heavily product-branded environment like a supermarket, simple visual communication that helps navigation is a welcome addition. Pão de Açúcar's identity is applied effectively throughout the stores.

► The identity and signage manual shows the range of pictograms developed.

Specifications outline the fabrication, placement guidelines,
and mounting details for pictographic signs (which are
created with PVC foam and medium-density fiberboard).

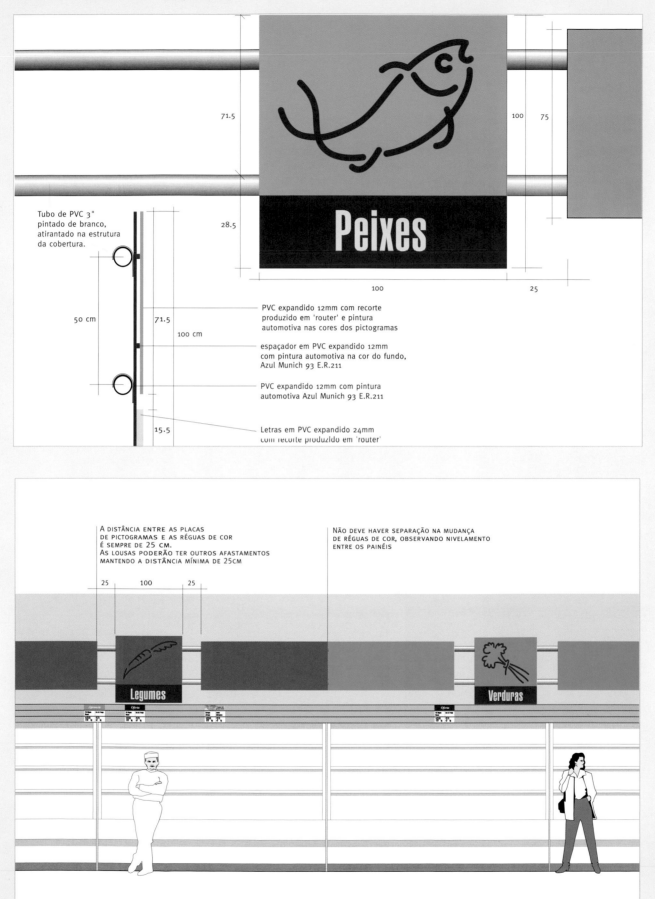

Tubo de PVC 3"
pintado de branco,
atirantado na estrutura
da cobertura.

Peixes

71.5

28.5

100

75

100

25

50 cm

71.5

100 cm

15.5

PVC expandido 12mm com recorte
produzido em 'router' e pintura
automotiva nas cores dos pictogramas

espaçador em PVC expandido 12mm
com pintura automotiva na cor do fundo,
Azul Munich 93 E.R.211

PVC expandido 12mm com pintura
automotiva Azul Munich 93 E.R.211

Letras em PVC expandido 24mm
com recorte produzido em 'router'

A DISTÂNCIA ENTRE AS PLACAS
DE PICTOGRAMAS E AS RÉGUAS DE COR
É SEMPRE DE 25 CM.
AS LOUSAS PODERÃO TER OUTROS AFASTAMENTOS
MANTENDO A DISTÂNCIA MÍNIMA DE 25CM

NÃO DEVE HAVER SEPARAÇÃO NA MUDANÇA
DE RÉGUAS DE COR, OBSERVANDO NIVELAMENTO
ENTRE OS PAINÉIS

25   100   25

Legumes

Verduras

design firm   GAD'DESIGN
art directors Hugo Kovadloff
              Valpirio Monteiro
designers   Peter Tang
              Suzi Ito

client   **CPFL Energia**

Renewed Energy

CPFL Energia is the largest private group in the Brazilian electricity sector; 100 percent nationally owned; and active in electricity distribution, marketing, and generation through its holdings, CPFL Paulista, CPFL Piratininga, CPFL Geração, CPFL Brasil, and Rio Grande Energia (RGE). The Companhia Paulista de Força e Luz (CPFL) was privatized in 1997, after which it experienced several years of stagnation. As it approached its nintieth anniversary, CPFL found itself "presenting a worn image" to its clients, staff, and the general public.

the brief GAD'DESIGN was engaged at this critical time of change to assist CPFL in the development of a new graphic expression for its trademark to symbolize the deep organizational transformations taking place.

the solution The project, developed by GAD'DESIGN, led from an initial defining of CPFL's new graphic expression to addressing the brand's complete architecture. This consolidation culminated in a trademark for CPFL Energia holding—an umbrella of distribution, generation, and marketing companies. With their focus firmly on the vision of creating a powerful image, the designers integrated design, architecture, and communication services and "immersed themselves in the world of CPFL." The project expanded with applications to print material, uniforms, fleet, communications, promotion, corporate marketing, and facility design—"in fact, the entire corporate identity." After four years of a deep, intense relationship with GAD'DESIGN, CPFL Energia's image has become the sector's benchmark. During this time, the company has also achieved significant results in terms of its key management indicators.

▲ The CPFL Energia logo is dynamic and energetic, appropriately signaling the client's core business and offering. Each of the regional holdings received a tailored identifier, differentiated by color and nomenclature.

▼ CPFL's identity has been applied thoughtfully and consistently across a large range of publicly visible applications, including generating stations, building exteriors, and fleets of vehicles. Although each individual installation has its own demands (as these examples show), the test of an effective corporate identity system is to have enough cohesive strength to ensure instant recognition in each iteration while possessing the flexibility to incorporate and compensate for a wide range of variables beyond the designers' control.

design firm   GAD' DESIGN
art directors Hugo Kovadloff
               Leonardo Araujo
               Luciano Deos
               Valpirio Monteiro
designers   Suzi Ito
               Claudio Nichetti
               Rodrigo Conde
               Peter Tang
               Fernando Angulo
               Leopoldo Leal

client   **Claro**

Claro Calling

Claro is the second-largest telephone operator in
Brazil. It arose from the merger and consolidations
of telephone operations ATL, Tess, Americel,
Clarol Digital, BCP Nordeste, and BCP São Paulo.
Controlled by the Mexican group Amèrica Movil,
the Claro brand was launched in August 2003.

The Claro logo in 2-D and 3-D.

the brief   GAD'DESIGN's challenge was to create a new trademark to compete with other established mobile phone operators (OI, TIM, VIVO) without having an exclusive competitive distinction. This required carving out a space for Claro in an already-saturated market.

the solution   The designers stated the strategy as follows: "Present a familiar company that better understands its clients and their needs. Launch a mark that symbolizes a change for the better to clients and a more convenient alternative to the general public." Describing the project concept and development, the designers explain, "The new Claro brand and identity was born from essential principles for positioning a company and its services. The attributes of the brand would have to be strength, simplicity, contemporaneity, force, brightness, and light. The personality would be local, happy, assertive, genuine, efficient, and simple. The concept of the new brand was the Sun and its rays. With the graphical synthesis of the sun and circle of its rays, the evolution toward the red circle and the solution of three rays to represent the whole was more than natural." The result of the brand launch has been impressive—Claro now has more than ten million customers, and the project was named Case of the Year in *About* magazine's festival of promotion, packaging, and design.

More than eighty suppliers from all parts of Brazil were involved in implementing the brand's logistics—from traditional trade sources to new vendors brought in by GAD'DESIGN with the aim of introducing new technologies and automating previously manual processes, thereby increasing scale, reducing production costs, enabling logistical processes, and "gaining time." Product packaging, retail store design, POS materials, and signage all integrate the strong visual palette developed for Claro—a great name (*claro* means "clear"), a strong logotype, a blue-sky attitude (with occasional wispy clouds), and an imbued energy and directness that form a comprehensive brand presence.

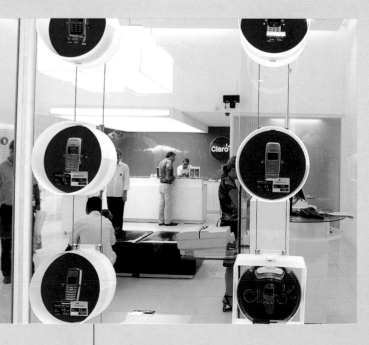

design firm 100% Design
art directors Renata Melman
Patricia Oliveira
designers Rosana Hepp
Patricia Oliveira
client **Drogaria Onofre**

Shaping Well-being

Onofre is a drugstore chain that for more than fifty years has offered a wide range of products at reasonable prices.

the brief The designers were commissioned to design identification and interior signage systems for Drogeria Onofre, the first medicine megastore in Brazil.

the solution The creative concept focused on consumers' well-being by creating a clean, emotionally calming in-store environment. As stated by the designers, "Onofre's positioning statement is expressed through a delicate composition of positive words such as *peace, beauty, health*, and *balance*." These keywords were applied on the façade as well as throughout the interior, along with a visual palette of cool blues, clean sans serif type (solid letters and delicate outlines), and fluid graphic backgrounds, all suggesting the calming movement of water. Lettering was applied to acrylic tubes in various configurations—suspended from the ceiling, acting as totems, providing directional navigation, and acting as section identifiers and merchandising displays.

On entering a Drogeria Onofre store, the consumer is immediately immersed in a clean, calming, and information-rich environment that aids navigation and contributes to her or his sense of well-being—an excellent example of a carefully designed visual palette being used to affect consumer experience and perceptions.

design firm | Book Company/Grafikz
art director | Andrei Polessi
designer | Andrei Polessi

client | **Brasreal Têxtil Ltda. (Lilás)**

Lilás is a new textile brand for a line of household products, such as table linens, bed and bath, and general kitchen accessories. The client wanted to "create a romantic, feminine feeling that could be at the same time modern, elegant, and practical." The brand's design involved the development of several distinctive components: an elegant serif logotype with wide-spaced, reversed letters framed in a black mortise; a series of well-lit, colorful, closely cropped photos of Lilás textiles and accessories; and a distinctive, energetic, pink-and-white-stripe pattern. The stationery, bags, and tags show how the three components weave together successfully to create the desired brand image.

design firm | Book Company/Grafikz
art director | Andrei Polessi
designer | Andrei Polessi

client | **Eric Santos**

Eric Santos is a freelance speaker (voice talent) who wanted to promote himself to audio studios and television/video production companies. He asked for low-budget stationery and CD graphics "with a personal feeling ... and with a little bit of humor." The designer's solution uses a "shouting kid" image to suggest "the irreverence of a new voice arriving in the market." An effective, consistent image is introduced to the two-color stationery and CD by means of the "kid" photos, reversed sans serif type, solid color bands, and the unexpected introduction of an orthodontic measurement scale (referencing the oral arcade, crucial to voice modulation).

design firm	Claudio Novaes Design
art director	Claudio Novaes
designer	Claudio Novaes

Blondie Hair

The client is described by the designer as "a hair stylist for cool people." The brief called for a strong, simple, communicative brand. The solution combines graphic and typographic elements drawn from the genre of the styling salons— a reversed comb acts as the letter *B* for Blondie, centered on a black circle.

design firm	BG Strategic Design
art director	Claudio Novaes
designer	Claudio Novaes

Jacaré do Brasil

The client is a Brazilian craft store looking to expand into São Paulo from Trancoso, Bahia. Because the market in São Paulo is more demanding, the firm needed to reposition itself and refine its identity. The designer's solution "rescues the alligator symbol from the existing identity and inserts it in a new context, aligned with the new store's positioning."

design firm	ZupiDesign.com
designer	Allan Szacher

House

House is a well-known building-management firm that was looking for "a logo that describes the idea of a relationship between a manager and his clients." As stated by the designer, "The solution is simple—two people shaking hands form the letter *H* for *house.*" The strong contrast between foreground and background helps ensure high visibility and reinforces recall.

design firm	100% Design
art directors	Renata Melman
	Patricia Oliveira
designers	Patricia Oliveira
	Angelica Ferreira
	André Viceconti
	Lilian Chiofolo

100% Design

100% Design provides strategic brand building, planning, and creative design services. The self-imposed brief: to show the unique way that 100% Design's brands work. The solution: a bold, colorful logo engages the viewer and triggers a synergy across a range of applications (not shown here) including print and environmental design.

design firm	100% Design
art directors	Renata Melman
	Patricia Oliveira
designers	Alessandro Ávila
	Rosana Hepp
	Vinicius Vieira
client	**Amyr Klink/Samello**

Brand Navigation

Amyr Klink is a well-known Brazilian sailor and navigator who wanted to enter the licensing business to leverage his image and reputation.

the brief The client needed a distinctive logo and a versatile brand identity that could extend to future licensed products. Brand attributes and values needed to encompass those of Amyr Klink himself—perseverance, entrepreneurial spirit, and determination.

the solution The designers explain, "The logo's graphics were inspired by a compass and visual elements showing the seriousness and honesty of Amyr Klink's personality." Distinctively styled letterforms were developed for the eponymous logotype and monogram in concert with the compass form and dominant navy blue color, creating a strong marine image that is both memorable and versatile.

▲ The brand signature consists of a monogram, the unique logotype, and a compass symbol.

▲ The unique business card shape emphasizes the brand signature. Latitude and longtitude references provide a clever reinforcement of the brand's source inspiration.

◄ The distinctive, versatile Amyr Klink brand lent itself well to effective application on signage, product labeling (as shown on these sport shoes designed by Samello), merchandising, and POS displays. Stands incorporated three-dimensional versions of the brand signature's compass element along with sail-like panel shapes bearing blue/black duotone photos of nautical settings and sailboats—an extremely effective application of the brand in a retail sales environment.

▼ A comprehensive visual identification manual provided guidelines for the correct application of the brand in a wide range of uses.

Canada—ever close to nature, its flag features a maple leaf, its national animal is the industrious beaver, and its money sports pictures of children playing outdoor hockey and glimpses of the vast country's breathtaking scenery.

Canada

area	9,976,100 km²
GDP, per capita	$29,000 USD
official languages	English, French
population	32.2 million

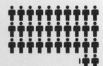

Canada is the second-largest country in the world and the most northerly. It occupies most of the North American land mass and is a land of vast distances, rich natural resources, and an extremely low population (population density is only 3.2 persons per km²). Economically and technologically, the nation has developed in parallel with the United States, its neighbor to the south with whom it shares the world's longest undefended border.

Inhabited by aboriginal peoples—known in Canada as the First Nations—for at least 10,000 years, Canada was first visited by Europeans around A.D. 1000, when the Vikings briefly settled at L'Anse aux Meadows in Newfoundland. More permanent European visits came in the sixteenth and seventeenth centuries, followed by numerous waves of immigration. Canada became a self-governing dominion in 1867, while retaining ties to the British crown. Today, Canada is a decentralized federation of ten provinces and three territories, governed as a parliamentary constitutional monarchy. Culturally, the country is a mosaic of First Nations and later immigrants from every corner of the world—a large picture made of many distinct pieces rather than a melting pot. A strong belief in the value of diversity has contributed to a multicultural milieu that forms a vibrant environment for commerce and creativity.

Canada is affluent, technologically advanced, and industrialized. It is largely self-sufficient in energy due to its relatively large deposits of fossil fuels, nuclear energy generation, and hydroelectric power capabilities. Its economy has traditionally relied heavily on the abundance of natural resources and trade, particularly with the United States, with which it has a long, extensive relationship. Although the modern Canadian economy has become widely diversified, exploitation of natural resources remains an important driving force of many regional economies.

Canada's vibrant design community is served by various associations, with the Society of Graphic Designers of Canada (GDC) being the national body for visual communicators. How could one describe Canadian graphic design? "Swiss with a twist and a sense of humor," is how one astute pundit put it.

♟ = 1 million

Island City, by Nature

design firm   Studio Allsorts
agency   Fisher & Associates
art directors   Don Fisher
Dennis Nagy
Dale Simonson
copywriter   Don Fisher
designer   Dale Simonson

client

City of Richmond, B.C.
The city of Richmond, B.C.—comprising seventeen islands in the mouth of the Fraser River in the Greater Vancouver Regional District on Canada's Pacific Coast, close to the U.S. border—wanted to deliver a key message about livability and locale. The design solution involved a wordmark and a positioning statement. The statement incorporates an image of the great blue heron (*ardea herodias*), a common sight on the city's shorelines and waterways, with the definitive line *Island City, by Nature* in support of the natural beauty of the city's environs.

design firm   The Farm/Supercapacity
art director   Alison Hladkyj
designers   Alison Hladkyj
Ian Mitchell

client

The Redwood
The Redwood is a refuge and support system for women and children fleeing domestic violence. This redesign for The Redwood goes beyond depicting a shelter and signals an ongoing support system for immigrant women and their children. The inspirational icon depicts a mother holding hands and playing with her two children, signaling care, safety, family unity, and racial diversity. It fulfills the client's wish of implying spiritual and emotional support to families of all races. The identity is successful with both the users (multiracial women) and the donors.

design firm   Communications Nemesis Inc.
art director   Luc Desaulniers
designer   Luc Desaulniers

client

Consensus Communication
This logo for a firm offering financial assistance information to rural clients consists of the letter *C* inside a circle. The visual form represents sheets of paper in motion and signals dynamic rotation.

design firm   Bounce Communication Design
art director   Evan Kuz
designer   Evan Kuz

client

Stick Strategy
Stick Strategy works with design firms and B2B clients to market their services, create campaigns, and provide business systems. The brief for this logo was clear: "Be unique. Make a statement. Have fun. Be memorable. Use metaphors if possible." The designer saw the client as aggressive yet playful, and that's where the dog image came in.

design firm | Karacters Design Group
art director | Maria Kennedy
designer | Lisa Nakamura

client

Shoppers Drug Mart

Shoppers Drug Mart, Canada's largest drugstore chain, wanted to establish a stronger brand proposition for their private label, Life Brand. They need to elevate the Life Brand bath and body line to a premium product offering through distinct and eye-catching design. The successful solution, named Fresh Blends, truly feels fresh and modern—new product reformulations infuse combinations of tropical fruit, vibrant liquid colors show through the clear containers, and photographic imagery depicts the representative fruit. Sales have exceeded expectations.

design firm | Mackay l Wong
art director | Kelly Moorhead
designer | Kelly Moorhead

client

4 on the Floor

A nostalgic, stylized chair logo that recalls the streamlined luxury of an earlier era acts as the identity cornerstone for this Toronto furniture manufacturer. The client wanted an identity that would convey the ability to quickly customize products and fill orders promptly. Their largest product lines are chairs, and with their name being 4 on the Floor, the chair was a natural choice for the icon. Enlarged details from the logo's illustration were used to tie together effectively a range of stationery and collateral materials, all printed in black and metallic green.

O'Dell Advertising

O!

design firm | Glenn Tinley Design
art director | Fran Carmichael
designer | Morris Antosh

client

O'Dell Advertising
The client, a copywriter and creative director, had a simple request: "Make me a cool logo!" Use of an exclamation point in place of an apostrophe suggests a positive reaction to the client's ad products.

LIFE IN THE WOODS™

design firm | Ross + Doell
designers | Alex Ross
Mike Doell

client

Life in the Woods
Life in the Woods is a Canadian manufacturer of 100 percent organic body care products. It uses only ingredients that do not require a plant to be uprooted, cut down, or otherwise damaged. The design solution fulfills the aim of adding a greater level of sophistication to the company's identity. An organic tree/leaf logomark combines with clean, geometric sans serif letterforms to create a distinctive identifier.

inkling press

design firm | Colberg Design
art director | Susan Colberg
designer | Susan Colberg

client

Inkling Press
This logo was designed for a small independent publisher of poetry books—a low-budget venture with a small but enthusiastic staff. Colberg states, "My client stressed the importance of a link with the literary past, which had been made with the selection of the typeface and a sense of the small, humble scale of the venture combined with the enthusiasm of its participants. The link was achieved by rendering the words in lowercase letters punctuated by small (but enthusiastic!) inkblots. The audience consists of lovers of poetry, especially poetry that might not otherwise be published." The logo is printed in black only because of a very limited production budget.

magpie pr°ductions

design firm | Colberg Design
art director | Susan Colberg
designer | Susan Colberg

client

Magpie Productions
This logo is designed for a small production house of poetry CDs (related to but separate from Inkling Press). The significance of the magpie as a symbol was described as "taking the best, shiniest poems and producing them on CD for listeners." The logo, therefore, shows the magpie stealing the *O* from the word *productions*. The O also echoes the shape of a CD. The typeface is the same as for Inkling Press; the two ventures are linked, but distinct from each other.

design firm   dossiercreative inc.
art director Don Chisholm
designer   Patrick Smith

client   **Phillips Distilling Ltd.**

Jinx Sour Citrus

the brief   Phillips Distilling wanted to launch a new ready-
to-drink beverage made from a blend of premium
vodka and Sour Puss liqueur.

the solution The brand's use of strong graphic imagery and
lighthearted overtones communicate both good
times and the product's great taste with a sour twist.
The name Jinx Sour Citrus evokes an emotional
connection with intrigue and nightlife—this feeling
was extended throughout the visual approach. The
logotype's edgy, unbalanced application hearkens
back to the beatnik graphic elements. The strolling
cat complements the bold, idiosyncratic typography,
reinforcing brand recognition with current Sour Puss
consumers and establishing a more sophisticated
brand that creates a character of its own.

▲ Unique, kinetic letterforms and strong contrast
make this mark stand out.

▼ Product labeling and packaging integrate the
brand's dynamic visual palette effectively.

design firm | Mackay I Wong
art director | Kelly Moorhead
designer | Kelly Moorhead

client | **Boom**

This strident restaurant logo makes good use of color and imagery to awaken a morning feeling—a crowing rooster in an egg-yolk yellow target shape with a cup of black coffee in the bull's-eye.

design firm | Colberg Design
art director | Susan Colberg
designer | Susan Colberg

client | **Friends of Printmaking**

This mark was designed for a group of printmakers at the University of Alberta, who were trying to raise funds through the production of portfolio prints to help them upgrade equipment and acquire materials. The solution shows the initials (F.O.P.) of the organization in a positive and mirror image configuration that relates to the printmaking process. The texture of rice paper and overall form of the mark relate to traditional print methods originating in Asia. The audience would be print artists and those with an interest in and some knowledge of the art form.

design firm | Pagemedia
art director | Hue White
designer | Hue White

client | **Brent Andrew Marshall**

Brent Andrew Marshall is an adventurous fashion and entertainment photographer. As the designer states, "Brent wanted a logo that matched his style of work … much more art than science. He has this classic rebel personality, and his photos are very human and organic. So, I focused my design to match—dynamic and organic at the same time. I like to think of the logo as that impulsive tattoo you wake up with after a crazy night." No further explanation needed.

design firm | Pagemedia
art director | Hue White
designer | Hue White

client | **Pagemedia**

Pagemedia is a design entity that provides a range of multimedia services—Web, print, and video. The designer's goal: "Design a logo that's not too literal. Avoid the typical ultra-high-tech flash." The solution: "The paperboy on the corner delivers facts to the people. The logo evokes a renaissance feel (what's old is new again) with whimsy. It also expresses visually the pun suggested by the name itself, Page and Media."

design firm	dossiercreative inc.
art director	Don Chisholm
designer	Eena Kim
client	**AG Hair Cosmetics**

The designer describes the product and challenge as follows: "ív cosmeceuticals, produced by AG cosmetics, are designed to reverse the effects of the environment and aging on hair. Spirited in this ideology, this is the first and only hair-care product with this purpose. The challenge was to communicate product benefits in a powerful, succinct way. The striking look of the brand represents the marriage of cosmetics and pharmaceuticals, a combination of serious efficacy and fashion cool."

The brand has a strong and medical presence, reinforcing the pharmaceutical-like benefits of the product. Unique packaging includes tamper-proof seals and a Zelzave dispensing system modeled on an intravenous drip.

design firm	Ion Design Inc.
art director	David Coates
designers	Rod Roodenburg
	Dawn Newton
client	**Left Bank Restaurants**

Left Bank Restaurants is a long-standing San Francisco–based client featuring *cuisine grand-mere* (French country cooking), elegantly served in an authentic French brasserie atmosphere at reasonable prices. Thanks in part to extensive work done by Ion since 1993, the client has grown from "a mere concept looking for investors" to a chain of five locations in the Bay Area. The brief was to create an identity program that reflected the mood of the 1920s-era Left Bank in Paris. The solution deployed bright, bold, and colorful graphics that recalled old French food labels and complemented the simple, fresh food served in the restaurants. The whimsical identity draws from the hanging signs found outside Parisian butcher shops.

design firm — HandyRandy Communications Inc.
art director — Randy Milanovic
designer — Randy Milanovic

client — **Hotchkiss Herbs and Produce**
This small organic grower specializes in heirloom tomatoes. The designer describes the design inspiration and process: "After stumbling over the family name a few times, I was reminded of a tongue twister I had known as a child. Modified slightly, I came up with, 'How many kisses could a Hotchkiss kiss, if a Hotchkiss could kiss kisses?' While holding hands with my technology associate, I sang the rhyme aloud and presented my identity comps. After setting the mood in such a way, it was obvious which the winning logo would be—it not only resembles the corner of a packing crate but also presented symbolically an iconic visual of the husband and wife team marching steadfastly forward, hand in hand. (Especially apt, because the growers had recently replaced all their plants because a virus had infected their legacy crop)."

design firm — MacMillan Lynch Multimedia
art director — Kerry Lynch
designer — John DeWolf

client — **Radiator Hosting**
The client is a progressive Web-hosting company based in Halifax, Nova Scotia, that provides safe hosting to clients around the world. The logo design is strong, literal, and memorable—and it won gold in the 2004 ICE awards for logo design.

design firm — Gustavo Machado Graphic Design
art director — Gustavo Machado
designer — Gustavo Machado

client — **Baião de Dois Filmes**
This small Brazilian production company produces broadcast design, film titles, and commercials. Their brief called for an identity that would "represent the industrial revolution that took place a century ago." The designer's logo solution combines distressed and distorted letterforms to re-create the output from an old 8 mm film projector, evoking both the past and today's kinetic mass media.

design firm — Sub Communications
art director — Sébastien Théraulaz
designer — Sébastien Théraulaz

client — **Patrick Masbourian/Empire of Baboon**
The Empire of Baboon is an underground collective of video artists and filmmakers concerned about social issues. The committed, aggressive nature of the images produced by its members is expressed clearly through the use of a baboon, the "chief of the gang." The challenge, as stated by the designer, was to "develop a baboon symbol expressing the idea of a kingdom, an empire that he rules … he is the head of something big but underground at the same time." The solution: "Playing with the baboon's hair, we ended up creating a mane that made the baboon look like a lion king. His face is showing at the same time a warrior, a wise person, and an emperor." Typical of work designed in Montréal, the collective's name is spelled out in both of Canada's official languages, English and French.

design firm | Subplot Design Inc.
creative directors | Roy White
| Matthew Clark
designer | Matthew Clark
photographer | Total Graphics

client | **Bright Nites USA**

Style, Sport, & Safety

StrideLite and CycLite products feature nanometer-thin electroluminescent lamps that are completely flexible and almost totally weightless: strobe-light safety gear for runners, walkers, and cyclists that is visible at night up to half a mile (800 meters) away.

the brief | The design challenge was to create a brand for fashion-inspired athletic gear with a clear safety proposition—style, sport, and safety all in one.

the solution | Taking its cues from hazard symbols and warning signs, the identity blends the idea of "safety + sport + light" in an icon for each product line. Prominent Product Feature Charts highlight the key product attributes and combine with the overall graphic sensibility to create a highly technical, but approachable, safety materials metaphor on every item of print and packaging. The personality of the brand goes even further, emphasizing the unique "illuminated" proposition with engaging wit and humor in such lines as "You will see the Lite," "You can run but you can't hide," and "Always wear protection when you go out at night."

The packaging and collateral use the ubiquitous reflective silver and fluorescent colors of safety materials in a modern, innovative design style.

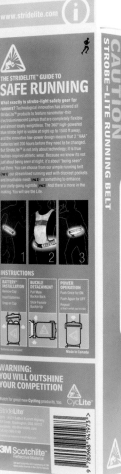

Vancouver International Writers Festival
presenting a world of words

design firm Ion Design Inc.
art director David Coates
designer David Coates

client **Vancouver International Writers (& Readers) Festival**
One of North America's premiere literary events, the Vancouver International Writers (& Readers) Festival attracts an audience of more than 11,000 annually and garners extraordinary media attention. Lacking a consistent identity, the client was looking for better visibility to help develop relationships with sponsors, governments, and the general public. This light, clever typographic approach helped convey the spirit of the festival. The smiling face (constructed of typographic letterforms) is fun and approachable, helping make accessible what some might consider a highbrow event.

design firm Agence Code
art director Jean Lesage
designer André Lavergne

client **Emergence Management Consulting**
Emergence is a high-tech consulting firm specializing in the manufacturing sector. Their comprehensive approach takes in analysis, planning, personalized software development, on-site implementation, and training. The brief involved creating a strong symbol to signal the start-to-finish scope of Emergence's problem-solving approach—a symbol that would inspire trust, be easily identifiable, and act as a lasting reminder. The solution is a bold, electric blue symbol built from a dominant lowercase e, combining smooth, curved lines with pictographic shapes, all in a form reminiscent of a computer screen or on/off button. The symbol communicates precision, process, and a spark setting things in motion—and, in the designers' words, acts as "an appropriate identifier that projects Emergence as the interface and catalyst for change and improved efficiency."

design firm Agence Code
art director Pierre Chapdelaine
designer Pierre Chapdelaine

client **Le Tour de l'île de Montréal**
Le Tour de l'île de Montréal has organized cycling-related events for all age groups since the early 1980s. Their main event brings together 30,000 cyclists for an annual, noncompetitive ride through the streets of Montréal. Other activities include a night ride, a children's ride, and conferences. In 1998, they decided to bring together all the activities under one name and identity—La Féria du vélo de Montréal, a one-week festival of cycling-related activities. The designer's solution was to associate the festival with Picasso's famous bicycle-inspired work of art, the *Head of a Bull'* sculpture. This approach worked well by connecting the Latin-sounding *Féria* with Spain's best-known artist. A modern, urban, two-dimensional rendition of the famous work was paired with heavy calligraphic brush strokes and brightly colored counters, also reminiscent of Miró, another well-known Spanish artist.

design firm Splash Design
art director Phred Martin
designer Phred Martin

client **The Impeccable Pig Eatery Oinc**
This clever restaurant logo takes a fresh approach from a different angle. In the designer's own words, "How do you create a memorable logo for a restaurant called The Impeccable Pig Eatery Oinc. without looking like other well-known pig icons? The solution: don't show the face." The successful symbol projects the restaurant's fun atmosphere in a memorable manner.

design firm	CFX Creative
art director	Carly H. Franklin
designer	Carly H. Franklin
client	**Filmwell Security Limited**

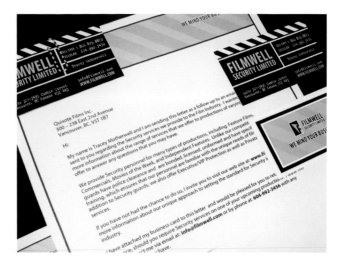

Vancouver's Filmwell Security Limited serves the unique security needs of the British Columbian film industry. The logo's solution ties the target audience (the film industry) to security through a dramatically lit *F,* carefully selected typography, and a caution-yellow highlight color. The visual vocabulary of the stressed typewriter-style font avoids an overly polished look and continues the theme of the caution-yellow stripe and clapboard-style graphics.

The mark applies well in reverse form on a dark background.

design firm	Ion Design Inc.
art director	David Coates
designer	Rod Roodenburg
client	**Ion Design Inc**

Ion is a well-known Vancouver-based design firm, founded in 1988. With clients mainly in the hospitality, education, and technology sectors, Ion offers a range of services from traditional print and exhibition design to Web, new media, and software development. Ion's logo had been in existence since 1995 and had built considerable brand equity. Rather than change it, the firm decided instead to completely redesign its business papers for a fresh look and greater impact. Using the existing palette and elements, they employed a bold use of color and innovative finishing techniques. Business cards were treated as a real sales tool by using Curious Touch paper; printed, embossed, and laminated to a full color back; and then die cut. Each staff member created his or her own image, personalizing the back of the cards and creating a collectable set.

design firm
Suburbia

art director Mary-Lynn Bellamy-Willms

designer Martin Aveyard

client **Suburbia**

Suburbia = Retail

Suburbia is a Victoria-based advertising firm.

the brief As the designers confidently state, "Suburbia gets shoppers. We understand them. So we know how to make our clients unforgettable. And then our clients get shoppers. That's why we're the leading branding agency in Western Canada serving midsized retailers." The challenge for this self-designed identity called for a bold, direct approach.

the solution To create an identity package that really "says retail," the designers "hijacked retail elements" such as price tags and credit cards to give their stationery a contemporary retail feel. A confident lowercase logotype, a distinct color palette, and clean sans serif supporting type round out a simple but effective corporate identity.

▲ Business cards in the form of a branded credit card really hit the retail-oriented message home. The back of the card contains full contact information.

▼ Suburbia's stationery makes a strong impression yet is deceptively simple. Die-cut hang tags reinforce the firm's shopping and shopper focus.

63

✛ Switzerland

area	41,300 km²
GDP, per capita	$31,900 USD
official languages	German, French, Italian, Romansh
population	7.3 million

Switzerland is a landlocked federal state in central Europe neighbored by Germany, France, Italy, Austria, and Liechtenstein. *Helvetia*, the country's Latin name, gained independence from Germany in 1499. It enjoys a strong tradition of political and military neutrality, as well as international cooperation—significant factors in its notable banking success. Although Switzerland is home to many U.N. agencies, international bodies (such as the International Red Cross, which uses the inverse of the Swiss flag as its identifier), and nongovernmental organizations, it did not officially become a U.N. member until 2002.

The Swiss Confederation is a parliamentary democratic republic consisting of twenty-six cantons. At the crossroads of several major European cultures, which have heavily influenced the country's languages and cultural practices, the Swiss landscape is characterized by the Alps, a high mountain range running across the south-central region of the country. Switzerland is a prosperous, stable, modern market economy with a per capita GDP higher than most of its neighbors. Besides banking, Switzerland is a popular tourist destination, capitalizing on its breathtaking scenery and varied seasons.

Most graphic designers are familiar with Switzerland's contribution to their profession—the renowned Gewerbschule Basel (its foundation program has likely influenced more design curricula around the world more than any other), the clean "international style" characterized by sans serif type (for example, Helvetica), finely articulated hierarchical grids, and a clean visual vocabulary that says "less is more."

🯅 = 1 million

design firm | CREACTIS
art director | Sébastien Canepa
designer | Sébastien Canepa

client

PIT'R PAN PROD
The client, an event-management agency, wanted to create a logo "around the imagination and dreams of the Peter Pan universe," in part to give meaning to the firm's chosen name, PIT'R PAN PROD. The designer chose to illustrate a symbolic fairy (remember Tinkerbell?) to represent the idea of—in his words—"…when the dream becomes reality. The symbolism of the fairy getting ready to jump evokes a festive spirit and a little bit of magic—four stars symbolize the four domains of the client's activities."

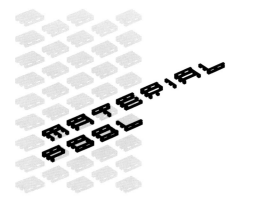

design firm | Mixer
art director | Erich Brechbühl
designer | Erich Brechbühl

client

Materialpool Zentralschweiz
The client is a technical equipment rental company for special events in central Switzerland. The logotype is based on the palettes and packaging used by the client to transport a wide spectrum of materials. A palette pattern, derived from the logotype, is used as a decorative visual element to support the identity.

design firm | Mixer
art director | Erich Brechbühl
designer | Erich Brechbühl

client

Detaillisten Sempach
Detaillisten Sempach is an association of small stores and businesses in the town of Sempach. The challenge was to create a common identity for all the members of the association. The logo uses two gate arches from Sempach's historical towers to form an S, which stands for Sempach as well as interlocking directional arrows. Red and green were used to express this unique identity, which was applied to a simplified street map showing the location of associated stores in "Sempach—your personal shopping center."

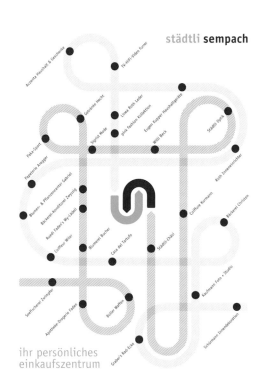

design firm | Mixer
art director | Erich Brechbühl
designer | Erich Brechbühl

client | **Wirtschaft zur Schlacht, Sempach**

To the Battle

The client is a restaurant named "To the Battle," which is located on the site where the historical battle of Sempach took place in 1386.

the brief | The challenge was to create a unique new identity for Wirtschaft zur Schlacht, while respecting the historical significance of the restaurant's name and location.

the solution | An archival search unearthed some engaging old prints and paintings of the historic battle. The logo takes the form of a circular crest, incorporating the restaurant's name and a detailed rendering of a mounted knight. Note that the knight's weapons have been replaced with kitchen implements.

Von nun an ... schwingt der Sohn die Kelle!

► The humorous logo and an advertisement announcing the restaurant's transition to fifth-generation family proprietorship sport a headline that reads, *From now on, the son wields the ladle!*

▼ This clever illustration expands on the depiction of the battle of Sempach—again, all the weapons have been replaced with kitchen implements.

Liebe Gäste
Die traditionsreiche Wirtschaft zur Schlacht geht in die 5. Generation. Nach über 30 Jahren Geschäftstätigkeit übergeben Sepp & Berta Wey-Meier den Betrieb an die nachfolgende Generation. Rolf Wey & Melanie Bürgi freuen sich ab Januar 2004 die historisch gelegene Gastwirtschaft weiter in die Zukunft führen zu können. Sie, liebe Gäste, sind herzlich eingeladen, an unserer grossen Uustrinkete / Aatrinkete am Wochenende des 9. / 10. und 11. Januar 2004 teilzunehmen.

Freitag, 9. Januar 2004
Grosser Unterhaltungsabend mit Schösu und den Schwyzerörgelifrönde Rast-Wiss. Begrüssungs-Apéro, kaltes und warmes Buurebuffet und Desserts à discrétion.

Samstag, 10. Januar 2004
Tag der offenen Beiz mit musikalischer Abend-Unterhaltung mit den Schwyzerörgelifrönde Rast-Wiss.

Sonntag, 11. Januar 2004
Ab 10 Uhr Brunch im Buureschopf mit der Dixieland-Jazzband "Les Moustaches". Gerne nehmen wir Ihre Reservation entgegen.

Wirtschaft zur Schlacht • 6204 Sempach • tel 041 460 19 33 • fax 041 460 47 33 • wirtschaft@schlacht.ch • www.schlacht.ch

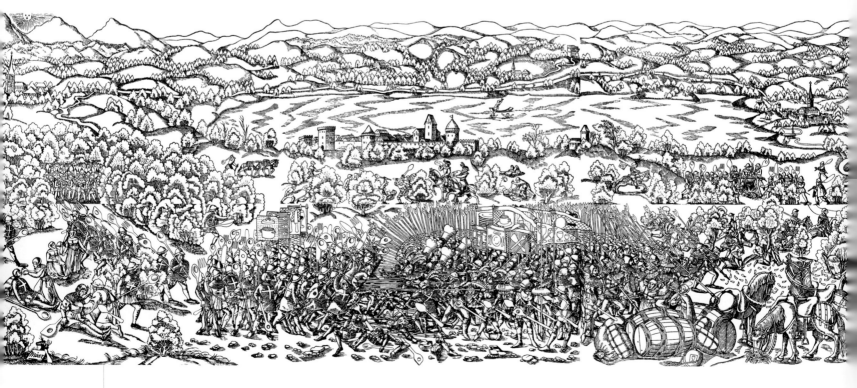

design firm	nothing
art director	Bastiaan van Rooden
designer	Bastiaan van Rooden
client	**nothing**

Something for nothing

The client, nothing, is a digital communication agency specializing in entertainment, website creation, and multimedia.

| the brief | The challenge was to create a complete new identity for nothing that would be applied to print and online functions. |
| the solution | According to the designer, the identity uses the outer space theme, giving freedom in a creative way—for example, "setting out on adventures, missions, planets, and so on." |

▲ Two versions of the nothing core identity show the Möbius-striplike *N*, stylized lowercase logotype, and strong orange color.

◄ The designer created a series of retro-futuristic rocket graphics to further the outer space concept and style palette developed for nothing.

▼ This image shows an example of the nothing identity applied to a promotional bag.

design firm | Team hp Schneider
art director | Hanspeter Schneider
designers | Hanspeter Schneider
 | Tina Grether
client | **Max Schweizer AG**

innen aussen
schweizer

Schweizer means Swiss

This firm of interior and exterior decorators, painters, plasterers, and insulation experts employs more than 150 specialist tradespeople who work on a wide variety of renovation and construction projects, from large public buildings to private homes. The name *Schweizer* literally means Swiss, in German.

the brief
The challenge was to create a cohesive, memorable, and versatile corporate identity that would engage and inspire confidence. The client prides itself on its cooperative management style; flat hierarchy; superior professional expertise; and open, collaborative approach to working with a discerning clientele. Applications of the identity would span print and promotional materials, online applications, livery vehicles, and construction signage.

the solution
A translation from the positioning brochure the designers created for the client clearly articulates the design rationale: "All-around Swiss. Our logo has numerous meanings—it stands for our care for both inner and outer values. It signals our well-rounded capabilities palette, the dynamic of our development process, and the interactive interplay among our various specialists." Indeed, it is not difficult to see this solution as quintessentially Swiss—from the symbol's distilled geometric form and red/white/gold simplicity to the use of lowercase Helvetica.

▲ This elegant and sophisticated mark graphically expresses the name's literal translation: "interior/exterior Swiss."

▼ ► The identity was applied to promotional giveaways, service vehicles, scaffold signage (for use on construction sites), and T-shirts in a simple Swiss manner that further exemplified the brand's essence.

▼ A theatrical portrayal of the range of decoration services the firm offers is used to communicate the key messages. A translated spread from the corporate brochure reads: "Ideas that inspire; best (trade) practices that convince; effort that truly achieves the goal: rooted in the trade tradition, open to the latest developments, and personally engaged—this is the posture that has signaled our essence and our commitment for more than 100 years…" The designers had great fun working closely with the client to design, build, orchestrate, and photograph the large indoor set. They noted, "The sparse, clean approach we used on the core identity allowed us to go over the top with this dramatic, creative representation of the client's capabilities. Both our client and our client's clients loved it."

design firm Team hp Schneider
art director Hanspeter Schneider
designer Hanspeter Schneider

client **Kulturverein Oxyd**

oxyd
oxyd

Oxidation as Identity

Oxyd is a unique culture club housed in an old, converted Swiss railway station, Bahhnof Wülfingen. Founded as a cooperative effort with sweat equity from local supporters, it has created a forum for contemporary art and a communication zone for cultural exchange. Featuring a gallery with four exhibit rooms, the repurposed building also boasts ten studios, three handcraft workstations, and a restoration service. During vernissages and exhibitions, visitors enjoy various culinary delights in connection with "conversations about art."

◄ Logo in Oxyd red and black.

◄ A certificate for members was created from laser-etched, rusted sheet metal.

► The corroded logotype fits perfectly on the weathered façade of the old railway station.

▼ House-brand labeling for Riesling and Sylvaner wines.

the brief

The challenge was clear and concise: "Oxyd is a place where content and structure evolve continually. The design task was to make this content manifest."

the solution

The designer describes the solution: "Photographs that contain oxidized materials will be used. The viewer's usual way of seeing will be disrupted intentionally. Values will be reassessed. It is an attempt to awaken memories, to free-associate, and to question things anew." In support of this stance, an appropriately "oxidized" logotype was created for use in black, white, and Oxyd red. The logotype always appears at a (slightly uncomfortable) 5-degree tilt. Other elements of Oxyd's visual palette include an Oxyd red mortise to hold definitive messages and miscellaneous information, and defined typography—only Boton Regular, Boton Bold, and the custom designed Oxyd font.

oxyd-font

ABCDEFGHIJKLMNOPQRSTUVWXYZ ÄÖÜ
abcdefghijklmnopqrstuvwxyz ß äöü çèàé
«» 0123456789
. , : , ! ? " ( ) _ - - — \ / ...

**Franz jagt im komplett
verwahrlosten
Taxi quer durch Bayern.**

The quick brown fox jumps
over the lazy dog.

Wofür hält mich die Dame?

Himmel – brennend

Tierversuche

Kasse

Getränkepalette

Weingenuss

Kunstmitbiss

Ein wegweisendes Geschenk:

oxyd **Gutschein**

Bestellungen: in der Galerie Oxyd oder Telefon 052 316 29 20

◄ Oxyd's house font provides an appropriate voice for the message.

◄ The designer also created beverage/wine and food menus.

▲ This ad promotes gift certificates—the translated headline reads, *A wayfinding gift.*

► An interior view of Oxyd shows the menus in use. Note the rusted member certificates lining the right wall.

China

area	9,597,000 km²
GDP, per capita	$4,700 USD
official language	*Putonghua* (Mandarin)
population	1.3 billion

The People's Republic of China (mainland China) is by every measure a giant. It's the most populous nation on Earth, inhabited by more than a fifth of all living humans. As the world's third-largest country by landmass, its resource-rich and varied terrain ranges from the world's highest mountains (Mount Everest in the Himalayas) to vast deserts (like the Gobi) to fertile plains—its diverse climates vary from subarctic in the north to tropical in the south.

To understand today's China, one must look back more than 3,000 years to the Bronze Age, when the roots of Chinese traditional class and social structure took hold and when a well-ordered societal framework was formed. Confucius (551–448 B.C.) and other philosophers of the time contributed doctrine aimed at providing harmony in thought and conduct, stressing virtue and natural order, love for humanity, ancestor worship, and reverence for parents. New ideas and new philosophies proliferated, including Taoism and legalism (featuring iron-fisted rule and suppression of dissent). As the class structures became legitimized, mutual societal obligations were defined, growing to become the "traditional" Chinese principles of ethics, morals, politics, and statesmanship.

With one of the world's greatest civilizations, China outpaced the rest of the world for thousands of years in the arts and sciences. It became a united independent empire in 210 B.C. at the dawn of the Iron Age. Chinese inventions included paper, printing, gunpowder, porcelain, silk, and the compass, to name just a few. In 2003, China became the third nation to send a human into space, a matter of great national pride.

In the nineteenth and early twentieth centuries, China was beset by civil unrest, major famines, military defeats, and foreign occupation. During the past one hundred years, China has experienced profound changes as it struggled through a transformation from a weak and defeated feudalistic society, distanced from the outside world, to a powerful, modern state with great global influence. Following the civil war of the 1940s, Mao Zedong was instrumental in transforming China into the collectivized Communist country it remains to this day.

Along with the remarkable social, industrial, and economic boom now taking place in China, graphic design is emerging as an exciting, new, and vigorous profession. It capitalizes on China's literate traditions and its expressive visual arts featuring a palette of riotous color and an intrinsic understanding of harmony (between point, line, surface, and textures) that informs use of contrast, symmetry, rhythm, and equilibrium. Differentiating much of Chinese culture (and design) is sensitivity to nature and a spiritual counterbalance in sharp contrast to the tactical intellectualism of European science and Western rationalism.

 = 1 million

design firm   Armstrong International Corporate Identity Co., Ltd.
art director   Zhang Wu
designer   Armstrong International Corporate Identity Co, Ltd.

client

China National Petroleum Corporation

China National Petroleum Corporation (CNPC) is the largest petroleum company in China and ranks forty-sixth in the top 500 corporations in the world. The designers were challenged not only to build an international image for the Chinese petroleum company but also to unite other branches and daughter companies. They were also asked to form a marketing strategy to unite the corporate and brand images. Using an image of Kunlun Mountain (the legendary source of all jade, the mythological ancestor to all other mountains, and the symbol of the Chinese nation) set against a rising sun, the emblem expresses the company's vision of "Starting from local, but facing international." To describe the mark as "Kunlun in sun rising" also emphasizes the corporation's core value—resources give us life and harmony.

design firm   Armstrong International Corporate Identity Co., Ltd.
art director   Zhang Wu
designer   Zhang Wu

client

New China Life Insurance Corporation

New China Life Insurance Corporation (NCL) is the first Chinese-foreign joint venture insurance company in China. The designer was tasked with building for the client a new image that would be effective in both the local and international insurance fields. The client asked that the design combine Chinese tradition and internationally advanced management systems. The solution characterizes the marketing style of the insurance company (stability and innovation) through the designer's use of a traditional Chinese artifact as well as "modern computer design language to exhibit modern technology and aesthetics." Here, the mark is shown in the form of a paperweight.

design firm · Armstrong International Corporate Identity Co., Ltd.
art director · Zhang Wu
designers · Zhang Wu
Liu Yue
Zhen Naixuan
Sun Yongjian

client · **The 6th Flower Exposition Committee**

Chengdu Flower Explosion

the brief · The designers were tasked with designing an identity to express the 6th Flower Exposition's thematic concept—flowers and the city of Chengdu. The client requested that the identity for the exposition have national and local characteristics as well as a festive, holiday image. This design submission was selected from some 3,000 designs.

the solution · Combining the Chinese characters for man (human being) and the number six, together with the city flower (lotus) of the exposition's hosting city, Chengdu, the designers created an image of an animated human and flower, appropriately representing the upcoming event and its anticipated success.

▲ The emblem/mascot developed for the festival combines Chinese characters and the lotus flower (representing the city of Chengdu), creating an interesting, colorful, and dynamic mark—undoubtedly suitable for this prominent flower festival.

◄ This poster for the festival literally expresses the concept of "dancing with flowers."

► This festival's poster keeps the color palette from the logo and uses an interesting cropping to capture the viewer's attention.

第|六|届|中|国|花|卉|博|览|会|
THE 6th CHINA FLOWER EXPO.

Chengdu 2005

Design by Wu Zhang   C.G. by Yongjian Sun   设计：张武   制作：孙永健

design firm   Armstrong International Corporate Identity Co., Ltd.
art director   Zhang Wu
designer   Guo ChunNing

client   **The 29th Olympic Games Committee**

The Olympics
Come to China

the brief   The challenge was to create a unique emblem that could represent not only the Olympic spirit but also China's long history. This emblem was chosen from 1,985 designs that were submitted by more than 500 well-known design firms.

the solution   The designer created an emblem imbued with meaning and possessing a very human quality (the character resembles a running man) to portray the joy and celebration of the Olympic Games. The red Chinese seal, which saw its origins in the Han dynasty (A.D. 206–220), bears the Chinese ideographic symbol for *Jing*, appropriately representing Beijing and China's rich cultural history. A bold brush-stroked logotype and the well-known Olympic rings round out the event's composite signature.

▲ This unique emblem was developed for the Beijing 2008 Summer Olympics.

► Design of an identity for the Olympic Games is a massive project spanning years of work and involving signage, promotional items, and identity applications. A sampling of various applications, including venue identification, festive signage, communications, licensed branding, and promotional items is shown at right.

Cuba—think Buena Vista Social Club, Cohiba cigars, Habana Club rum, warm smiles, and sunsets along the Malecón.

Cuba

area	110,900 km²
GDP, per capita	$2,700 USD
official language	Spanish
population	11.3 million

Cuba is the largest island nation in the Caribbean—actually, an archipelago of two large islands and 4,195 keys, islands, and islets. Its original Amerindian population (Taino, Siboney, and Guanajatabey) came under Spanish control in the sixteenth century and were soon exterminated and replaced with African slaves. These slaves provided the workforce for the extraction of gold and minerals and for labor to run the massive sugar, coffee, and tobacco plantations. The colony's struggle for independence from Spain began in 1868, and continued until independence was granted in 1902, though the United States then dominated Cuban affairs until popular uprisings resulted in a rebel army victory for true independence in 1959. (The United States still occupies Guantanamo on the eastern tip of the island.) Influential in this overthrow of foreign control was the guerilla movement led by Che Guevara, Camilo Cienfuegos, Raul Castro, and Fidel Castro—the latter has held the country together to this day under what is still called the revolutionary government.

Following the failed Bay of Pigs invasion attempt (an attack by expatriots supported by American warships and the C.I.A.), Castro turned to the Soviet Union for support against further aggression from its giant neighbor. This in turn led to the Cuban Missile Crisis of 1962, and the country's formal adoption of Communism. The U.S. embargo of Cuba began in 1961 and continues to this day, a factor that has polarized much of Latin America (and socialist sentiment around the world) in favor of the Cuban underdog.

Life in modern Cuba is an enigma. Though the population is poor and lacks the consumer goods found elsewhere, Cubans can boast the best education in Latin America, have universal health care, and have developed a remarkable resilience in the face of economic difficulties. When the billions of dollars of Soviet subsidies ended in 1990, Cuba found itself in a deep recession—tourism has been developed in compensation, with the country's exquisite beaches, rich historic sites, and Old Havana providing attractive destinations. Cuba's answer to the withdrawal of Soviet agricultural chemical imports led to a total restructuring of the country's formerly large-scale, mechanized, chemical-dependent agricultural model. A massive organic initiative has converted the entire country to strictly organic production—by law, only organic farming is now permitted.

Cuba enjoys a remarkably rich and varied flora and fauna, supported by the archipelago's warm waters, favorable currents, winds, and migratory patterns of bird species. When Columbus landed in Cuba in 1492 (thinking that he had found Asia), the aboriginal people were already growing tobacco. Today, Cuba is world famous for its cigars, rum, coffee, music (habanera, son, guajira, samba, timba, Latin jazz), and eco- and health tourism. As well as its revolutionary zeal, the country has been exporting medical, educational, and nutritional aid to underprivileged nations in Latin America and Africa since the 1960s.

✦ = 1 million

art director Santiago Pujol
designer Santiago Pujol

client

Doctor Café
This privately owned restaurant and specialty coffee shop requested that the design have a handmade feel and reflect qualities of coffee, such as color, taste, and aroma. The solution met the client's needs through a calligraphic logotype, swash capitals, and interlacing ornaments. A drop shadow emphasizes the desired effects and adds dimensionality.

art director Santiago Pujol
designer Santiago Pujol

client

Anima Ensemble
Anima Ensemble is a chamber music group that plays classical as well as Cuban music with a "different flavor." The brief called for a logo that represented the spirit of the group to be used on CDs, programs, posters, and other print materials. The solution uses an old-fashioned typeface with an enclosing form, rendered in rich, warm tones and accented with a drop shadow.

designer Osué Rodríguez

client

San Lechon
San Lechon (Saint Lechon) is a Cuban cafeteria serving typical Cuban pork sandwiches as its main attraction. The logo uses a simple illustration and a compelling tag line to differentiate the establishment—"Angelic pork sandwiches."

designer Osué Rodríguez

client

Jazz Association
Coco Fest is a jazz festival in Coco Keys, a tourist resort in northern Cuba. The logo comprises a unique, multicolored, and outlined logotype with an engaging festive type treatment.

designer	Liber Lannes
client	**Centro Promotor del Humor**

The Center for Humor Promotion is an agency for actors and their projects. The logo uses the comic symbolism of a banana, partially peeled to represent a court jester's hat.

design firm	Grafos Design
designer	Liber Lannes
client	**Cubalse Company—Multimarcas**

Multimarcas is an automotive dealership. Their logo uses a monogram *M* reversed inside a blue circle, which is placed above the name set in all cap sans serif type—bold, timeless, and functional.

art director	Liber Lannes
designer	Liber Lannes
client	**Premios Lucas**

Premios Lucas (the Lucas Award) for the best Cuban music video clips is an annual ceremony. The event's logo uses an attitude-rich illustration depicting a black sheep along with a pixellated typeface to create an interesting, memorable mark.

design firm	Consejo Nacional de las Artes Plásticas (in-house design department)
art director	Laura Llópiz
designer	Laura Llópiz
client	**Consejo Nacional de las Artes Plásticas (National Visual Arts Council, Ministry of Culture)**

The National Visual Arts Council needed a logo for a visual arts editorial house. The logo had to be easy to reproduce in various sizes and on various surfaces. The in-house designer's solution uses a square to represent the "piece of art" and surrounding text to represent the "editorial approach"— a clean, simple, and effective solution.

CUBADEPORTES s.a.

art director | Luis Alonso
designer | Luis Alonso

client

Cubadeportes

Cubadeportes commercializes the knowledge of Cuban sportsmen "based on the tradition, experience, and prestigious knowledge of Cuban sport all over the world." The design challenge was to portray the competitive spirit of the enterprise and its Cuban origin and also to imply that Cuban advisers and trainers are the best in each of their specialties. The solution builds on the letter *D* from *Deporte* (Sport) and shows the silhouette of a racer, signaling speed, agility, and readiness to win the gold. The additional colors of red, blue, and white represent the Cuban flag.

Sol Meliá

art director | Luis Alonso
designer | Luis Alonso

client

Sol Meliá

Sol Meliá is one of the most important Spanish tourism investors in Cuba, administering hotels in various areas—the cities, the countryside, the beaches, and the keys. The challenge was to show the special spirit of the *Cayos* (Keys) destination—waves, happiness, and holidays. The solution uses expressive calligraphy to showcase the initial capital *C* as a wave form and a representation of the jagged seashore. Colors represent the main attractions: the sea and the extensive beaches.

Mitos en el Caribe

design firm | Casa de las Américas (in-house design department)
art director | Pepe Menéndez
designer | Pepe Menéndez

client

**Casa de las Américas—
Mitos en el Caribe (Myths in the Caribbean)**

Casa de las Américas is a cultural institution that promotes the culture of Latin American and Caribbean countries. Mitos en el Caribe is an event centered on the culture of the Caribbean region. The diversity of activities included theoretical debates on literature, music, sociology, and plastic arts exhibitions. Representation of the event's broad scope and of Caribbean culture itself were the main challenges of the project, along with the fact that the audience consisted of artists, researchers, and a learned public. The design solution uses a human element (the hand) to link the topics of myths with the lives of people, their traditions, and their relationship with nature. The hand's decoratively colored curve forms recall the sea that flows between the islands of the Caribbean.

art director | Pepe Menéndez
designer | Pepe Menéndez

client

**Instituto Superior Latinoamericano de Ajedrez
(Latin American Chess Institute)**

Instituto Superior Latinoamericano de Ajedrez (ISLA) is a chess school created to develop the talent of young players. The school director, a prestigious Cuban Grand Master, wanted the logo to show the abstraction of chess, not the game's pieces. The design solution attempts to express the complexity of spatial relations and the strategies of chess. The combination of the acronym's four letters integrates the white

A popular tourist destination, the Czech Republic is renowned for its architecture, art, poetry, castles, Prague's ornate structures (like the world-famous Charles Bridge), and, of course, Pilsen, where Pilsner beer originated.

Czech Republic

area	78,900 km²
GDP, per capita	$15,300 USD
official language	Czech
population	10.3 million

The Czech Republic (or *Czechia*, as the Ministry of Foreign Affairs prefers) is a landlocked country in Central Europe bordered by Poland to the north, Germany to the northwest and west, Austria to the south, and Slovakia to the east. Historic Praha (Prague) is the capital, the largest city, and a major tourist attraction. The country is composed of two older regions, Bohemia and Moravia, and part of a third one, Silesia.

A democratic parliamentary nation, the Czech Republic became independent in 1993 after a peaceful split with the Slovak Republic, its counterpart in the former Czechoslovakia. In 1989, Czechoslovakia gained its freedom through a peaceful "Velvet Revolution." Czechoslovakia was first formed following the Austrian-Hungarian state after World War I in 1918, and then was reconstituted within the Soviet sphere of influence after World War II, after being occupied and annexed by Germany from 1938 to the end of the war. Much of the world remembers the (televised) 1968 invasion by Warsaw Pact troops that ended the efforts of the country's leaders to liberalize party rule and create "socialism with a human face" during the Prague Spring.

The Czech Republic joined NATO in 1999, and the European Union in 2004. Long one of the most stable and prosperous of the post-Communist states, the Czech Republic has been recovering from recession since mid-1999. Current growth comes from exports to the E.U. (especially Germany) and foreign investment, and domestic demand is reviving. Moves to complete banking, telecommunications, and energy privatization are adding to foreign investment, alongside intensified restructuring among large enterprises and banks and improvements in the financial sector.

= 1 million

designer Kateřina Šachová
client   **Faculty of Applied Arts and Design**
          University of J. E. Purkyně, Ústí nad Labem

The Art of Chemistry

the brief The challenge was to develop a conceptual image for an academic catalog to attract students and to clearly project the character and atmosphere of the art school.

the solution The concept draws on the school's locale of the Czech city Ústí nad Labem, which is known for its chemical industry. The solution builds on this "chemical" inspiration—experiments, actions, and reactions. Experimentation is the basis of all art schools, so the school could be positioned as a type of laboratory where students and teachers search, create, and experiment. The design approach uses an open, colorful system of scientific elements, symbols, and molecules, representing various elements that are independent yet work together and influence each other—much like studios and individuals in the art school.

The conceptual image developed for the school's recruitment literature uses "the language of science" inspired by the city's core industry in an engaging, colorful, and unexpected manner. Shown above, below, and at right are a minifolder, a catalog cover, and a series of catalog spreads.

design firm | Studio Najbrt, s.r.o.
designers | Zuzana Lednická
Pavel Lev
Mikuláš Macháček
Ales Najbrt

client | **Magistrát hlavního města Prahy
(The Municipal Council of the City of Prague)**

The logo developed for the city of Prague, featuring the city's name in four languages.

A Capital Identity

the brief The designers' task was to develop a logo and visual corporate identity for Prague, the capital of the Czech Republic. This identity was to project the city in a contemporary manner yet needed to work well alongside the historically established heraldry. A specific condition set by the client was the necessity to use Prague's heraldic colors, red and yellow.

the solution The designers developed a logo using four variations of the city's name. These variations represent all of the languages using the Latin alphabet, representing the way *Prague* would be pronounced in each language. As stated by the designers, "The logo and the corporate identity project the 'approachability' of the city and its desire to communicate with the visitors and guests. We also meant to express that Prague has always been a center where many cultures and nationalities meet."

City of Prague

Rada hlavního města Prahy
Primátor hlavního města Prahy
Kancelář primátora
Zasedací síně
Reprezentační prostory primátora

City Hall of Prague

Ředitel magistrátu
Technická správa komunikací
Městská hygienická stanice
Městská policie
Hlavní podatelna
Tiskové středisko
Odbor Public Relations
Hospodářská správa

Hlavní město Praha

Rada hlavního města Prahy
Primátor hlavního města Prahy
Kancelář primátora
Zasedací síně
Reprezentační prostory primátora

Magistrát hlavního města
Prahy

Ředitel magistrátu
Technická správa komunikací
Městská hygienická stanice
Městská policie
Hlavní podatelna
Tiskové středisko
Odbor Public Relations
Hospodářská správa

More samples of the identity in application
are shown here—pylon signage in front
of municipal buildings, sewer (manhole)
covers, and information kiosks.

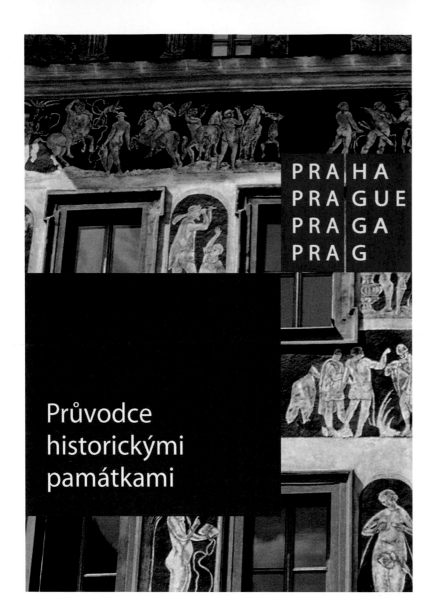

PRA HA
PRA GUE
PRA GA
PRA G

Průvodce
historickými
památkami

◄ The identity appears in many applications—municipal publications, annual reports, and brochures.

► The identity was also applied to fleet vehicles, waste services, and municipal buildings.

PRA HA
PRA GUE
PRA GA
PRA G

Průvodce
městskou
hromadnou
dopravou

Průvodce
technickými
památkami

PRA HA
PRA GUE
PRA GA
PRA G

Germany—think Oktoberfest, the Black Forest, Autobahns, the Volkswagen (and its highly engineered cousins Porsche, Mercedes, Audi, and BMW), Rhineland wines, lager beer, hearty food, and jovial times.

Germany

area	357,000 km²
GDP, per capita	$26,200 USD
official language	German
population	82.4 million

Germany is a prosperous, industrious country in Western Europe and a founding member of the European Union. Germany has the continent's largest economy and is its most populous nation. As such, the mainly Christian federal parliamentary democratic republic plays a key role in the continent's economic, political, and defense organizations. Measured by gross domestic product Germany is the world's third-largest economy, following the United States and Japan. As of 2004, Germany was also the world's largest exporter for the second year in a row, despite the skyrocketing strength of the euro. Germany's major trading partners include France, the United States, the United Kingdom, Italy, and the Netherlands.

Germany became a united empire in 1871. European power struggles then immersed the country in two devastating world wars in the first half of the twentieth century and left Germany occupied by the victorious allied powers of the United States, United Kingdom, France, and the Soviet Union in 1945. In 1949, it was split into the Federal Republic of Germany and the German Democratic Republic (GDR). The GDR rejoined the Federal Republic of Germany in 1990s unification—many will recall the ensuing fall of the Berlin Wall. Since then, Germany has expended considerable funds to bring eastern productivity and wages up to western standards.

Germany has a rich artistic and creative history, which factors large in recent design history, thanks to influential movements such as the Bauhaus. German manufacturers are renowned for their well-designed and efficiently engineered products (for example, Krupp, Braun, Siemens, and Porsche).

= 1 million

design firm   Helmut Langer Design
art director   Helmut Langer
designer   Helmut Langer

client   **United Nations Educational Scientific and
Cultural Organization (UNESCO)**

UNESCO's world campaign *Freedom of Expression, Press, and Democracy*
called for a corporate identity to "symbolize freedom of expression, press, and
democracy for global use." The solution was a "super symbol" comprising a
dove, for freedom; a pen, for expression, writing, and the press; and a hand,
representing voting. Primary colors, plus black and white, represent the five
continents (à la the Olympic rings), and the overall composition signals global
interconnection through diverse elements forming a common whole.

design firm   Nina David Kommunikationsdesign
art director   Nina David
designer   Nina David

client   **Nina David Kommunikationsdesign**

Telling Her Own Story

the brief   The challenge for this young designer was to develop a corporate
identity—using only type—for her independent studio.

the solution   The designer chose to limit her identity to a highly typographic approach,
reflecting the main focus of her work—developing typefaces and
typographic projects. She chose the color pink "as a modern derivative
of the former 'typographic red.'" To make the identity more personal, she
developed a unique typeface, Mein Schatz (My Darling), and applied this to
all stationery elements.

Nina David's stationery is distinct and visually
engaging. Pink, gray, and white dominate, and
typographic patterns adorn the various print pieces.
Rounded, die-cut corners on cards and a series of
small "enclosure chips" bearing individual messages
(Many Greetings, RSVP, and so on) further the
stationery's tactile interest. A small booklet entitled
Font Report displays typographic fonts developed by
the designer and continues her pink theme.

design firm   sh&r
art directors   Daryl Roske
    Bernd Sanmann
designer   Daryl Roske
client   **Advocard**

Fully Covered

Advocard, a twenty-year-old German legal-protection insurance company, offers insurance for private individuals, covering expenses of attorneys and legal fees resulting from court cases. Its target audience is broad, ranging from young professionals to senior citizens.

the brief

Advocard sales figures had been declining in recent years, and intensive market research indicated a need to strengthen appeal to a younger market. Therefore, the objective was to reposition the brand with stronger appeal to a younger and more progressive audience. A new corporate identity was to be a visible starting point for this process.

the solution

As described by the designers, "The use of cards is familiar to everyone, from customer cards to credit cards. They just work. And so does Advocard. Advocard was the first player in the market to give out cards to its customers, to represent its insurance services. So we made the card the symbol for the brand. The shape of the logo—a mental link to the always ready-to-use card itself—is integrated into all Advocard communications."

▲ Shown above is the Advocard customer card, front and back.

▼ Advocard print applications and environmental signage further the Advocard card concept. The color palette and typeface is consistent throughout to provide a cohesive and memorable identity, and the card shape communicates effectively, regardless of size or medium.

design firm | SIGN.ID
art director | Dirk Nolte
designer | Dirk Nolte

client | **SIGN.ID**

Outside of the Box

SIGN.ID is a small, creative design agency specializing in corporate identity and corporate design with a highly creative aspect.

the brief
The self-imposed challenge: "To inspire companies to think outside the box and establish an agency known for its creative approach to designing identities and other tasks."

the solution
The solution, as described by the designer, was "to build a world in which one could immerse oneself—if only for a few seconds—during which time you encounter the company." This solution was achieved by means of a whimsical, creative, and unexpected palette of visual elements, graphics, and typography, all woven together with scamless fluidity to create "a world outside of the box."

design firm   Peter Schmidt Studios Group GmbH

client   **Design Zentrum Nordrhein Westfalen**

reddot design award

reddot design museum

Top Awards

The Design Zentrum (Center) Nordrhein Westfalen is a promotional design entity situated in Essen, Germany. Since 1955, the Center has held an annual award (named the Red Dot Award in 1992) for product design and design excellence. Today, it is one of the oldest, most renowned design competitions in the world. Since 1997, the Center and the Red Dot Design Museum have been housed in the former boiler house of the remarkable Zeche Zollverein, an outstanding Bauhaus-era mine complex recently named a UNESCO World Cultural Heritage site—one of only ten modern architectural projects in the world to be accorded this honor. The unique Red Dot Design Museum displays the world's largest and most unusual exhibition of contemporary design. More than an acre (4,000 square meters) of floor space provides a showcase for approximately 1,000 products from across the globe—all of them winners of the Red Dot Award. Each year, 120,000 visitors explore designed artifacts of daily life, such as kitchen utensils, furniture, cars, office furnishings, fashion accessories, and tools.

▲ The internationally recognized seal of quality for award winning product and communication design is the Red Dot, designed by Peter Schmidt in 2000.

► These images show the gift shop and bookstore/café at the Red Dot design museum and exterior views of the Red Dot design museum's entrance in historic Zeche Zollverein.

Design Zentrum
Nordrhein Westfalen

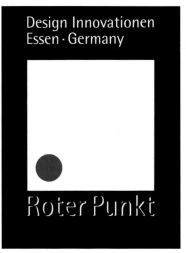

▲ The logo of the Design Zentrum Nordrhein Westfalen was designed by Otl Aicher in 1991, and the first Red Dot symbol for awards conferred by the Design Zentrum Nordrhein Westfalen as designed by Kurt Weidemann in 1994.

the brief

In 1992, the design prize warded by the center since 1955 gained a face: the Red Dot. The first award symbol designed by the renowned Otl Aicher integrated the signet of the center and the stylized red dot taken from it. To distinguish the competition's award symbol from the center's signet, Kurt Weidemann reworked the Red Dot symbol in 1994. Then, the competition grew to span the world. Increased internationalization and the convergence of the disciplines of product and communication design finally encouraged the center to unify the brand marks of the two competitions for global use. What had begun in Germany as the Roter Punkt was quickly accepted throughout the world, spawning a host of national variants: "Punto Rosso" in Italian, "Point Rouge" in French, and, of course, the "Red Dot" in English. So many local variants made maintaining a uniform image difficult for the center and its award on the international design scene. So, at the end of the 1990s, it became clear that a single international name would be needed to preserve the identity and profile of the competition. In 2000, communication designer Peter Schmidt of Hamburg was commissioned by the center to provide the Red Dot with an internationally recognizable and coherent brand image.

the solution

The new Red Dot was created in a distinctive world-encompassing visual form and was systematically developed into a brand, meeting with almost immediate worldwide acceptance. The new logo was especially striking and dynamic in new media, where the mark lends itself to an animated presence. The two (previously separate) competitions for product design and communication design were subsequently brought together under the single umbrella of the Red Dot Award. Today, manufacturers and designers use the Red Dot both nationally and internationally as a successful communication tool to promote their award-winning products and to position themselves as quality and design leaders.

Design
Innovationen
Jahrbuch
2004

reddot edition

reddot award: product design

◄ These images feature some views of the exhibition and display spaces at the Red Dot design museum.

▲ The cover of the Red Dot's annual Design Innovation Yearbook features a detail of the award-winning Adidas soccer shoes.

► An exhibition of the Red Dot's "best of the best" showcases Adidas soccer shoes and Buchstabenmöbel's letter-shaped storage units.

design firm	Ständige Vertretung
art directors	Nick Kapica
	Andy Lawrence
designers	Nick Kapica
	Andy Lawrence
client	**SXF Flughafen Berlin Schönefeld** **(Berlin Brandenburg Airport)**

Berlin's Airport Takes Off

the brief   The challenge was to create a new identity and rebranding for Berlin's rapidly growing international airport. The identity would be applied to building signage, the environment, advertising, and collateral. The identity was also to be integrated into a new sign system in and around the airport.

the solution   As described by the design team, "The aim was to communicate movement and dynamism. A dot matrix was produced to generate the logotype and other elements, such as the pictograms. This matrix enabled the SFX logotype to be animated. Dots were used to create lines, arrows, and patterns, hinting at runway lights and modern communication systems." All graphic elements were based on a 21- by 21-unit dot grid. A six-color palette was selected (red, bright blue, dark blue, green, gray, and yellow), and the designers defined three font weights of Foundry Sterling as the official typographic voice for the airport.

SXF
berlin
brandenburg
airport

▲ The SXF airport logo was constructed from the core dot matrix.

▼ A concise leaflet introduces the airport's new look and feel and explains the identity's intent—to develop a persona seen as "competent, dynamic, fast, clever, and smart."

◄ Spreads from the identity standards manual show the dot matrix construction of the airport's new visual vocabulary and instructions for use of navigational signage.

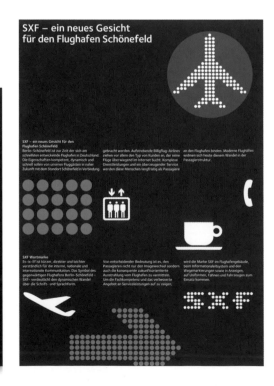

Applications of the bold new identity include signage, banners, airport livery, and environmental graphics.

Denmark

area	43,100 km²
GDP, per capita	$28,800 USD
official language	Danish
population	5.4 million

Formerly the seat of Viking raiders, and later a major northern European power, the Kingdom of Denmark has evolved into a modern, prosperous nation that is participating in the general political and economic integration of Europe. Denmark's thoroughly modern market economy features high-tech agriculture, up-to-date small-scale and corporate industry, extensive government welfare measures, comfortable living standards, a stable currency, and a high dependence on foreign trade. Denmark is a net exporter of food and energy and has a comfortable balance-of-payments surplus.

Geographically the smallest Nordic country, this largely Christian state and parliamentary democratic monarchy gained its independence around A.D. 800. Bordering the Baltic Sea and the North Sea, Denmark consists of a peninsula attached to Northern Germany, named Jutland, and many smaller islands. Denmark is north of Germany and Poland, southwest of Sweden, and south of Norway. The Faroe Islands and Greenland are autonomous overseas dependencies of the Kingdom. Denmark joined NATO in 1949 and the E.E.C. (now the E.U.) in 1973.

Danes are famous in many fields of endeavor, including writer Hans Christian Andersen, known for his fairy tales such as *The Emperor's New Clothes* and *The Ugly Duckling*. Influential individuals such as architect and designer Arne Jacobsen and designer Georg Jensen have left a rich design legacy. A powerhouse of modern design, Denmark has become renowned over the past century for its art, architecture, interiors, furniture, appliances, housewares, jewelry, and other designed objects.

= 1 million

RAR LYD®

design firm   Designbolaget
art director   Claus Due
designer   Claus Due

client

Rar Lyd
The client is a record company that concentrates on acoustic, singer/song writing, and folk music. Rar Lyd, which means "feel-good sounds," targets people who don't like modern music, hip-hop, and heavy rock—people who want to relax when they listen to music. The designer explains: "We liked that the client told us his audience were people who did not like modern music. We found that funny, so we made the ear plugs."

taburet®

design firm   Designbolaget
art director   Claus Due
designer   Claus Due

client

Taburet
Taburet, a furniture retailer, wanted a logo that was unique, and humor was important to them. They also wanted a logo that could be printed on T-shirts and mugs. In the designer's words, "Taburet means "stool" (*tabouret*, or three legs). The audience is people who buy designer furniture. When we thought of furniture, we thought of shapes and textures. Combine that thought with a friendly looking mascot and you have a sheep. The name of the company represents 'tabouret,' so the sheep has only three legs."

TIM BUY

design firm   Goodmorning Technology—GMTN
art director   Jacob Thuesen
designers   Jacob Thuesen
Kristian Bengtson
Frederik Andersen

client

Tim Buy
Tim Buy is a Danish company that buys, sells, and distributes lumber. The designer was asked to create a logotype to reflect the company's profile. The solution is a logotype with an industrial look and arrows depicting the flow of lumber transactions. A white zigzag line cuts through the letters, "telling the story of the sawmill and the cutting of lumber." The colors reference the green of leaves and the black of tree trunks.

HJERTEFORENINGEN

design firm   Krogh & Co.
art directors   Lene Perez
Dorte Krogh
designers   Lene Perez
Dorte Krogh

client

Danish Heart Foundation
For almost fifty years, the Danish Heart Foundation, Hjerteforeningen, had used the same logo to represent the support organization for patients with heart disease. The designers state that, "This redesign of the logo is modern, possesses energy and dynamism, but is still recognizable to those familiar with the former version. The little heart icon has taken on a new form to reflect the physiological circulation of the heart."

design firm	Designbolaget
art director	Claus Due
designer	Claus Due
client	**First Booking**

First Booking for Talent

First Booking is a talent agency that represents stylists, makeup artists, and special-effects people. Their audience is creative people, mostly advertising agencies, photographers, and film/movie companies.

the brief
The identity had to be appealing to creative people, the firm's clients. First Booking is run by a woman, so "a feminine touch" was requested.

the solution
As described by the designer, "We liked the idea of having a link between the stylists and the creative client. When stylists approach an assignment, they begin with an empty sheet. They then bring in the 'color'—the same as when we were kids and painted-by-number in our children's books. Creatives should feel the need to fill in the fields. It starts with number one, 1 = first, as in First Booking." The design solution engages the audience to explore further and to "fill in the colors."

▲ The wordmark replaces the number "1" in place of the first "I."

▼ The logo is shown in application along with the paint-by-number concept and the floral graphic representing the "feminine touch" requested by the client. The distinctive artist's book is a deck of notched, two-sided talent cards held together with a wide black rubber band.

design firm | Kontrapunkt

client | **Danske Bank—Danish Bank Group**

Typography You Can Bank On

the brief | The challenge was to create a consistent visual identity for the Danske Bank Group that could be applied readily to a wide range of materials so that the bank could differentiate itself visually from other players in the market.

the solution | Kontrapunkt developed a unique presence for the bank by using a distinctive typographic voice, Danske (Danish). As described by the designers, "The typography is an essential identity-bearing element in the visual presence of the entire group and is a stringent, relatively easy way for the bank to differentiate itself. Danske, which represents an entire font family, expresses the fundamental concept of the entire design program by virtue of its simplicity, its horizontal design, and its subdued and timeless expression. The typography is used throughout the group, thereby ensuring visual coherence and unity. Danske brings identity and ownership to all of the bank's written messages and is a refined way to brand the group—as well as in cases where the Danske Bank logo does not appear."

The Danske typeface acts as the bank's identifying DNA, forming its modular logo, and is equally effective in detailed print applications and environmental signage.

design firm	VIA
art director	Sune Kjems
designer	Sune Kjems
client	**Hotel Pro Forma**

Design Pro Forma

Hotel Pro Forma is a Danish performance art group that displaces the notion of traditional theater, blurring the line between art and nonart, theater and nontheater, between the physical and metaphysical expression. Their performances involve not only content but also space.

the brief — The designer was approached to design an identity for a performance by Hotel Pro Forma, *Jesus_C_Odd_Size*, an exhibition of international contemporary art. The identity would be applied across multiple media.

the solution — The typographic solution sets large, sans serif green type against a black background. In addition to providing strong contrast, this combination evokes an association with technology and the computer screen. The color palette and typographic identifier were kept consistent in all applications to create a cohesive overall identity.

▲ The performance by Hotel Pro Forma was accompanied by an aggressive guerrilla advertising campaign combining street posters and trash bin "wraps."

◀ The typographic identifier for *Jesus_C_Odd_Size*, a performance by Hotel Pro Forma.

▼ For the exhibition, the event's typographic identity was projected onto the side of a building—a highly appropriate solution for the nature of the client's activities.

▼ Here, the typographic identity for the performance is applied to a flyer.

A PERFORMANCE BY HOTEL PRO FORMA
JESUS_C_ODD_SIZE
AN EXHIBITION OF INTERNATIONAL CONTEMPORARY ART

design firm | Krogh & Co.
art directors | Heidi Kure
| Dorte Krogh
designer | Heidi Kure
client | **Royal Copenhagen porcelain factory**

Updating a Classic

the brief | The designer was commissioned to redesign the name and product identity of a thirty-five-year-old classic dinner service made by the Danish Royal Copenhagen porcelain factory.

the solution | The designer explains, "The original name of the service, 'White Pot,' has now become 'White Pot—Urban Living.' The dinner service is a market success in an extended range with matching items like shopping bags and a cookbook."

▲ The redesigned name and identity of the classic dinner service has a clean, updated look, appealing to the tastes and sensibilities of young, contemporary executives.

▼ The identity is applied to a range of materials, from shopping bags to product packaging. The monochromatic palette, photographic treatment, and refined typography are kept consistent throughout to provide a visually cohesive product identity.

design firm   Kontrapunkt

client   **Danish State Institutions (various)**

The Crowning Touch

"If a piece of paper carries the crown, the Danish state vouches for it," explain the designers. "Only state institutions may use the crown, a symbol of supreme authority and the sovereign Danish nation." The "living symbol" of the Danish crown saw its introduction in 1671 with King Christian V; since that time, it has been identified by its five visible braces, orb, and cross. New versions of the crown require the approval of the heraldic consultant at the National Archives of Denmark.

The work shown here is a small sampling of design for Danish state institutions and crown agencies by Kontrapunkt's principals Bo Linnemann and Kim Meyer Anderson, supported by a group of participating designers too long to list. The work that began in the early 1990s still continues—Kontrapunkt recently developed the identity for the police intelligence agency and is now working with the Ministry of Defense.

▲ A sampling of the crowns designed for the various Danish institutions. The crown for the Danish Ministry for Education incorporates an open book, and the Ministry of Housing and Urban Affairs has roof gables. Each institution has its own crown, and each crown is imbued with individual meaning. The crowns work as a whole to clearly signal the authority and identity of the Danish nation, yet at the same time become living symbols that identify and relate to specific topics or functions.

◄ Shown here is the application of the logo designed for the Royal Theatre on corporate stationery.

Master Brand

Administrators

Services

KULTUR
MINISTERIET

NATIONALMUSEET

UNDERVISNINGS
MINISTERIET

DSB

UDENRIGSMINISTERIET

DET
KGL
BIB
LIO
TEK

BY & BOLIG
MINISTERIET

DET KONGELIGE TEATER

FINANSMINISTERIET

POST

KUL
TUR
ARV

PET

ØKONOMI- OG ERHVERVSMINISTERIET

An organizational chart shows the public brand architecture and the relationship of the master brand to administrative bodies and public services for which Kontrapunkt has provided identity design services.

the brief

This process—"not just a project," as Linneman explains—began in the early 1990s, with the desire of several state institutions to move from the prevailing, bureaucratic perception of civil servants as unquestionable authorities to being more accurately projected as responsive providers of public services. The individual institutions now had more accountability, and they desired more visibility, so "individualized identity" became important. Driven by massive growth of the public sector, a shift to decentralized power, a perceived need for a Danish identity (among other things, in the face of the internationalizing influence of the European Union), and a movement described by some as a "lightness of democracy," Kontrapunkt began branding Danish institutions "with a contemporary expression combining openness with natural authority." The massive popularity of the royal family played a role, as did the succinct realization that "the modern-day Dane is in search of an identity. We are not equipped for a life as nationless modernists," as stated by the designers. It's important to understand the context for this process. Unlike neighboring Sweden, which has always been known as "a planning culture," Denmark has a history as an oft-conquered, adoptive "trading nation," without a fixed concept for governmental institutions.

the solution

As stated by the principals in the introductory sentences of *The Crowning Touch*, a book illustrating this remarkable body of work, "Our approach used the powerful expressiveness and idiom of heraldry in a new way, giving the crown a new content. The crown used to signal unrestricted power, and later, stuffy departments, but it now signals a dialogue-seeking democratic state—the property of the people. The crown has also become a symbol of Danish identity in a time of internationalism and rootlessness." The crown is a symbol of quality, one that many private companies would love to be able to use. As stated by the Linnemann, "We have been participants in creating a paradox: that a monarchic symbol can be evolved to represent a democratic state. This 'closing of the gap' between the state and its constituents could be seen as a natural Danish trait. For example, you can meet our prime minister while he is bicycling through the center of Copenhagen." Today, the crown has truly become a symbol of Danes and the Danish—it is experienced daily by the citizenry and is woven into their social and cultural fabric. Widely recognized for the fundamental change that their work has made in the public perception of the role of Danish institutions and their impact on everyday life, Kontrapunkt's work was lauded by the late Jens Bernsen, director of the Danish Design Centre, as follows: "No other design company has understood the nature of the task (of creating distinction within organizational identity) and embraced it more closely than Kontrapunkt has. Over the years, this [understanding] has produced a royal parade of design programs appearing both obvious and unquestionable, the marks of the true master. Only one ministry could have a logotype that is handwritten with a matchstick dipped in ink. And only one national institution could have a logo that features a crown with connotations of the jester's cap and bells, of dignity and comedy combined, so that is what they got." Linnemann is more modest in acknowledging the work's success when he explains, "Other Danish design firms respect the approach we have taken, and the work that they do now (for crown institutions) is indistinguishable from Kontrapunkt's."

► *The Crowning Touch*, published by the Danish Design Centre, chronicles a decade of identity design by Kontrapunkt for Danish ministries and crown corporations. The crown on the cover (top) is the identifier designed in 1996 for the Royal Theatre—look closely, and you will see the hat of a court jester in the braced crown.

► The identity developed for Post Denmark, an independent public corporation that emerged from its former role as a government service in 1995, is shown here as signage and the ubiquitous postal boxes that now punctuate Denmark's cities and towns.

▲ This logo was developed for the Ministry of Culture. In explaining the rationale for the expressive signature, the designers say, "The handwritten 'culture' refers to top athletes and performers handing out autographs, painters signing pictures, and graffiti freaks leaving their tags. But it also includes the 'man on the street' or 'Joe Six-Pack,' spontaneously and hastily jotting down something." The crown; the official state colors; and the classical, centered typography refer both to the ministry's status as a state authority and to a veneration for tradition and Danish culture. "The direct and expressive logo makes the letter stand out from the stack of mail. The logo signals that the ministry is an active, dialogue-seeking sender, and consequently, the linguistic style must be open and direct as well."

► This monumental sign for the National Museum serves a distinct function— a good example of the thoughtful, innovative attention to detail evident throughout the range of projects Kontrapunkt has undertaken for Danish institutions. As explained by the designers, "The yard in front of the entrance to the museum needed 'furnishing.' The solution was a monumental granite stone that welcomes visitors—a landmark and a guide that acts as the museum's handshake with the guests. The noble, durable materials express quality and history, whereas the shape and the composition speak a more modern tongue. The crown is cast in bronze, the stone is polished, and the map that shows the museum's overall layout is sandblasted into the granite." The massive slab of black granite from Zimbabwe was carved and processed in Pietrasanta, Italy.

◄ The Royal Library was founded more than 350 years ago. Kontrapunkt's design of its crown identity and logo is described by the designers: "The solution was modern classicist: a combination of the stylized crown and the historical typography in an untraditional setup—a logo that is easy to decipher and, in its simplicity, is reminiscent of the stamp on the back of a book. The basic elements of the design are the logo, the dark green, and the typeface Trajan. The logo contains the initials KB. The K resembles an open book, and the B is shaped as a crown, reflecting the library's status as a state institution. The green has literary reference, for example, to the glass shades of the lamps in the study hall and to the felt cover of the traditional Danish examination table."

Spain brings many different things to mind—armadas and conquistadors, the Inquisition, a rich artistic history (Picasso, Gaudí, Miró, Dalí, and others), bullfights and matadors, paella, fine wines, and the sound of castanets.

Spain

area	504,800 km²
GDP, per capita	$21,200 USD
official languages	Spanish, Catalan, Basque
population	40.2 million

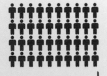

Spain lies in southwestern Europe and shares the Iberian Peninsula with Portugal, Gibraltar, and Andorra. Along the Pyrenees mountain range in the northeast, it borders France and the tiny principality of Andorra. Spain includes the Balearic Islands in the Mediterranean Sea, the Canary Islands in the Atlantic Ocean, the exclave cities of Ceuta and Melilla in the north of Africa, and a number of minor uninhabited islands on the Mediterranean side of the strait of Gibraltar.

In 1037, Castillia became an independent state—it merged with Aragon in 1479 to form Spain. Its powerful world empire of the sixteenth and seventeenth centuries (which drew great wealth from its conquered colonies) ultimately yielded command of the seas to England. Subsequent failure to embrace the mercantile and industrial revolutions caused the country to fall behind Britain, France, and Germany in economic and political power. Spain remained neutral through both world wars but suffered a devastating civil war between fascist and socialist forces from 1936 to 1939. In the second half of the twentieth century, Spain has played a catchup role in the Western international community.

Modern Spain remains predominantly Catholic and has been a constitutional monarchy and parliamentary democracy since the Spanish constitution was approved in 1978. Strong postwar economic growth and an expansion in trade following membership of the European Union in 1986 made the country's economy the tenth largest in the world in 2002. Life expectancy, public transportation, sanitation, infrastructure, and health care are first-rate, although the GDP per capita remains at 87 percent of that of the four leading European economies.

= 1 million

design firm   Estudio Manuel Estrada
art director   Manuel Estrada
designer   Manuel Estrada

client

Ministry of Culture
Commissioned by the Spanish Ministry of Culture and Alcalá de Henares University, this identifier was created for the Premios Cervantes writer's award. The task was to create a strong graphic and literary icon to serve as the image for the prize that carries the name of the author Cervantes. The designer drew the face of the writer with the letters that spell out his name. The mark obtained a diploma from the Art Director's Club in Europe.

design firm   Estudio Manuel Estrada
art director   Manuel Estrada
designer   Manuel Estrada

client

Madrid's City Hall
Bibliometro is a project developed by Madrid's City Hall to create a system for borrowing books in the subways of Madrid. The task was to "create a distinguishable image that remains easily in the user's mind." The logo uses the project name's initial letter, *B*, turned on its side to represent the subway's tunnels as well as two wide-open eyes.

design firm   Estudio Manuel Estrada
art director   Manuel Estrada
designer   Manuel Estrada

client

IFEMA (Madrid Trade Fair)
Feria de Emprendedores (entrepreneur's fair), a new trade fair that takes place in IFEMA (Madrid's fair grounds), is a "meeting point for young businessmen and entrepreneurs." A logo was needed that could express "the decisive spirit of the young businessman." The lowercase *e* represents the first letter of the fair's name and, as stated by the designer, acts "as the representation of a small entrepreneur that walks in a daring manner."

design firm   Estudio Manuel Estrada
art director   Manuel Estrada
designer   Manuel Estrada

client

Simple Informática
Simple Informática is a small I.T. company that not only creates software and hardware but also does consulting work for companies and professionals. As stated by the designer, "They make the complicated world of technology simple and easy, hence the name 'Simple' that I proposed for the company. The image uses the metaphor of the (computer) mouse with a tail that clearly forms an *S*." In 2000, the logo was awarded a prize by A.E.P.D., the Spanish Association of Design Professionals.

design firm | GMI/Grupo Memelsdorff Ibérica
art directors | Frank Memelsdorff
| Gabriel Martínez
designer | Gabriel Martínez
client | **gráfica**

gráfica

Communicate to Exist

Agencia Gráfica (gráfica) is a company specializing in graphic production and project management that offers consultation and services to designers.

the brief | The designer was given the task of designing "a sophisticated, simple, but powerful mark."

the solution | The designer developed a typographic solution and a unique logotype for gráfica made of friendly lowercase letterforms. The typographic treatment introduces accents evoking "perked eyebrows" on a face, inviting the viewer to delve further into the agency's services.

▲ Here, the simple, yet effective, logotype developed for Agencia Gráfica.

▼ The typographic logo was applied to a folding poster, conceived as a promotional mailing. The newly developed identity for the agency along with the key message is explained in the mailer: "In a competitive marketplace, if you don't communicate, you don't exist." Graphic elements from the logotype are used as a background palette to reinforce the memorable nature of the mark and to demonstrate the agency's competency—graphic production services.

design firm · Javier Glez. Solas
art director · Javier Glez. Solas
designer · Javier Glez. Solas

client

Fundación Universidad—Empresa

This logo, developed for the Centro de Evaluación de Impacto Ambiental (EIA), uses a juxtaposition of contrasting letterforms (hand-drawn versus stenciled) and contrasting colors to suggest the impact of human activity on the environment.

design firm · Rafo Hdez.
art director · Rafo Hdez.
designer · Rafo Hdez.

client

FUNED

This colorful logo for Intervención Psicoterapéutica, a graduate school for psychotherapy, makes effective use of "eye contact" to engage the viewer. The imposition of a grid on the human figure suggests a gestalt composed of distinct parts—a highly appropriate graphic expression to suit the subject matter.

design firm · LSD
art directors · Sonia Díaz
Gabriel Martínez
designer · Gabriel Martínez

client

E space

E space is an art gallery, formed to create "an alternative space for new and emerging artists." As stated by the designers, "It is the space that isn't—an open space to new people." The effective, minimalist logo solution fulfills the mandate: "Simple and radical, space + E. In this case, we can really say less is more."

design firm · Santamarina Diseñadores
designer · José Santamarina

client

Principado de Asturias Govertnment

This logo commissioned by the government of Asturias is for the local public health service. The logo, a combination of a cross—internationally associated with health—and a human figure, is friendly yet corporate, which is highly appropriate for a public health service.

design firm | The Design House
art director | Jorge González
designer | Segundo Leria

client | **Coca-Cola España**

agua mineral natural
BONAQUA
Marca Reg.

The Joy of Simple Things

Coca-Cola launched Bonaqua (still bottled water) to expand its offering in the noncarbonated beverage category and to assure itself a large share of the bottled-water market. This product segment is at a stage of rapid growth in Spain and Europe. The target audience is universal—the intention was to extend consumption to all times of the day, stated as "drinking Bonaqua becomes a good, healthy, routine habit."

the brief | Previously, all bottled water offerings in Spain were marketed based on the intrinsic values of the water: healthy, natural, and thirst quenching. The aim with Bonaqua was to provide the brand with more extrinsic values, summarized by the positioning of the brand: "The joy of simple things."

the solution | As the designers explain, "To embody this positioning, a research phase was carried out using brainstorming techniques to seek concepts and situations that may represent the positioning. Finally, the positioning was conceptualized through the simplest act related to water: its origin. The origin is embodied in its allegoric representation: Poseidon and a highly visual image explaining that origin, birth/the flow of water. It is all dealt with in a most elegant, premium manner, with clear, classical typography and a color palette of intense blues, whites, and silver tones that emphasize the vectorization strength of the Q in red, as a typographic nod to the Coca-Cola Company."

▲ The typographic logo for Bonaqua bottled water and an example of a vending machine graphic.

◄ In the Bonaqua brand's application to promotional materials, the color palette and typography is kept consistent to provide a cohesive visual identity.

◄ The Bonaqua bottle ranges in sizes from ¾ pint (330 ml) to 1 ⅓ gallons (5 L). The bottle label shows the logo superimposed on a classical representation of Poseidon.

el vallé
de Almodóvar

design firm	The Design House
creative director	Jorge González
designers	Jorge González
	Miguel Ortiz
client	**QUALIA, Slu**

Pure Cheese

Quesos del Valle is a company that sells cheese under its own national brand, but it claimed a market share of less than 1 percent. Although distributors consider its products to be of high quality, the firm's image was seen as "very diffused and lacking in content."

the brief The designers were approached to "convey new values of the brand in keeping with the new business strategy—clarity, nearness, and thoroughness—as distinguishing attributes of the brand in its competitive environment. This strategy is linked to an image showing the natural origin (the Valley of Almodóvar), because of the relevance of the trade name to the company." The brand redesign would entail naming, a logotype, a corporate identity, packaging, and brand architecture.

the solution The solution encompasses all of the client's requests through what the designers describe as "the creation of a robust identity, simple and pure in its lines—a feature shared by natural colors and white—that provides visual cleanliness and aids legibility." Also, "typographic play on the use of handwritten letters (quality, thoroughness) and more sober, serene typefaces, with straight lines (simplicity, nearness). Graphic composition points to the green horizon of a valley, in which the natural elements (grass, leaves) are the protagonists."

▲ The expressive, personality-rich logo incorporates a simplified leaf graphic. Note the hand-drawn quality shown in the enlarged detail.

▲ In keeping with the client's new positioning, the designers also developed the tag line "a taste for life!" rendered in an expressive calligraphic hand.

▼ Here, the new brand applied effectively to full-color labeling, product packaging, and an advertisement featuring the tag line.

Finland

area	337,000 km²
GDP, per capita	$25,800 USD
official languages	Finnish, Swedish
population	5.2 million

 The Republic of Finland is a predominantly Christian country in Scandinavia and a member of the European Union (it was the only Nordic state to adopt the euro at its initiation in 1999). It has land frontiers with Sweden, Norway, and Russia, a maritime frontier with Estonia, and is bordered by the Baltic Sea to the southwest, the Gulf of Finland to the southeast, and the Gulf of Bothnia to the west.

Finland was first a province and then a grand duchy under Sweden from the twelfth to the nineteenth centuries and an autonomous grand duchy of Russia after 1809. It finally won its complete independence from Russia in 1917. During World War II, it successfully resisted invasion attempts by the Soviet Union and defended its freedom, although at the cost of some territory. In the last sixty years, the Finns have made a remarkable transformation from a farm/forest economy to a diversified modern industrial economy with a per capita income on par with Western Europe.

Finland has a highly industrialized, largely free-market economy and enjoys a high standard of living. Its key economic sector is manufacturing—principally in wood, metals, engineering, telecommunications (for example, Nokia), and the electronics industry. Trade is important, with exports equaling almost one-third of the GDP. Because of its cold climate, agricultural development is limited to maintaining self-sufficiency in basic products. Forestry, an important export earner, provides a secondary occupation for the rural population.

= 1 million

design firm Kari Piippo oy
art director Kari Piippo
designer Kari Piippo

client **Ballet Mikkeli**
This expressive symbol is for the Ballet Mikkeli, an international ballet festival held annually in the town of Mikkeli, Finland. The designer describes the brush-stroked logo as "a dancer, light as a butterfly."

design firm Kari Piippo oy
art director Kari Piippo
designer Kari Piippo

client **Et-Savon mestarikokit (Master Chefs)**
This illustrative mark for Et-Savon mestarikokit, an association of the province's best chefs, aims to promote regional cuisine culture through what the designer describes as "chefs for better food." The strong figure-ground contrast and confident stance of the cutlery-wielding cook provide a strong identifier.

design firm Kari Piippo oy
art director Kari Piippo
designer Kari Piippo

client **Mikkelin musiikkiopisto (Mikkeli Music Institute)**
"Learning music with happy spirits" is the designer's rationale for this self-explanatory, anthropomorphic symbol representing Mikkelin musiikkiopisto, a music school for children and young people.

design firm Kari Piippo oy
art director Kari Piippo
designer Kari Piippo

client **Kuopion seurakunta
(Kuopio Congregation/Church)**
In celebration of its 450th anniversary, the Kuopio Congregation/Church wanted a symbol that related to water. Water is an important symbol for life, and the congregation is located in Finland's lake district. As the designer explains, "The key to the image is a local specialty, a bread with little fish baked inside. In this way the symbol combines the water, bread, and fish themes of the Bible with the regional tradition." Following the anniversary year, the mark was adopted as the official symbol of the congregation.

Hong Kong—think Cantonese food, opera, Bruce Lee, Hong Kong tea culture, Chinese mythology, and innumerable festivals.

Hong Kong

area	1,100 km²
GDP, per capita	$26,900 USD
official languages	Cantonese, English
population	7.4 million

Hong Kong today consists of Hong Kong Island, Kowloon, and the New Territories. The Kowloon Peninsula is attached to the New Territories in the north, and the New Territories are, in turn, connected to mainland China across the Sham Chun River. In total, Hong Kong has 236 islands in the South China Sea, of which Lantau is the largest and Hong Kong Island the second largest and most heavily populated.

Occupied by the United Kingdom in 1841, Hong Kong was formally ceded by China the following year and various adjacent lands were added later in the ninetheeth century. According to an agreement signed by China and the United Kingdom in 1984, Hong Kong became the Hong Kong Special Administrative Region (SAR) of China on July 1, 1997. In this agreement, China has promised that, under its "one country, two systems" policy, China's socialist economy will not be imposed on Hong Kong and that Hong Kong will enjoy a high degree of autonomy in all matters, except foreign and defense affairs, for the next fifty years.

Hong Kong has its own legal system, currency, customs, immigration authorities, and own rules of the road—traffic continues to drive on the left, as it does in the United Kingdom. It has a bustling economy highly dependent on international trade, is one of the world's freest economies, the tenth-largest trading entity, and eleventh-largest banking center. This makes it an attractive seat and Asian headquarters for many multinational corporations. Natural resources are limited, and food and raw materials must be imported. Hong Kong has extensive trade and investment ties with the People's Republic of China.

The culture of Hong Kong is characterized by the bustling mix of Asian (mainly south Chinese) and Western influences, as well as the status of the city as a major international business center.

= 1 million

design firm | Steiner & Co.
art director | Henry Steiner
designer | Henry Steiner

client

The Hong Kong and Shanghai Banking Corporation
The designer describes the creation of this highly visible and memorable identity launched in 1983, now recognizable worldwide: "By 1980, the Hong Kong and Shanghai Banking Corporation was emerging as a major force in international finance, albeit one lacking a consistent, distinctive visual identity. I was appointed as branding consultant and immediately set about creating a single, authoritative identity, one that would serve as a powerful brand for an international audience. A bold symbol was designed referring to the shapes and colors of the bank's flag—a variant of the Scottish Saint Andrew's cross. It has proved durable and central to the rebranding of 'the world's local bank.'"

design firm | Steiner & Co.
art director | Henry Steiner
designer | Henry Steiner

client

The Hong Kong Jockey Club
"After the Royal Hong Kong Jockey Club voted to delete the *Royal* from its name, I was approached in early 1996 to advise on how to alter the signs of their numerous off-track betting centers," explains the designer. "I suggested that this occasion presented a perfect opportunity for an ambitious professional design program to clarify and consolidate the venerable, but inconsistent, corporate identity. On July 1, 1996, the new system was launched. We refined the former set of whip, horseshoe, and bridle (HJC) and placed them in an oval ground to be used consistently on printed and architectural applications. The shortened Chinese name was repositioned above the English wording, all in more elegant typography and with a new color scheme."

design firm   Alan Chan Design Co.
art director   Alan Chan
designers   Alan Chan
   Peter Lo

client   **Coca-Cola (China) Beverages Ltd.**
The arrival of the Year of the Ram (2003) marked a milestone
for Coca-Cola in China—the launch of a brand new Coca-Cola
graphic featuring "refreshing modernity and the first new
Chinese script logo for Coca-Cola since 1979." The designer
explains his design approach, "Coca-Cola's original Spencerian
English script is an icon that has made an indelible impression
in the hearts and minds of people around the world. I sought to
create a Chinese equivalent with the unique Spencerian style
fluidity while imbuing it with a modernistic touch."

design firm   Steiner & Co.
art director   Henry Steiner
designer   Henry Steiner

client   **SearchBank Ltd.**
SearchBank is an executive recruitment firm headquartered
in Hong Kong with offices in Asia and North America. The
designer explains, "They had been operating for about a year
when they approached me to give them a new brand identity.
There was little in the way of guidelines except that they felt
strongly about not using the traditional blue or 'business suit'
palette; they wanted to look dynamic and youthful. The eventual
solution came out of a brainstorming session where the idea of
'opening doors' for their clients arose. I interpreted this as an
opening, or unpeeling, in a mark that makes the most of their
name."

design firm   Steiner & Co.
art director   Henry Steiner
designer   Henry Steiner

client   **Radio Television Hong Kong**
Radio Television Hong Kong's English language radio service
(Radio3) wanted a distinctive identity to reflect its multicultural
audience. The designer's solution strikingly combines three
versions of the number 3 in Arabic, Chinese, and Roman
characters.

design firm	Alan Chan Design Co.
art director	Alan Chan
designers	Alan Chan
	Peter Lo
client	**Kirin Beverage Ltd., Tokyo Japan**

Mr. Chan the Master of Tea

the brief Kirin Beverage Ltd. launched its new Chinese Tea in October 1999 with massive media support. Named after the well-known Hong Kong graphic designer Alan Chan, Mr Chan Tea is now distributed nationwide in Japan. In what was no doubt a world first, the designer was tasked with creating the tea's brand identity based on his own persona.

the solution The brand identifier features a sensuously styled gestural hand presenting a single tea leaf, centered in a circular seal that defines the product's pedigree. This image is accompanied by a uniquely distressed uppercase logotype. Product packaging features the logo, Alan Chan's distinctive silhouette, his signature, and the title "the Master of Tea." In addition, Alan Chan appeared as Tea Master in the product-launch TV commercial shot in Vietnam.

The distinctive logo works well in positive form as well as in reverse. On product labeling, it appears reversed out of a graduated tea-colored sphere, with a glow added to the gestural illustration.

design firm	Alan Chan Design Co.
art director	Alan Chan
designers	Alan Chan
	Charlie Kim
	Annie Leung
client	**Airport Authority Hong Kong**

An Identity Takes Flight

the brief

The client required a corporate identity that would project a sophisticated and global image for the newly constructed Hong Kong International Airport. The unique identity is inspired by the new passenger terminal's vaulted, soaring, wavelike roof structure. The new logo embodies the essence and the spirit of Hong Kong's magnificent international airport—its flowing line symbolizes movement, flight, and dynamic energy. The designer explains, "I wanted the design to make a statement about Hong Kong, so I opted for the fluidity of a stylish Chinese brush stroke, which also symbolizes the previously mentioned criteria. The more simple the design is in its execution, the more memorable the impression."

the solution

The letterforms are basic, simple, and contemporary in design, reflecting the simplicity and elegance of the airport. A clean-looking and highly legible typeface combines with the wavelike symbol to create a logo with global appeal. The vertical line between the Chinese and English characters acts as a divider between the two languages and initiates a systematic approach for the visual identity's implementation program. A bluish gray was chosen to complement the interior of the new airport.

▲ The distinctive logo comprises an expressive waveform on top of the airport's name, spelled out in both Chinese and English.

▼ A glimpse of the Hong Kong International Airport's passenger terminal leaves no doubt regarding the appropriateness of the identity's iconic form.

▼ Two-color stationery furthers the clean, sophisticated impression lent by the airport's new identity.

design firm | Alan Chan Design Co.
art director | Alan Chan
interior designers | Alan Chan
 | William Lim (CL3 Architects Limited)

client | **Hunan Baishayuan Cultural Development Co. Ltd.**

Redesigning the Teahouse

Located in Changsha, the capital of Hunan province in China, Bashayuan is a Chinese teahouse developed by Baisha Group for the purpose of enhancing and promoting its corporate image. Baisha Group is one of the five largest Chinese cigarette brands.

the brief Baishayuan Tea House is situated in Baisha Park at the site of a well-preserved "thousand-year-old well" that has provided an ample supply of mineral water to nearby inhabitants of Changsha for many generations—in fact, since the Ming Dynasty the well has been a "fount of life," providing water for drinking, the making of tea, and bathing. The structure's architecture is based on the design of traditional Suzhou Gardens with the intent of preserving the cultural uniqueness of the locale. The design challenge entailed creating a new, contemporary look that would well serve a high-profile clientele, including government officials, artists, designers, cultural workers, and tea lovers. In collaboration with a partnering architectural firm, the designer was tasked with creating a distinctive visual identity and interior design for the teahouse.

the solution The Baishayuan Tea House is divided into three main areas: the retail portion, the walkways, and a two-story building. Along the walkways lined with full-height red and clear glass, an exquisite sofa-seating area provides stylish, yet relaxed, sophistication. At nighttime, one experiences an intimate, cozy feeling of comfortable ambience. The upper floor of the two-story building is for guests, whereas the ground floor provides a contemporary seating environment looking into the garden, where live performances take place during the Chinese festive seasons. The use of various linear elements such as screens and columns is in harmony with the existing traditional Chinese architecture, capturing the cultural spirit of "East meets West" and providing a reinterpretation throughout the unique style of this contemporary Chinese teahouse.

白沙源
baishayuan

▲ The logo block, reminiscent of a Chinese seal, incorporates a welcoming, round portal in the form of a lowercase *b* along with the name in both Chinese and English.

▼ The impressive design of the teahouse's spaces, interiors, and surfaces uses a repeating palette of graphic elements, forms, patterns, lighting effects, and muted colors (in addition to the ubiquitous and identifying red) to create the desired image—a facility to impress the visitor with the esteem, success, and sophistication of the Baisha Group.

Croatia claims a distinct role in the history of neckwear—it is the home to the necktie (cravat is derived from the eponymous Croat, or Hrvatska).

 # Croatia

area	56,600 km²
GDP, per capita	$9,800 USD
official language	Croatian
population	4.4 million

 The parliamentary democratic Republic of Croatia is a young country with old roots at the intersection of the Mediterranean, Central Europe, and the Balkans. It seceded from former Yugoslavia in 1991, amid several years of sporadic and bitter war. Yugoslavia was initially formed in 1918 as a kingdom of Croats, Serbs, and Slovenes and became known as Yugoslavia in 1929. Following World War II, Yugoslavia became a federal independent Communist state under the strong hand of Marshall Tito.

Croatia has an economy based mostly on services and light industry. Tourism has become a notable source of income, and recent years have seen faster economic growth as the country prepares for membership in the European Union, its most important trading partner.

Croatia has a long artistic, literary, and musical tradition. Its culture is rooted in a thirteen-century history that gave birth to many brilliant individuals (three Nobel winners), significant monuments, unique cities, and numerous inventions (such as the fountain pen). Croatia now includes six World Heritage sites and eight national parks. The country's capital is the ancient city of Zagreb.

= 1 million

Hrvatska udruga za pomoć
osobama koje mucaju
Hinko Freund

Croatian Association
For People Who Stutter
Hinko Freund

design firm   Likovni Studio
art director   Danko Jaksic
designer   Danko Jaksic

client

Hinko Freund

Hinko Freund is the Croatian Association for People Who Stutter. The designer was asked to develop a logo that would communicate clearly the client's profile. The solution is simple: a knot.

design firm   Elevator
art director   Tony Adamic
designer   Tony Adamic

client

Elevator

Elevator is a Croatian advertising agency and design studio. The self-imposed design brief called for a logo with impact to reflect its mission—a commitment to excellence, constant striving for better solutions, and "bringing things to the next level." The solution features an upward arrow "referring to a state of mind where constant betterment is sought" and a powerful lowercase logotype.

design firm   Studio International
designer   Boris Ljubicic
designer   Boris Ljubicic

client

HRT—Hrvatska Radio Television (Croatian Radio Television)

This logo for the national broadcaster HRT uses the alternating square motif as a visual code to signify its Croatian origin. Red, white, and blue are Croatia's flag colors. The identifier is clean and memorable and is easily applied to numerous applications.

design firm   Studio International
designer   Boris Ljubicic
designer   Boris Ljubicic

client

Croatian Tourist Board

The designer describes this widely seen identity for Croatian tourism as follows: "The names for Croatia in different languages (Croatie, Kroatien, Croazia, and Hrvatska) all share a common fourth letter—A—which is also the initial letter for the Adriatic Sea. Alternating squares represent a visual code for Croatia (the checkerboard pattern appears in the nation's official emblem and flag), whereas red, blue, and white are its national colors. The sun shines from the red square, and on the blue square is a sailing boat. The logo was created in watercolor and calligraphy and is applied easily to all sorts of tourist items."

design firm | Parabureau
art director | Igor Stanišlević
designer | Igor Stanišlević

client | **Black Box Berlin**

Black Box is a Berlin-based art organization that stages art festivals and similar events. The designer was asked to create an identity that was simple, young, and modern. The solution is a human being with a black box replacing his head. The designer's rationale is straightforward: "We're all black boxes containing our histories."

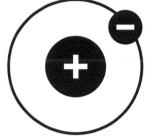

design firm | Laboratorium
art directors | Orsat Franković
Ivana Vučić
designers | Orsat Franković
Ivana Vučić

client | **Energy Clinic**

Energy Clinic is a health and beauty center, as well as a brand of cosmetics and aromatherapy products. The designer was asked to create a logo that would "signify the revitalization of both body and soul, as implied by the name: Energy Clinic." The solution is obvious to anyone familiar with the concept of recharging batteries.

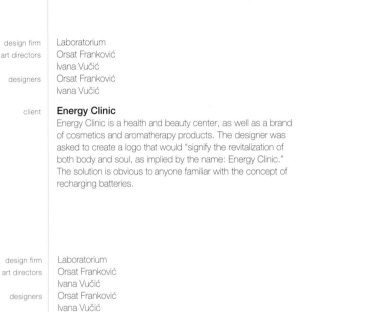

design firm | Laboratorium
art directors | Orsat Franković
Ivana Vučić
designers | Orsat Franković
Ivana Vučić

client | **MIV**

The client, MIV, is in the textile industry and is focused on large-scale production and outsourcing fashion designers for its collections. The challenge was to design a simple logo for a brand that can "go" with different subbrands (fashion labels). The solution, as described by the designers, "Find the letters (initials) in a stitch."

design firm | Laboratorium
art directors | Orsat Franković
Ivana Vučić
designers | Orsat Franković
Ivana Vučić

client | **Vivendum**

The client is a property planning and hospitality business involved with project development and modern architecture related to the integration of nature and the Mediterranean tradition of harmony with Dalmatian sights and resorts. The designers were tasked with creating a visual identity that would imply the synthesis of nature and ecology, science and technology. The solution is a geometric rendition of a natural form—precise, structural, technical, and multidimensional on one hand; soft, emotional, and natural on the other.

VIVENDUM

villa eugenia

design firm　Manasteriotti Design Studio
art director　Igor Manasteriotti
designer　Igor Manasteriotti

client　**ETO D.O.O.—Villa Eugenia**
Villa Eugenia is a small, high-class hotel and international conference center. The designer was tasked with designing a logo to reflect a sophisticated, high-class establishment. The design solution is both modern and traditional, imbued with a delicate sense of class.

istragrafika

design firm　Bruketa&Zinic
art directors　Davor Bruketa
　　　　　　　Nikola Zinic

client　**Istragrafika**
The designers were asked to create an appropriate, eye-catching visual identity for Istragrafika, a printing company. The result is a simple graphic image reminiscent of a modernist landscape, colorful and clean. It can also be seen as a bird's-eye view of a lift of colorful paper, an impression implied by perspective introduced by the angled lower-right corner.

art director　Dubraveo Papa
designer　Dubraveo Papa

client　**Dubraveo Papa**
This personal identifier created by independent designer Dubraveo Papa forms an interesting graphic composition constructed from his interconnecting initials, *d* and *p*.

design firm　Elevator
art director　Tony Adamic
designers　Tony Adamic
　　　　　　Jova Dodig

client　**Pivac**
Pivac Brothers Vgorac is a producer of quality smoked meats. Their product is differentiated by a traditional family recipe and by a unique geographic location—both essential for the renowned flavor. The designers created a logo that depicted the producer's geographic region as well as the company's "tradition." The designed solution displays the family name in a bold signature, with a supporting graphic depiction of the hilltop Fortress of Vgorac and the Vgorac name. Chosen colors reflect the elements that contribute to the uniqueness of the smoked meat product: dry soil, hot sun, and pure sea air.

design firm | Laboratorium
art directors | Orsat Franković
Ivana Vučić
designers | Orsat Franković
Ivana Vučić
client | **Dubrovnik Museums**

The Museums' New Look

the brief
The client is a museum institution with six different museum members that depict the history of Dubrovnik in different ways. The designers were challenged to develop "a unique code" to communicate six unique museums as being part of one single institution—Dubrovnik Museums.

the solution
The corporate identity for Dubrovnik Museums is a pure, simple typographic logo. The individual logos developed for the six separate museums are symbols that may be interpreted as parts of one significant system. They stand on their own, but sometimes they appear together.

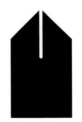

The logo designed for the House of Marin Drzic (Drzic was a famous pre-Shakespearean writer) combines of the silhouette of the actual house and a pen nib.

The logo designed for the Archeological Museum features a buried *A* for *archeology.*

Shown here, the logo designed for the Rupe/Ethnographical Museum. Rupe (means "holes" in English) is an old city-state granary now housing the museum. The logo is made of a simplified ground plan.

DU'M

Here, the typographic corporate identity designed for Dubrovnik Museums— pure, simple, and clean.

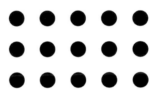

The logo design for the Rector's Palace, a Cultural-Historical Museum, is based on the characteristic monumental front of the Rector's Palace—a Renaissance arcade with six arches.

IXXI

▲ The logo designed for the Contemporary History Museum, housing historical artifacts from the nineteenth, twentieth, and twenty-first centuries, represents the relevant centuries written in Roman numerals.

◄ The logo developed for the Maritime Museum shows a simplified drawing of an old ship that was built in Dubrovnik.

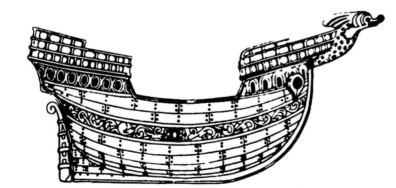

design firm | STUDIO GRAFIČKIH IDEJA
art director | Melina Mikulić
designer | Iva Čular

client

Tarol

Tarol is a beauty salon offering makeup and hairdressing services for female clientele. The designer was approached with the task of designing an identity that would be "original, elegant, and perhaps a little extravagant." The identity also had to emphasize the identity of the owner, a well-known public personality. The logo combines a powdery, stylized flower (representing the Greek goddess of beauty, Aphrodite) with an unconventionally styled signature. The identity was applied to various applications—shown here is a promotional leaflet.

design firm | STUDIO GRAFIČKIH IDEJA
art director | Melina Mikulić
designers | Iva Čular
| Melina Mikulić

client

Naklada MD

Naklada MD is a publishing company that organizes literary events as well as international festivals. The designers were asked to design an identity for the European Festival of Short Stories. The highly recognizable logo uses a comma, ever present in novel writing, graphically shortened to become a period. The identity solution supports the festival's title (set in a typewriter-like font) to literally "make a long story short."

This logo/concept was used effectively in various applications including posters, flyers, bookmarks, and ads.

design firm STUDIO GRAFIČKIH IDEJA
art director Melina Mikulić
designer Melina Mikulić

client **0800DOSTAVA (0800DELIVERY)**

Door-to-Door Service

0800DOSTAVA is a door-to-door delivery service.

the brief The designer was asked to create a recognizable, versatile, and memorable identity using graphic elements derived from the visual vocabulary of traffic symbols. The identity had to perform well in stand-alone applications, as well as lend itself to the projection of a dynamic presence when seen as a whole.

the solution The proposed design solution consisted of a galloping zebra as a core identifier, selected for its traits of flexibility, urgency, speed, and obvious connections to traffic. The black and white stripes tie together the entire identity with a visually powerful leitmotiv, creating a clear and distinctive corporate presence and ease of application.

▲ Here, the zebra logo developed for the client, using the bold contrast of white, black, and red to create a dynamic, recognizable presence. The name is also the phone number and a call to action—0800DELIVERY.

▼ ► The distinctive logo and dynamic visual palette of zebra stripes and bright red are shown in action: livery vehicles, motorcycle helmet (for couriers), business cards, promotional items, specialty items, and a corporate newsletter.

designer | Branimir Lazanja

client | **Mimice**

Mimice is a seafood restaurant specializing in "*srdela*—the delicious blue fish" (sardines). The design brief was clear and to the point: "Mimice is not a pretentious restaurant. Sardines are available to everyone. Quick and simple, it's also light food, so you can eat a lot of it." The designer's solution and rationale are equally concise. "Simplify the way sardines look. Use more than one. Keep it blue."

designer | Branimir Lazanja

client | **King Kong Ping Pong**

King Kong Ping Pong is a creative shop producing design and communication ideas for both large and small clients. The graphic identifier, as described by the designer, "The gorilla plays table tennis"—unexpected but effective.

design firm | Cvetković & Poturica
art directors | Morana Cvetković
Nina Poturica
designers | Morana Cvetković
Nina Poturica

client | **Adeco Australia Export/Import Pty Ltd.**

Adeco, an Australian exporter/importer situated in Sydney, required a logo that would identify their Australian origin and reach out to an international audience, representing them as a serious and professional company. The solution melds the human hand, the shape of the Australian continent, and the name set in Gill Sans caps, creating a memorable mark appropriate to the client's business.

design firm | STUDIO GRAFIČKIH IDEJA
art director | Melina Mikulić
designer | Barbara Galant

client | **Berny**

Berny is a salon with three unisex offerings: hairdressing, massage, and pedicures. The designer was approached with the challenge of creating an identity to unite the three offerings into a single maxim, imbue an expression of nurturing, and reflect classical beauty. The solution is a symbol with emphasized art nouveau overtones—classical beauty; an androgynous face; and emphasis on a creatively brash, curly hairstyle. Uniquely colored hairstreaks provide three symbol variations.

SOHA

design firm STUDIO GRAFIČKIH IDEJA
art director Melina Mikulić
designer Iva Čular

client **Croatia Liber—Soha**
The designers were challenged with branding Croatia Liber's (a literary and publishing company) Soha line of notebooks and journals. The solution transforms the name's significance (*soha* is a Y-shaped branch) into graphical form supported by appropriate colors—the "wood motif" suggested by the name is linked naturally to paper products.

MEMOAIDS

design firm STUDIO GRAFIČKIH IDEJA
art director Melina Mikulić
designer Melina Mikulić

client **Ministry for Health and Welfare**
MEMOAIDS is an AIDS-education campaign of the Ministry for Health and Welfare, targeted at youth. The designer explains: "The logo shows high school students posed as superheroes in an all-knowing sense—attractive to youth because it clearly sends out the message of the competency of young people in promoting awareness and education on this important health issue."

AGROTEKA

design firm STUDIO GRAFIČKIH IDEJA
art director Melina Mikulić
designer Melina Mikulić

client **Agroteka**
Agroteka is a wholesaler with operations relating to two specific branches: Agro for agricultural products and Teka for office materials. The demanding job for the designer was to develop an identity that would unite the two different types of products represented. The solution is a minimalist depiction of a pen combined with a root vegetable, thus fully uniting the two areas of concern while presenting a meaningful, memorable, and highly comprehensible logo.

Hoteli VODICE

 Hotel OLYMPIA   Villa GLORIETTE   Hotel PUNTA

design firm STUDIO GRAFIČKIH IDEJA
art director Melina Mikulić
designer Melina Mikulić

client **Hoteli Vodice**
Hoteli Vodice is a company in the tourism/hospitality sector consisting of several subgroups, each independent from the others. The designer was charged with creating an identity that could be used to signify the independence of each segment of the firm while also representing the parent company. The solution employs the symbol of a stylized sun divided into quadrant sections. Each section, accompanied by a specific logotype, represents one specific facility. A unique color is used for each subgroup, and a common color (the golden sun) represents the parent firm, Hoteli Vodice, acting as a common denominator.

Hungary

area	93,000 km²
GDP, per capita	$13,300 USD
official language	Hungarian
population	10 million

The Republic of Hungary (also known as the Magyar Republic) is a landlocked European nation bordered by Austria, Slovakia, Ukraine, Romania, Serbia, Croatia, and Slovenia. Hungary seceded from the polyglot Austro-Hungarian Empire in 1918, at the end of World War I, and fell under Communist rule following World War II. In 1956, a revolt and announced withdrawal from the Warsaw Pact met with massive military intervention from Moscow. In 1968, Hungary began liberalizing its economy and introduced so-called "goulash Communism."

Following the dissolution of the Soviet Union, Hungary initiated a free-market economy in 1990, and then joined NATO in 1999. The country is a parliamentary democratic republic and has demonstrated strong economic growth as one of the newest members of the European Union (since 2004). The private sector currently accounts for more than 80 percent of GDP. Foreign ownership of and investment in Hungarian firms is widespread, and both inflation and unemployment have declined substantially in recent years.

= 1 million

designer   Laszlo Lelkes

client   **Speakeasy Music Club**
The designer was approached by Attila Taborszky, the club's owner, to design an identity that "would capture the essence of the Capone-era and the style of U.S. comic books." The designer's interpretation of the brief and creative response resulted in a richly illustrated, engaging, and memorable visual identity loaded with iconic references borrowed from an earlier era and a faraway place.

TEXTBOOK PUBLISHERS

designer   Laszlo Lelkes

client   **Hungarian Textbook Publishers' Association**
The brief for this project was to create a new emblem for the client that was "simple and based on the formal qualities of a book." The solution, as described by the designer, "Textbooks are cheap and humble. In addition, they are constantly used. A typical aspect of the book was reinterpreted by virtue of the simplicity of a couple of basic forms and colors."

designer   Laszlo Lelkes

client   **Bonté Advertising**
The client agency wanted to communicate two things through their identity: first, the firm's owners are French, and second, "successful advertising always hits the target." The designer's solution was to use the French tricolor as a target, supported by an expressive logotype.

designer   Laszlo Lelkes

client   **"Molnár Ferenc" Hungarian Authors' Theater**
"This new identity incorporates the idea of theater and the special character of the early nineteenth-century Budapest secessionist style," according to the designer. "The curtain is the stereotype of European theaters. A secessionist ornament from a neighboring building provides a specific cultural reference, and the playful typography is in harmony with the not-too-serious profile of this particular theater."

Ireland

area	70,300 km²
GDP, per capita	$29,000 USD
official languages	English, Gaelic
population	3.9 million

The isle of Ireland is the third-largest island in Europe, consisting of the Republic of Ireland, which covers five-sixths of the island (south, east, and west), and Northern Ireland, a region of the United Kingdom. The predominantly Catholic Republic of Ireland seceded from the United Kingdom in 1921—following several years of guerrilla warfare—withdrew from the British Commonwealth in 1948, and joined the European Community in 1973. In recent decades, Ireland has developed a remarkably robust, high-tech economy, the envy of many nations.

Celtic tribes settled on the island as early as the fourth century B.C. Invasions by Norsemen began in the late eighth century and were finally ended when King Brian Boru defeated the Danes in 1014. English invasions began in the twelfth century and set off more than seven centuries of Anglo-Irish struggle, marked by fierce rebellions and harsh repressions.

For its small size, Ireland has made a disproportionate contribution to world literature, the visual arts, and music. Irish poetry provides the oldest vernacular poetry in Europe, with early examples dating from the sixth century. The early history of Irish visual art traces back to early carvings found at sites such as Newgrange and is seen in Bronze Age artifacts, particularly ornamental gold objects, and the religious carvings and illuminated manuscripts of the medieval period. During the nineteenth and twentieth centuries, a strong indigenous tradition of painting emerged.

Ireland's traditional folk music and dance is also widely known. A 1960s revival of traditional folk music triggered renowned artists such as The Dubliners, The Chieftains, Sean Ó Riada, later mixing with the rock genre, including the Horslips, Van Morrison, Thin Lizzy, and then U2, Sinéad O'Connor, and The Pogues.

= 1 million

design firm **Sharpshooter Design**
art director Philip Byrne
designer Philip Byrne

client **Sharpshooter Design**
This Dublin-based designer used a stylized image of a speeding bullet to communicate his own clean, sharp, graphic style. He caters to the local business community and also provides outsourced services to the local graphic design and advertising industry.

HUDSON KILLEEN

design firm **Design Factory**
art director Conor Clarke
designer David Rooney

client **Hudson Killeen, Fine Lithographic Printers**
This identity was created to signal the Hudson Killeen's change from being a medium-sized "jobbing" printer to becoming a full-scale commercial color-printing house. The logo, full of references and visual jokes that were personal to the firm's two owners, reinterprets the iconography of technological advances and travel from early-twentieth-century postage stamps to create an over-the-top scene that would challenge all but the very best of printers.

design firm **Design Factory**
art director Conor Clarke
designer Conor Clarke

client **National Safety Council**
The National Safety Council promotes road and fire safety in Ireland, implementing safety programs, media campaigns, and community activities. The logo sets the organization's name on top of the single word *safety*, thereby making the two synonymous and signaling safety as a top priority. The implied white shape surrounding the name ensures that it is read first.

orphan
International Aid Ireland

design firm **Design Factory**
art director Stephen Kavanagh
designer Stephen Kavanagh

client **International Orphan Aid**
The logo presents the viewer with the name of the organization that has apparently been altered by a child's handwriting. This gesture alerts the viewer to the urgency of the orphan's needs and presents a stark contrast to the necessarily anonymous bureaucratic typography of an international organization.

Israel—historical Jewish homeland, source of the Bible, legendary holy land of milk and honey, site of the Dead Sea (lowest point on Earth's surface), an embattled history, inspiration for Crusaders, and a kibbutzim success, as well as upscale shopping, pristine diving, and a seemingly permanent position in the world's headlines.

Israel

area	20,800 km²
GDP, per capita	$19,200 USD
official languages	Hebrew, Arabic
population	6.1 million

Israel is a parliamentary democratic republic in the heart of the Middle East (actually part of West Asia). Formed at the end of World War II when the U.N. partitioned the former British Trust Territory into Jewish and Arab states (in an agreement rejected by most Arabs), Israel has experienced a subsequent series of wars that has not ended the tensions between the two sides. The Palestinian territories have been occupied by Israel since 1967, an ongoing point of contention and conflict in the Palestinian-Israeli violence. Geographically, Israel is situated along the Western edge of the Mediterranean and surrounded by Arab neighbors.

Jews have long considered Israel to be their spiritual home—as a Holy Land and their Promised Land. The Land of Israel holds a special place in Jewish religious obligations, including the remains of the Second Jewish Temple. It is also the birthplace of Christianity and contains many other sites of great spiritual significance in Judaism, Christianity, and Islam. Modern Israel's two major religions are Judaism and Islam, the latter practiced primarily by the country's Arab minority.

Since its formation, waves of immigration from around the world (in particular, Europe and former Soviet-bloc nations) have brought a mix of ideas and talents to this new, yet ancient, land. Jewish communities around the world provide active support for, and exchange with, the nation as well. Israel enjoys a thriving, modern economy with an accomplished high-tech sector. Tourism is a significant economic contributor, with the ancient religious sites and modern resorts providing the major attraction for pilgrims and vacationers alike.

= 1 million

design firm	Rotem Design
art director	Ruthi Rotem
designer	Ada Wardi
client	**Ankori Education System**

Right on Target

Ankori is a corporation that specializes in methods of education, directing high schools, offering preparatory courses for matriculation examinations and psychometric tests, and publishing textbooks.

the brief The client requested a logo design and graphic identity concept that would be applied to the various services it offers. The identity had to appeal to the corresponding target groups. The design aims were to highlight the novelty and dynamism of Ankori's educational methods, its schools and extracurricular courses, which offer students a "warm home" for high achievements.

the solution As described by the designer, "A target was chosen as the corporate symbol. The logotype font is rounded, bold, and italic (dynamic). The orange conveys optimism—it and the regal violet color both support the graphic image of the corporation as a stable and ambitious institute."

▲ The identity was applied to a wide range of printed materials, including stationery, presentation literature, brochures, and catalogs. Consistent use of two match colors helps lend the array of materials a family look.

▼ This bag shows the target symbol used in a repeating pattern and together with the logotype as part of the corporate signature. Note that Hebrew is read from right to left.

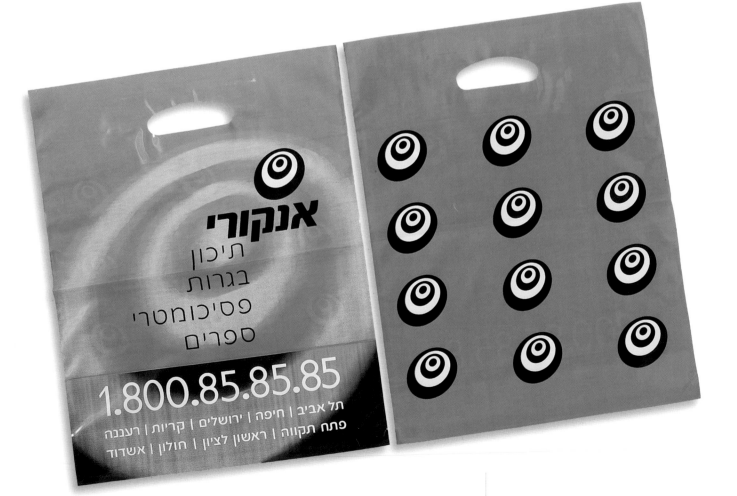

design firm | Jason & Jason/Wolff Olins
art director | Dalia Inbar (visual brand rollout)
designers | Nikki Jason (naming)
Dalia Inbar (visual rollout)
Vered Rosen Zvi (logo)

client | **Colbar**

EVOLENCE

Wrinkle-free Branding

the brief

Colbar is a biotech company that produces Evolence, a product that reduces facial wrinkles and is aimed at the "filler" market. "Working in association with Wolff Olins in the United Kingdom, we developed the name and logo. Wolff Olins developed the brand guidelines, and we were tasked with applying it to the full range of the Evolence rollout campaign," say the designers. "The project was to produce a promotional campaign for the product release."

the solution

"We developed a series of product promotional collateral and user guides geared at medical professionals and end users."

▲ The Evolence logo features classic typography with an engaging focal point that provides a timeless look.

▼ Product promotional collateral and user guides geared at medical professionals and end clients incorporate the Evolence identity with quiet confidence and understated style. Custom studio photography is by Miri Davidovitch.

EVOLENCE™

Long lasting by nature

Restore your true beauty, naturally

Why Choose EVOLENCE™?

EVOLENCE™ – restore your true beauty, naturally

During the natural aging process, the collagen layer which supports your skin gradually diminishes, giving rise to wrinkles, lines and folds. You can now counteract these effects. EVOLENCE™ restores your natural youthful appearance by replenishing the lost collagen, adding volume and smoothing away unwelcome wrinkles.

How does EVOLENCE™ remove wrinkles, lines and folds?
EVOLENCE™ is injected just below the skin surface, where it replenishes lost collagen and adds support to your skin's own remaining collagen network. It restores shape and smoothes away wrinkles, lines and folds, quickly and effectively, to give your skin texture a soft even tone.

How long do the effects of EVOLENCE™ last?
EVOLENCE™ restores the skin's tone for a period of at least 12 months. This means repeat procedures may not be needed for at least a year – unlike other treatments that tend to need repeating 2 or 3 times a year. Most importantly, the visible effect of the improved facial contour is maintained throughout the 12 month period.

immediate results,
long-lasting effect

design firm	Jason & Jason Visual Communications
art director	Jonathan Jason
designer	Tamar Lourie
client	**Business Layers**

Creating Value
through Look and Feel

Business Layers, "the e-Provisioning company" (today called Netegrity), provides a software solution for assigning or provisioning digital resources to employees, contractors, and business partners, ensuring that these resources can be allocated and decommissioned as quickly, efficiently, and securely as required.

the brief The designer was tasked with creating a visual identity that would strongly communicate the product's value propositions of return on investment (ROI), productivity, and security.

the solution The designer states, "This software solution is expensive, so we needed to communicate value in the look, feel, and finish of the material to support this. Using typography as the main graphic element and repeating the main product benefits using upscale finishes such as embossing and selective UV helped position the company as a leader in its market and communicate its value successfully."

▲ A concise visual palette of clean sans serif typography, duotone photography, metallic inks, embossing, and selective UV varnishes combine to evoke the desired effect in this business-to-business literature.

India is a sensual kaleidoscope—vibrant colors, a cacophony of sounds, Sari and Dhoti-clad throngs, bustling tuk-tuks (taxi rickshaws), the Taj Mahal (and many other Mughal legacies), memories of Mahatma Gandhi, sacred cows, spicy vegan cuisine, and exquisite sweets— all in a land of remarkable tolerance and respect.

India

area	3,287,600 km²
GDP, per capita	$2,500 USD
official languages	Hindi, English, and seventeen others
population	1.05 billion

The Republic of India has the world's second-largest population and its economy is the world's fourth-largest in terms of purchasing power parity. It also has the world's second-fastest growing economy. It is the largest democracy and the seventh-largest country by size. In the last twenty years, it has also grown in strategic importance, emerging as an important regional power with one of the world's largest military forces and a declared nuclear weapons capability.

Constituting most of the Indian subcontinent, India straddles many traditional trade routes. It shares its borders with Pakistan, the People's Republic of China, Myanmar, Bangladesh, Nepal, Bhutan, and Afghanistan. Sri Lanka, the Maldives, and Indonesia are nearby island nations in the Indian Ocean. Home to some of the most ancient civilizations, India has also given birth to four major world religions: Hinduism, Buddhism, Jainism, and Sikhism.

The 5,000-year-old Indus Valley civilization is one of the oldest in the world. Aryan tribes from the northwest invaded about 1500 B.C., and their merger with the earlier inhabitants created the classical Indian culture. Arab incursions from the eighth century on, and Turkish in the twelfth century, were followed by European traders beginning in the fifteenth century. By the nineteenth century, Britain had assumed political control of virtually all Indian lands. In 1947, nonviolent resistance to British colonialism led to independence. The subcontinent was then divided into the secular state of India and the smaller Muslim state of Pakistan.

Most of India's industrial regions are centered on the major cities. Mumbai (formerly Bombay) serves as the nation's financial capital and nerve center. Although many Indians live in poverty, a large middle class has emerged along with the growth of a promising I.T. industry. The economy has shed much of its historical dependence on agriculture—important industries are mining, petroleum, diamond polishing, films, textiles, information technology services, and handicrafts. In recent years, India has emerged as the global leader in software and business process outsourcing services. India's major trading partners are the United States, Japan, and Europe.

India has a rich and unique cultural heritage, having preserved its established traditions through-out history. Living in a pluralist, multilingual, and multicultural society, Indians are largely tolerant and peaceful. Religious practices of various faiths are an integral part of everyday life in society. Education is highly regarded by members of every socioeconomic stratum, and traditional family values are highly respected. India produces the world's highest number of films annually (think Bollywood) and is widely known for its Carnatic, Hindustani, and Filmi music; dance forms such as Bharatanatyam, Odissi, Kuchipudi, Kathak, and Kathakali; and a rich oral literary tradition and sacred Hindu works such as the *Vedas*, epics of the *Mahabharatha* and *Ramayana*, as well as Sangam literature from Tamil Nadu.

 = 1 million

design firm National Institute of Design
art director Anil Sinha
designer Anil Sinha

client **Agricultural and Processed Food Export Development Authority, Ministry of Commerce, Government of India**

According to the designer, the challenge was "to create an image of freshness of agricultural products and longevity of processed foods" while at the same time "conveying an inherent Indian-ness" in a symbol suitable for application to an entire range of identity materials. The solution entailed an outward-radiating form, derived from an ear of wheat that denotes export activity. The symbol also resembles a peacock, India's national bird.

design firm National Institute of Design
art director Anil Sinha
designer Anil Sinha

client **National Human Rights Commission, India**

The designer was asked to create an identity that could project justice, hope, and equal treatment for all for this national body that monitors human rights issues and intervenes "at the people's level, to ensure justice and to keep hope alive." The designer's explains, "the Ashok Chakra, the central disc on the Indian flag, is the representative icon. The top half represents the Sun—a symbol of hope and equality for all. The inward-facing palms symbolize care and nurturing—the commission's role in India."

BHOOMI
An offering to the Earth in you..

design firm   Elephant Design Private Limited
art director Ashwini Deshpande
designers   Shantanu
              Nitin

client   **Nirlep/Duraware Private Limited**

Cookware from the Earth

Nirlep, the pioneer of the Indian nonstick cookware market, is acknowledged to have revolutionized the cooking habits of the Indian housewife. Nirlep means "nonstick" in Sanskrit. In India, this company enjoys a 40 percent market share and clear leadership in branded cookware, and exports cookware to European and African markets as well.

the brief The client was about to launch new terra-cotta cookware that "would address the modern enlightened woman, who expects the best in all her possessions, trying to reconcile her modern lifestyle with her concern for nature." The requirement was "for a premium product brand to innovate and create an exclusive lifestyle offering in a market crowded with many unorganized players in all segments."

the solution As described by the designers, "Our main task was to find an appropriate name and design the brand identity. The name chosen was Bhoomi, which means "earth" in Hindi. The Bhoomi brand was given a handcrafted style. The letter *i* is designed as a free-spirited human figure, supported by the tag line, *An offering to the Earth in you*. To add to the handcrafted touch, we used hand-painted Warli (tribal art) motifs on the first edition. This treatment will be followed by other art forms such as Phulkari, Saora, and other tribal and folk art from different states in India. Every edition of Bhoomi will be limited to a small number and, therefore, will be unique. We decided on an ecofriendly offering. This range has collaterals such as recipe booklets, posters, and tags, all with a unified look of the brand's persona."

▲ The expressive logo and tag line were developed for the launch of Nirlep's new terra-cotta cookware.

▼ The set of two terra-cotta pots comes with jute coasters and coconut-shell wooden spoons packed in corrugated cardboard. The Bhoomi identity applies well in both positive and reverse—an appropriate solution for this premium earthenware product.

design firm   mCube
art director   Rachana Mehta
designers   Nena Mehta
               Rachana Mehta

client   **Kanika Mehra, Fashion Designer**

Capturing the Client's Spirit

The client is a high-end designer of Indian and Western clothing that are full of color and feature unique embroidery.

the brief
The designers were approached to develop an identity that would help Kanika launch a design label under her own name, highlighting her distinct personality—a learner, a thinker, and a fashion designer. As stated by the designers, "The challenge was to create a distinguished symbol that would set Kanika apart from other Indian designers who use mainly type-treatment logos."

the solution
The designers explain, "The solution was to emphasize the word *Ka*, which in Egyptian means soul, spirit, and life. The word *Ka*, which is part of the client's name, reflects her personality. The solution was to use the symbolism of the butterfly, a form she could relate to, which also stands for free spirit, life, launch of creative thought, transformation, and metamorphosis. To encapsulate her personality and the clothes she designs, a versatile color palette was created and applied to the collateral pieces."

Stationery, promotional literature, and collateral materials incorporate the unique butterfly symbol and stylish sans serif logotype developed by the designers. Blind embossing and a distinctive color palette impart a unique and visually engaging quality.

design firm   Elephant Design Private Limited
art directors Sudhir Sharma
               Partho Guha
designers   Vandana
               Prashant
               Rahul

client   **Bajaj Auto Limited**

Two-Wheel Revolution

Bajaj Auto Limited is the flagship company of the Bajaj Group, the world's fourth largest two- and three-wheel vehicle manufacturer. The Bajaj brand is also well known in more than a dozen countries in Europe, Latin America, North America, and Asia.

the brief — As described by the designers, "Bajaj Auto was on a cusp of revolution on various fronts—design, research and development, modern products, new channels of distribution, and global markets. The sweeping changes needed an identity that truly represented the new philosophy—dynamic, vibrant, exciting, and confident. An identity change for a multiproduct, multichannel corporation meant a huge change. It called for a change in every tool, die, and mold of each one of the 2,000-odd components that makes an automobile. It also meant a change in graphic representation at every point of contact, be it buildings and showrooms, websites and advertisements. The business objectives of the new identity design are to instill faith in the brand Bajaj in the minds of younger audiences, thereby bringing in consistent sales growth in the future."

the solution — "In a country where public transportation systems are inadequate, the motorcycle is the most preferred and affordable form of mobility. A rugged, fuel-efficient two-wheeler also has a popular acceptance in rural India," explain the designers. "This identity program helped this giant corporation align its philosophy with its image. The design solution made the new values and brand essence visible. It brought excitement into every product, every communication, and every point-of-sale interface. Bajaj Auto sells a little fewer than two million two-wheelers every year. The impact of changing the mindset of internal and external audiences from an old-economy manufacturer to that of a modern, market-savvy corporation is refreshing and welcome."

"The new symbol retains a hint of the hexagonal form from the old identity of Bajaj Auto, yet makes a pronounced quality statement of speed and perfection. The flying B symbol represents style and technology. The open space around the flying B suggests vastness and transparency. Unlike the condensed lowercase letters in the earlier logotype, the new identity uses a bold, confident uppercase logotype. The blue color represents stability and strength and also connotes high technology and process engineering."

◄ The new flying *B* brand signature developed for Bajaj.

▲ The new flying *B* logo appears in multiple applications, such as buildings, showroom signage, and environmental graphics.

► Shown here, the new flying *B* brand as it appears on a Bajaj motorcycle.

Iran—ancient historical sites; intricate antique artifacts; exquisite calligraphy; bustling Tehran; strict Islamic traditions; fresh flowers; and the flavors of dates, pistachios, and Persian spices.

Iran

area	1,648,000 km²
GDP, per capita	$6,700 USD
official languages	Farsi, Azerbaijani, Kurdish
population	68.3 million

Known as Persia from 1499 to 1935 (from when it regained independence from the Mongol Empire until it was renamed), Iran became an Islamic republic in 1979 after the ruling shah was forced into exile. Today, the central Asian country has a mixture of theocratic rule and democratic government, with dominant influence of the clergy. In the 1980s, Iran fought a bloody, indecisive war with Iraq over disputed territory. In the past decade, popular dissatisfaction with the government, driven by demographic changes, restrictive social policies, and poor economic conditions has created pressure for political reform.

Iran is OPEC's second-largest oil producer, holding 10 percent of the world's proven oil reserves. It also has the world's second-largest natural gas reserves (after Russia). Iran's economy consists of a mixture of central planning, state ownership of oil and other large enterprises, village agriculture, and small-scale private trading and service ventures. The country's current administration continues to follow earlier market reform plans in pursuit of diversification of Iran's oil-reliant economy. Large-scale irrigation schemes, together with the wider production of export-based crops, produced the fastest economic growth of any Iranian sector through the 1990s, and agriculture continues to be one of the largest employers.

= 1 million

design firm Did Graphics Inc., Tehran
art director Majid Abbasi
designer Majid Abbasi

client **Doran Publication**
The designer was commissioned to design for a logo made of
Persian (Farsi) letters that at the same time would incorporate
the image of a large, powerful tree. As specified, the logotype
solution for this literary publisher weaves together five Persian
(Farsi) letters to create the name *Doran*.

design firm Ashna Advertising
art director Iraj Mirza Alikhani
designer Iraj Mirza Alikhani

client **The Friendship Association of Iran & Switzerland**
The Friendship Association of Iran & Switzerland is active in
cultural and social exchange between the two countries.
The design challenge was to combine symbols of both
countries in a logo. The solution is a combination of the
countries' respective flags, rendered in an expressive hand.
The colors red and white are shared by both nations, and
the white cross (from the Swiss flag) is used to symbolize
the cooperation between the two countries.

design firm Ashna Advertising
art director Iraj Mirza Alikhani
designer Ladan Rezaei

client **Jahahn Pahlavon Foundation**
The Jahahn Pahlavon Foundation is an Iranian nonprofit
cultural organization based in the United States. The client
needed a memorable logo that would appeal to all Iranians
and that would help make the foundation more visible.
The design solution uses traditional Iranian calligraphy,
Nasta'liq, in a modern, attractive composition that is both
familiar and memorable to Iranian audiences.

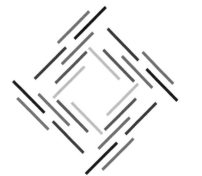

design firm Did Graphics Inc., Tehran
art director Majid Abbasi
designer Majid Abbasi

client **Behrizan Company**
Behrizan is one of the major manufacturers of door handles
in Iran, with a 25 percent share of the market. They organize
The World Pavilion, an architecture and urbanism competition
featuring a pavilion that can be located anywhere in the world
that represents a symbolic, poetic space—a progressive,
conceptual multicultural reference landmark that can be a space
of remembrance, pluralism, and beauty. The designer's logo for
the competition/event focused on "human experience through
constructive contacts between various civilizations." Multiple
colors were used to show various cultures and their diversity.

design firm	Eshareh Advertising Agency
art director	Alireza Mostafazadeh
designer	Alireza Mostafazadeh

AM Studio

AM Studio is a graphic design consultancy involved in a wide range of commercial and cultural work. Their clients are drawn to them by "their different point of view, inflective nature, and peculiar style." The designer, who was asked to design an identity and stationery that would project this attitude appropriately, selected the red-hot pepper image in keeping with "the pungent style of work produced by the studio. The layout is like a rising flame, accentuating the hot feeling."

art director	Saed Meshki
designer	Saed Meshki

Constantinople

Constantinople is a musical group from Canada that composes and plays music from the Middle Ages using period instruments, including Persian instruments. The designer explains, "For the logo I designed a bird in a frame, which resembled a musical instrument, such as a harp. For the logotype I altered an ancient Persian text. I spent a lot of time thinking about how to combine European painting and engravings from the Middle Ages with those of the same era from Iran. I wanted the mark to seem both ancient and modern."

CONSTANTINOPLE

design firm	Eshareh Advertising Agency
art director	Alireza Mostafazadeh
designer	Alireza Mostafazadeh

Eshareh Advertising Agency

This advertising agency is one of the most recognized in Iran. The challenge was to design a promotional identifier for the agency that would be prominent and visually engaging and would signal the scope of the firm's activities. The lively solution combines various graphic elements representing the agency's scope in a dynamic composition. Four match colors were used to ensure consistent reproduction quality across a range of applications, including T-shirts, mugs, and print materials.

design firm	Ashna Advertising
art director	Iraj Mirza Alikhani
designer	Ladan Rezaei

Noori Textile Ltd.

The client is a textile manufacturer that produces various textiles. The client wanted a modern logo but wanted to retain the image from its previous logo of a horse standing on two legs. As described by the designer, "The solution uses a modern style of design, such as free watercolor lines, to modernize the old logo."

design firm | Did Graphics Inc., Tehran
art director | Majid Abbasi
designer | Majid Abbasi

client | **Mehr Publications**

Folded Papers Transformed

the brief | Mehr Publications specializes in cultural and artistic books, with art students as their main audience. The designer was tasked with creating an appropriate identity for use as the imprimatur and on collateral materials.

the solution | The designer explains how his logo design evolved: "This logotype design is based on Persian (Farsi) letters. I was writing down the publisher's name. By complete accident I understood that the movement of folded papers can be transformed to the word *Mehr*." (Author's note: Many designers have experienced similar instances of what could truly be called "happy accidents"—one of the joys of working in a creative profession.)

The logotype based on Persian (Farsi) letters developed for the publisher was arrived at through purely accidental experimentation. The identity applies well in both positive and reverse, as seen here on wrapping paper.

Iceland is known for its active volcanoes, glaciated landscapes, adventure tourism, thriving Rekjavik (its capital city), fine fish exports, the idiomatic pop singer Björk, and avant-garde rock bands.

Iceland

area	103,000 km²
GDP, per capita	$30,100 USD
official language	Icelandic
population	280,800

The Republic of Iceland is a borderless nation in the northern Atlantic Ocean, situated between Greenland and Scotland, northwest of the Faroe Islands. Originally settled by Norwegian and Celtic immigrants during the late ninth and tenth centuries, Iceland boasts the world's oldest functioning legislative assembly, the Althing, established in A.D. 930. Following 300 years of independence, Iceland was subsequently ruled by Norway and Denmark. Fallout from the Askja volcano of 1875 devastated the Icelandic economy and caused widespread famine, and over the next quarter century, 20 percent of the island's population emigrated—mostly to Canada and the United States. Limited home rule was granted by Denmark in 1874, and complete independence was again attained in 1944. Today, Iceland is a parliamentary democratic republic.

Measured against world standards, literacy, longevity, income, employment, and social cohesion are first-rate in this dominantly Christian European nation. The economy depends heavily on the fishing industry, which provides more than 60 percent of export earnings. In the absence of other natural resources (aside from abundant hydroelectric and geothermal power), Iceland's economy is sensitive to declining fish stocks as well as to drops in world prices for its main exports: fish and fish products, aluminum, and ferrosilicon. The only natural resource conversion is the manufacture of cement, so most buildings are made of concrete, with expensive imported wood used only sparingly and where necessary.

In the last decade, Iceland's economy has been diversifying into manufacturing and service industries, and new developments in software production, biotechnology, and financial services are taking place. The tourism sector is also expanding, fueled by recent trends in ecotourism and whale watching.

= 1 million

design firm   Ó!
art director   Einar Gylfason
designer   Einar Gylfason

client   **Yogi B**

This identity was created for a yoga instructor. The brief was to create a spiritual and humble logo, suitable for a yoga instructor. The solution takes the form of a human hand, stylized to resemble the spirit of a bird, along with an idiosyncratic logotype set against a woodgrain background.

design firm   Ó!
art director   Einar Gylfason
designer   Einar Gylfason

client   **Thoromar**

The client is a film director who required an identity for use on his website. The logo: "An eye with burning desire."

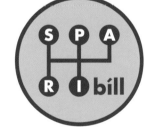

design firm   Ó!
art director   Einar Gylfason
designer   Einar Gylfason

client   **Sparibíll**

Sparibill is an automotive importer that asked the designer to create a visual identity that would represent their business of offering new cars at discount rates. The solution is the image of a gear-stick shifter using the word *Spari* (to save) in place of the gear numbers and *bill* (a car).

design firm   Ó!
art director   Einar Gylfason
designer   Einar Gylfason

client   **Olís**

Olís, an oil company, approached the designer to develop an identity for a program funded by the client to preserve wild forests. The solution is a simple graphic combination of man and nature.

Italy

area	301,200 km²
GDP, per capita	$25,100 USD
official language	Italian
population	58 million

Italy (*Italia* in Italian) comprises a boot-shaped peninsula and two large islands in the Mediterranean Sea: Sicily and Sardinia. The southern European nation shares its northern alpine boundary with France, Switzerland, Austria, and Slovenia, and encircles the independent enclaves of San Marino and Vatican City. A dominantly Catholic nation, Italy became a united state in 1861, and is today a parliamentary democratic republic. Following the defeat of Fascist dictator Benito Mussolini in 1945, Italy became a charter member of NATO and the E.E.C. With its subsequent economic revival, it has been at the forefront of European unification.

Italy has a diversified industrial economy with roughly the same total and per capita output as France and the United Kingdom. Its capitalistic economy remains divided as a developed, industrial north dominated by private companies, and a less developed, agricultural south, with high unemployment. In comparison to its Western European neighbors, Italy has a high number of small to medium-sized enterprises (SMEs). Most raw materials needed by industry and more than 75 percent of energy requirements are imported.

The Renaissance began in Italy during the fourteenth and fifteenth centuries. Literary achievements, such as the poetry of Dante, Petrarch, Tasso, and Ariosto and the prose of Boccaccio, Machiavelli, and Castiglione, had a lasting influence on the subsequent development of Western culture, as did the architecture and art by the likes of Filippo Brunelleschi, Leonardo da Vinci, Raffaello, Botticelli, Fra Angelico, and Michelangelo. Contemporary Italian artists, filmmakers, architects, composers, and designers are likewise renowned, as are the country's monuments (such as the leaning tower of Pisa and the Roman Coliseum), its food (pizza, pasta, and so on), wines, lifestyle, cinema, theater, music (notably opera), public holidays, elegance, and, generally speaking, its "taste." The plastic arts and design factor large in Italy—from the pinnacle in automobiles (Pinninfarina's styling and Ferrari's racing dominance) to housewares (Alessi), and Milanese fashion ramps (Armani).

= 1 million

design firm · Iliprandi Associati
art director · Giancarlo Iliprandi
designer · Monica Fumagalli

client · **Vitali spa**

Civil Power

Vitali spa is a leading Italian construction and civil engineering firm.

the brief · The designer was approached to design a cohesive visual identity system that would extend to a number of divisions and subcompanies across a wide range of applications.

the solution · The solution creates an industrial framework for a logotype that uses bold black on white contrasting sans serif capitals to present the corporate name boldly. Bold frames in primary colors create a family look while allowing for differentiation by corporate division and activity.

costruzioni
strade|autostrade

demolizioni speciali

ambiente

engineering

▶ The logotype is bold, highly visible, and unmistakable. A palette of primary colors and unique defining denominators extends the core image, presenting a consistent, cohesive identity. This cement truck demonstrates the visual power of this simple but powerful solution.

Italy

155

design firm   Gaetano Grizzanti
designer   Gaetano Grizzanti
designer   Gaetano Grizzanti

client   **Salmoiraghi & Viganò—VistaSì**

A Different Way of Seeing a Brand

Salmoiraghi & Viganò, the top Italian chain of opticians, decided to enter the premium-price ophthalmic segment to further expand its market share. To avoid a positioning conflict between medium and medium-high pricing, Salmoiraghi & Viganò decided to create a new retail chain with a separate identity and completely different characteristics.

the brief   The primary values the new brand had to transmit were "simplicity and clarity," secondarily "innovation," and finally "professionalism." The project's starting point was to develop a suitable name and branding—the result being VistaSì, and the slogan *Vedi chiaro, spendi meno* (see clearly, spend less).

the solution   The design solution communicates the twin values of transparency and improvement in eyesight, plus that of "delivering good value for your money," as the designers explain. "The symbol accentuates the impact of visual communication with the twin forces of image and gesture: a pair of hands, joining thumb and forefinger to form two circles that represent a pair of glasses, behind which a virtual smiling human face is perceptible. The brandmark image can also be read as a double 'okay' gesture."

▲ The logotype is functional and effective in various color combinations and across a wide range of applications. A defined color palette of green and light blue was chosen to connote the VistaSì brand—"light and relaxing, with a familiar sense of being Italian."

▼ A graphic standards manual spells out the application guidelines for VistaSì. The effectiveness of the solution is demonstrated through the samples seen here: storefront signage and an engaging advertisement.

design firm	Gaetano Grizzanti
art director	Gaetano Grizzanti
designer	Gaetano Grizzanti
client	**Salmoiraghi & Viganò**

Good Optics

Salmoiraghi & Viganò is a well-known leading Italian optical brand, tracing its roots to the late 1800s. Today, it enjoys market brand awareness of 70 percent in Italy, and offers 230 points of sale across the country.

the brief The client approached the designer to develop an entirely new visual identity that would communicate a strong change and that could leverage its leadership role versus competitors by moving beyond being a distribution chain to becoming a brand.

the solution Only the well-known name was retained from the previous identity, written in a custom-designed font, Optica. The design solution centers on an eye symbol constructed of a series of visually engaging circles. The color choice is a refined chromatic pairing of blue and silver—authoritative, elegant, and avoiding ephemeral trendiness.

The bold new visual identity developed for Salmoiraghi & Viganò is applied with consistency and style across a wide range of media, such as this font CD, customer card, retail storefront, website, and a carry bag.

design firm	Jekyll & Hyde
designers	Marco Molteni
	Margherita Monguzzi
	Francesca Bozzia
	Serena Brovelli

Hukapan

Hukapan is a music production and management company created by the rock/pop band Elio e le storie tese, well known for its surreal and ironic lyrics. The client's stated need was to create "a simple and neat image" for the company to reflect both the provocative personality of the band as well as the professional and reliable attitude of the company. The design uses the word *Hukapan* from what the designers describe as "a gross phrase from the title track of the band's first album, *Elio Samaga Hukapan Kariyana Turu*, translated in an Indian dialect" along with the international H sign for hospital used outside of its usual context—appropriately ironic and a solution to the client's requests.

design firm	Jekyll & Hyde
designers	Marco Molteni
	Margherita Monguzzi

Antonio Maniscalco

The client is an architect and photographer, specializing in contemporary art and architecture photography. He approached the designers to create a new identity that would reflect his way of working. The designers explain, "He loves harmony and neatness and exploring space from different points of view." The solution is a monogram rendition featuring the client's initials in a contemporary style. The letter used for *a* rotates to become the *m*, reflecting the photographer's ability to "change his point of view and to give reality a new and different meaning."

design firm	Martina De Rui & Chiara Mangione
art director	Martina De Rui
designer	Martina De Rui

AHSI

AHSI is a leading firm in the field of scientific refrigeration and the supply of microbiological appliances for the health industry. The design brief called for a brand identity that was "cold, aseptic, and clean with technical appeal" and that could extend to various affiliates and subcompanies. The solution is a smooth, fluid shape inspired by the capital *A* in AHSI. It suggests the movement of water and, according to the designer, "pureness is emphasized by using pure cyan as the brand color."

design firm	Martina De Rui
art director	Martina De Rui
designer	Martina De Rui

Hammam

Hammam is a new Turkish bathhouse situated in the heart of Palermo, Sicily. The logo design and corporate image needed to relate strongly to North African Arabian culture and its influence on Sicily. A rhomboidal diamond, the decorative element typical of Arabian writing, was chosen by the designer to suggest a link with Islamic architecture. The blue and beige symbolize deep water and sand, respectively.

FONTEGRAFICA

A.RI.BI.

design firm · Cacao Design
designer · Cacao Design

client · **Fontegrafica**

Fontegrafica is a top-level printer, known worldwide for the Sappi International Printer of the Year 2003 awards and for the recent Sappi European Printer of the Year 2004 award. The design firm was tasked to rebrand the client to more adequately represent the firm's worldwide leadership and the top-quality orientation. The client requested that the designers create a prestigious image that would "be hard to print," allowing them to demonstrate their capabilities. The solution was to play with the initial *F*, making Fontagrafica recognizable immediately by means of classic lettering and innovative reproduction and packaging techniques, including mirror-effect foil stamping and embossing.

design firm · Luca Galessi
art director · Luca Galessi
designer · Luca Galessi

client · **Semeraro Arredamenti—L'Osteria**

The client, an Italian furniture retailer, asked the designer to create a complete identity for a new restaurant chain called L'Osteria (The Tavern), to be located inside the furniture stores of Semeraro Arredamenti. The simple, effective image combines a lowercase logotype in classic serifs with a chalklike, gestural image.

design firm · studiocharlie
art director · studiocharlie
designer · studiocharlie

client · **A.RI.BI.**

Associazione per il Rilancio della Bicicletta (Association for the Relaunch of the Bicycle, A.RI.BI) is a nonprofit organization in Bergamo that periodically organizes events "to sensitize public opinion about the bicycle." The designers were tasked with creating a mark and graphic concept for applications ranging from print to Web. The image "had to be happy and communicate a sense of freedom." The illustrated bike is reminiscent of a roadway symbol, and the solution works well in one color, to ensure frugal reproduction. The distance between the logo's two elements produces the effect of "a flying bicycle, which communicates happiness and freedom."

design firm · no.parking
art directors · Elisa Dall'Angelo
Sabine Lercher
Caterina Romio
designers · Elisa Dall'Angelo
Simone Piva

client · **Holimites Tour Operator**

The client is an online tour operator that organizes ski, snowboard, and trekking holidays for young people in the Dolomites (Italian Alps) under the tag line *Holimites—dynamic holidays in the Dolomites*. The logo had to be trendy, dynamic, and relevant to the world of snowboarding, skiing, free climbing, and youth sports. According to the designers, the solution is "a strong image with a little red logo" that applies readily to print, the Web, and various promotional gadgets. "It shows a young spirit and, at the same time, the good organization of the product."

Jekyll & Hyde
Marco Molteni
Margherita Monguzzi

client

Warner Music Italia

Lollipop Design

the brief

the solution

Lollipop is an all-girl Italian pop group, formed by the winners of a television show.
For the band's first album, the designers were approached by Warner Music Italia to design the band's logo and first CD. The request was to give the group a young and international appeal. The chosen logo is simple and sophisticated. It's based on the repetition of the same two graphic elements that form the letters of the band's name, Lollipop. The designers then developed a matching lowercase font based on the logo's letterforms that was used to write the singers' names. This project was selected and recognized in *ADI Design Index 2002* annual, showing the best Italian design of the year.

▲ The clean, strong logotype designed for the Italian all-girl band Lollipop is featured on the band's first CD package and the insert featuring the font based on the logotype's letterforms.

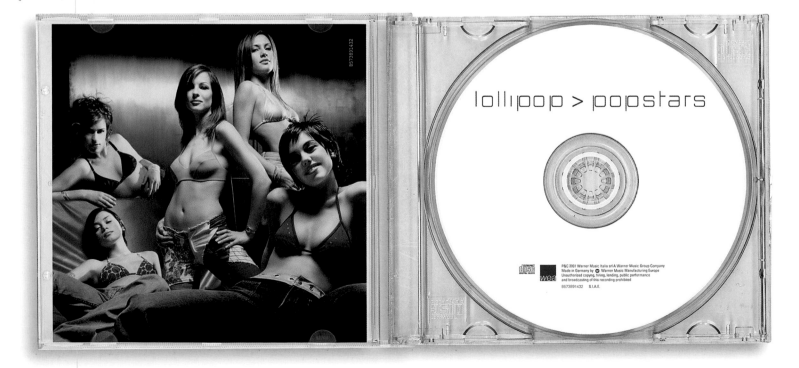

design firm | Studio Laura Moretti
art director | Laura Moretti
designer | Laura Moretti

client | **Castello Di Monsanto**

CASTELLO | 𝔐onsanto

1962 | 2002

Forty Years of Monsanto

"The roots of Castello Di Monsanto's history go back to the years of its first vintages, beginning in 1962. Today, every sip of Monsanto wine contains reminders of a history that can be summed up in a cluster of dates," reads the designer's description of this venerated Italian vintner.

the brief | The designer was commissioned to create an identity to celebrate the fortieth anniversary of Castello di Monsanto's prestigious winery. A main point in the identity was to be the magnificent wine cellar, a 820-foot (250 meter)-long gallery housing 1,200 barrels of wine.

the solution | The celebration logo was the first step. The designer explains, "The antique and the modern combine with equilibrium, telling the story of the historic roots of the company and the new generation's wish to experiment." Sophisticated visuals and careful attention to detail throughout the selection and development of supporting applications maintained a formal, communicative balance in all materials produced in conjunction with the celebration.

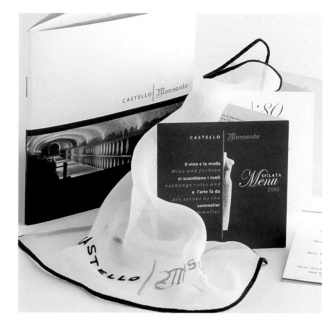

▲ The two-color logo developed for the fortieth anniversary celebration of Castello di Monsanto features two contrasting typographic styles set in contrasting quadrants.

▲ The identity was applied effectively to a wide range of promotional literature and collateral materials, such as these invitations, cards, and menus.

▼ This anniversary brochure cover shows the client's impressive wine cellar and features the anniversary logo reversed out of a regal, dark blue background.

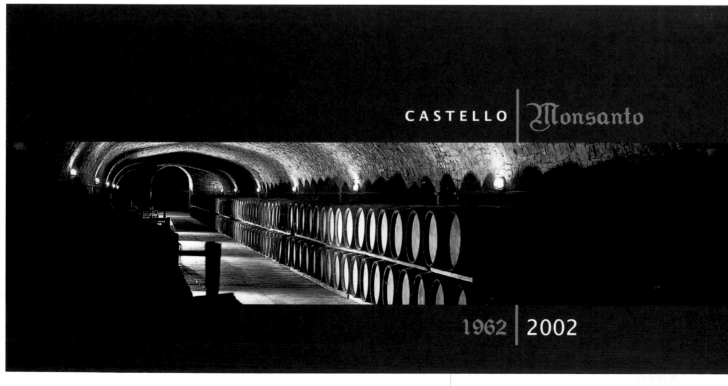

CASTELLO | 𝔐onsanto

1962 | 2002

design firm	Publicis Design
creative director	Fulvio Caldarelli
brand stategist	Paolo Romano
design director	Massimiliano Sagrati
project manager	Alessia Crisarà
designers	Massimiliano Sagrati
	Hanna Lehtinen
	Alfredo Laneve
copywriter	Gianluigi Biagini
client	**Sogin**

Communicating Reactive Thinking

Sogin is a state-owned company with the mission of carrying out safety maintenance activities involving radioactive materials and the dismantling of nuclear power plants, while ensuring the preservation of the environment.

the brief
In 2003, the company decided to launch a new communication plan. Publicis Design was charged with repositioning Sogin's identity. "Ability and reactive thinking" were the keywords to describe this high-powered company.

the solution
The designers describe their approach: "The revitalization of the company starts by taking a direction away from the idea of nuclear energy. So, the new logo design represents the concept of the natural environment. Environment, technology, and safety—these three words form the payoff and communicate immediately the core identity values and the core idea of the company's personality."

► The new visual identifier designed for Sogin—the symbol's *S* in rotation—takes on the form of a leaf and, together with a refined lowercase logotype and a blue/green color palette, represents concepts of the natural environment.

▼ Detailed application guidelines for the fresh new identity appear in a concise graphic standards manual. Stationery and print applications show implementation of the refined Sogin identity.

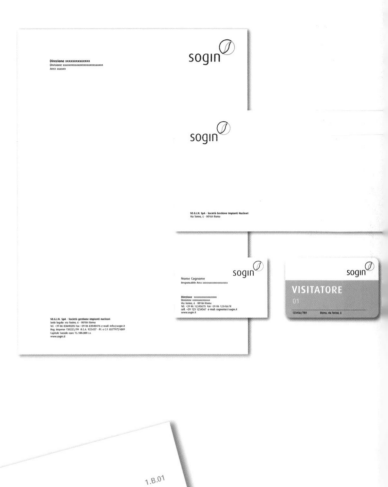

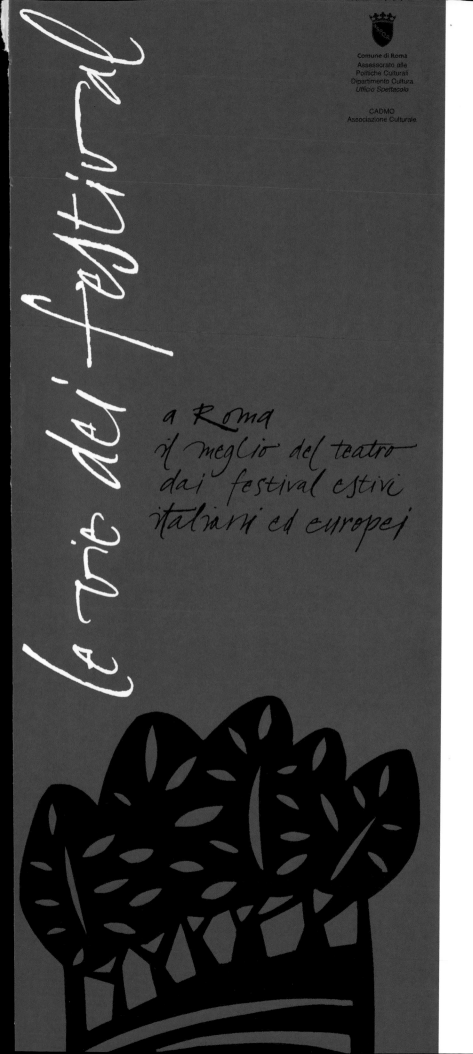

Comune di Roma
Assessorato alle
Politiche Culturali
Dipartimento Cultura
Ufficio Spettacolo

CADMO
Associazione Culturale

design firm	Studio Amato
art director	Silvana Amato
designer	Silvana Amato
illustrator	Francesca Biasetion
client	**Cadmo Le Vie Dei Festival**

Celebrating the Theater

| the brief | The client is a theater festival in Rome. The designers were tasked with developing an expressive image, stationery, and promotional print materials for this tenth annual festival featuring the best in Italian and European theater. |
| the solution | The illustrative logo developed for the festival combines a woodcut illustration with expressive, gestural calligraphy to create an engaging, organic, and "human" image for the festival. |

◄ Effective use of two-color printing in
rust-orange and black helps tie together a
powerful, graphic impression across the
range of stationery and promotional printed
applications. Shown at left is the visually
striking event poster.

Korea's many great scholars and philosophers are not well known to outsiders, due to the country's early isolationism. Most outsiders know South Korea for its powerful brands (Hyundai and Samsung), its distinctive Taeguk flag (representing the center of the universe and all creation), Taekwondo, and Korean cuisine.

South Korea

area	99,300 km^2
GDP, per capita	$19,500 USD
official language	Korean
population	48.3 million

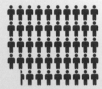

The Republic of Korea—or South Korea, as it is commonly known today—comprises the southern half of the Korean peninsula. To its north lies North Korea, with which it formed a single nation until 1948, a division entrenched by the Korean War of 1950 to 1953 through the establishment of a demilitarized zone near the thirty-eighth parallel. Following World War II (and the end of Japanese occupation in 1946), a republic had been set up in the southern half of the Korean peninsula whereas a Communist-style government was installed in the north. South Korea shares its traditional culture with that of North Korea. Throughout history, Korean culture was greatly influenced by that of China and its Buddhist, Taoist, and Confucian traditions. Today, the roles are reversing, with an increased Korean influence in China in terms of popular music, fashion, and television drama.

Seoul is the busy capital city of this parliamentary democratic republic whose main religions are Christianity, Confucianism, and Buddhism. As one of the four East Asian Tigers, South Korea has achieved an impressive record of growth and integration into the global economy, making South Korea the eleventh largest economy in the world, with a GDP per capita equal to the medium economies of the European Union.

† = 1 million

design firm | Ahn Graphics Ltd.
designer | Ahn Sang-Soo

client | **Icograda Millennium Congress, Oullim 2000 Seoul**

The world congress of the Icograda was held in Seoul, South Korea, in October 2000. The remarkable gathering brought together more than 1,500 visual communicators from forty countries.

Ahn Sang-Soo, the event's orchestrator, explains the event's thematic core: "*Oullim*, a Korean word meaning 'the great harmony,' is proposed as an open design concept that can break through the closed design concept of the industrial society—beyond the modern project of the twentieth century and enlightenment ideals of design. We hope that the concept of design can be elevated to an autonomous language and, at the same time, be expanded into the public realm. Oullim is proposed as an alternative to dualism, a modern concept of the West that divides—rather than harmonizes—North, South, East, and West."

"Oullim promises to tune nature, humans, and machines, to harmonize past, present, and future. Oullim knows no demarcation between the whole and the individual, or between principle and substance. The spirit of Oullim emanates from putting on an equal footing all individuals and people and nature, and all things and nature," he explains. The holistic identifier that formed the core of all of the event's applications provides a visual expression of these stated ideals.

icograda millennium congress oullim 2000 seoul

Typo Janchi
seoul typography biennale

design firm | Ahn Graphics Ltd.
designer | Ahn Sang-Soo

client | **TypoJanchi—Seoul Typography Biennale**

The first biennial TypoJanchi was held at the Seoul Arts Center Design Gallery in 2001. Its stated mandate was to "introduce a new stream of typography and to gather together excellent typographic works from around world in a single place, so that Seoul will be reborn as a city of typography." *Janchi* is a Korean word meaning "open festival." The event's logotype consists of an engaging typographic construct and the name spelled out in English and Korean (using the Hangul alphabet).

South Korea

South Korea 165

design firm   Interbrand Korea
art director   Yong Woo Shin

client   **Korean Overseas Information
Service/Government Information Agency of Korea**

Dynamic Korea

the brief   As outlined by the designers, "The 'Dynamic Korea' campaign was originally created to stir international interest in promoting the 2002 World Cup. However, since the successful completion of the games, the Korean government realized a need to revamp the existing image to appeal to a wider global audience and to project the overall attributes of Korea—from its long cultural heritage to its recent prominence as a leader in the high-tech industry. Thus, the challenge became how to evolve from a sporting campaign image to that of a sophisticated, sustainable national brand identity. Interbrand Korea was selected to conduct a comprehensive identity program that started with a visual audit of the existing logo, as well as research of other related national branding programs, to define current problems and find effective solutions. Based on these findings, the designers formulated a communication strategy that simultaneously embodied assets of the existing logo with the ideals and images of a 'New Korea' in this fast-paced global community."

the solution   The identity components are described as follows: "Meaning: the transition from 'Land of the Morning Calm' to 'Land of Morning Activity and Vigor.' Function: a visual tool to aid in promoting Korea to a global audience, conveying a consistent national image through a diverse range of media, expressing Korea's unique national brand, and differentiating it from other countries. Symbol Concept: a design approach based on a modern refinement of the Taeguk mark symbolizing the center of the universe and all creation. 'The New Korean Wave' is a forward-thinking design philosophy. With the *A* as the focal point, the word *Dynamic* expands out in both directions, symbolizing the expansion of Korea in today's global community. Color: the traditional red that shoots forth from the mark symbolizes Korea's vigor and energy as well as its rich history and vibrant future. The blue, which provides the foundation for the energetic Taeguk mark, symbolizes the sky and sea that surrounds the Korean peninsula. This color is also indicative of Korea's development into a forerunner of technological innovation. This relationship between red and blue symbolizes both the distinctive Taeguk mark of Korea and the present and future of the Republic of Korea. The gray denotes a tranquil calmness as well as a modern, intellectual image. This new design aptly symbolizes the spirit of the Korean people."

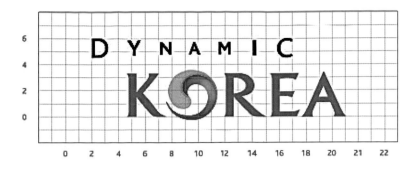

▲ The logomark developed for Dynamic Korea is a composition full of energy.

▼ The identity is seen on promotional clothing, posters, banners, and print materials. A powerful image is created through consistent use of the effective core identity adapted appropriately to individual viewing contexts and media.

Lebanon

area	10,400 km²
GDP, per capita	$4,700 USD
official language	Arabic
population	3.7 million

Lebanon is a parliamentary democratic republic bordered the Mediterranean Sea, Israel, and Syria. It is considered to be one of the fifteen present-day countries that comprise the ancient "Cradle of Humanity." Its main religions today are Islam and Christianity.

The French League of Nations Trust territory of Lebanon became independent in 1943. Since that time, Lebanon has known much strife and sectarian friction among Christians, Shi'a Muslims, and Druze. The devastating 1975 to 1991 civil war seriously damaged Lebanon's economic infrastructure, cut national output by half, and nearly ended Lebanon's long-held position as a Middle Eastern entrepot and banking hub.

Peace has enabled the central government to restore control in Beirut, collect taxes, and regain access to key port and government facilities. Economic recovery has been helped by a financially sound banking system and resilient small- and medium-scale manufacturers, with family remittances, banking services, manufactured and farm exports, and international aid as the main sources of foreign exchange. Modern Lebanon has a competitive, free-market regime built on commercial tradition. The economy is service oriented, with main growth sectors including banking and tourism.

= 1 million

design firm   Mayda Freije Makdessi
art director Mayda Freije Makdessi
designer   Mayda Freije Makdessi

client

Ghada Ghanem

The client, Ghada Ghanem, is a soprano who performs in Lebanon and abroad, as well as acting as a voice teacher. She required an identity with a contemporary look that would reflect her musical background as well as her Lebanese heritage. The logo is the Arabic initials of her first and last names intertwined in a musical arabesque. The unconventional size of the delicately embossed business card complements the identity's classical elements.

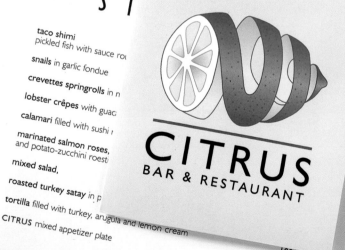

design firm   Rima Rifai
art director Rima Rifai
designer   Nathalie Irani

client

Irani—Citrus Bar and Restaurant

The designers were commissioned to create an identity for Irani that would compete with trendy restaurants in the newly developed downtown Beirut. The solution, as described by the designers, is "a simple yet zesty approach, combining an image for a 'fusion' cuisine restaurant and clubbing."

le charcutier aoun
لو شركوتيه عون

designer · Jimmy Ghazal

client · **Le Charcutier Aoun**

Meat Market Design

the brief · Le Charcutier Aoun is the largest supermarket chain in Lebanon—*Charcuterie* is French for butchershop. The designers were tasked with creating an identity for a series of supermarkets that operated as a chain, but retained individuality.

the solution · The solution was a complete visual identity that was introduced gradually over a three-year period, enabling a cost-efficient move to a uniform identity for all outlets. The logo is a highly stylized crown, inscribed in a circular shape. Its purpose is to convey the aims of this corporation—"quality, service, speed, and good prices," and to emphasize the slogan, *Because our customer is king*. The corporate color is orange, "a friendly color by its nature, full of energy and movement." The Latin logotype is set in a medium weight of Frutiger, using lowercase characters "to prevent visual distractions." The Arabic text was created especially to comple- ment the Latin logotype and to give it a harmonious, balanced look and weight.

dairy
الالبان والاجبان

milk
حليب

pasta
معكرونة

- The Le Charcutier Aoun logotype was created in both Latin and Arabic alphabets.

- The strong use of the corporate orange makes for a striking supermarket façade.

▼ A unique "personalized signage system" comprising custom-designed icons was developed to represent all the symbolic needs and product categories of the supermarket. The orange icons are used throughout the supermarket, imbuing the shopper's experience with the chain's identity and aiding navigation in the stores.

rice
ارز

wine
النبيذ

tools
عدة

home appliances
ادوات منزلية

diapers
حفاضات

baby food
اكل للاطفال

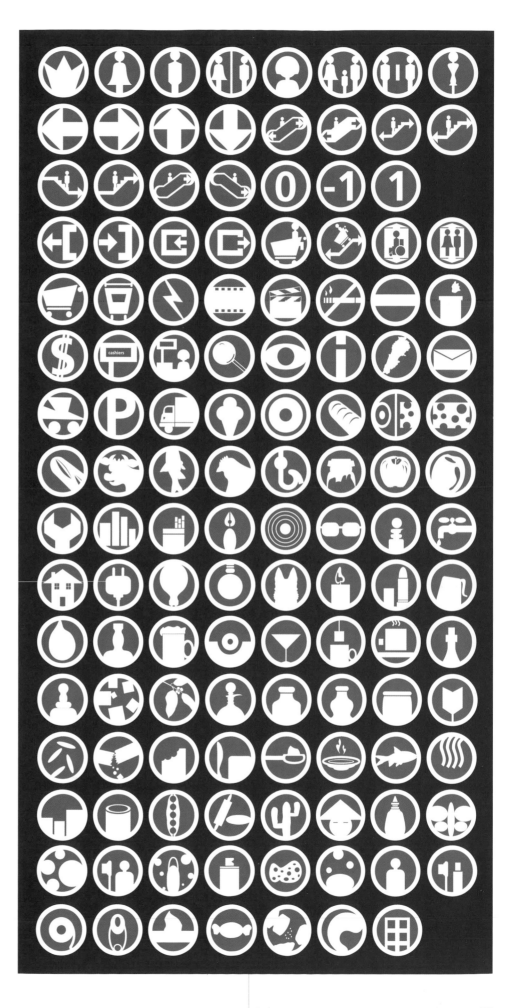

design firm | Taketwo [Designhaus]
art director | Leila Musfy
designers | Leila Musfy
 | Nisreen Fayad
 | Nadia El Hage

client

Fadi Ashkar—BlueFin (Import/Export)

The client is an importer and distributor of Japanese foods and products. The brief called for a logo and a corporate identity that would "maintain a reputation of freshness and reliability." The logo is a playful logo; the introduction of Japanese characters gives BlueFin a sense of authenticity. The color palette is fresh and vibrant, reflecting water and the colors of raw fish.

design firm | Taketwo [Designhaus]
art director | Leila Musfy
designers | Leila Musfy
 | Nisreen Fayad
arabic calligrapher | Samir Sayegh

client

Beiteddine Festival Committee

The designers were approached to design a new identity for this annual cultural festival. The logo solution incorporates both Arabic and Latin alphabets, using calligraphy and typography, respectively, to establish "a cultural, festive feel." A colorful supporting palette of graphics and duotone photography extends the logo's expression across a range of print applications, as seen on the cover of this folder.

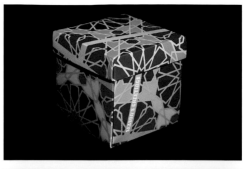

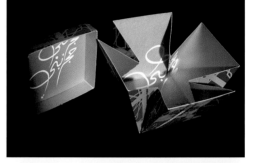

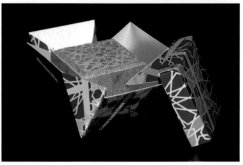

design firm   Taketwo [Designhaus]
art director   Leila Musfy
designers   Leila Musfy
                Nisreen Fayad
arabic calligrapher Samir Sayegh
client   **South for Construction (SFC)**

Building Capacity

A construction company based in Lebanon
since 1982, SFC is involved primarily in building,
rebuilding, and renovating Lebanon's infrastructure.

the brief   The designers describe the job as "bringing the
company into the twenty-first century without
eliminating its original cause. Arabic language
must be the primary language, and the arabesque
logo needed to be studied and its proportions
corrected."

the solution   The design solution introduced Arabic calligraphy
in combination with the delicate arabesque design
to provide a clean, fresh corporate identity.

► Shown here is the identity applied to colorful packaging for
a "Season's Greetings" paperweight brick. Note the cleverly
constructed box that opens itself with a gesture when the lid is
removed and assembles without glue.

▼ Coordinated stationery items feature the intricate arabesque logo
and two-language identity. A delicate paper stock with a laid finish
enhanced the tactile feel of the print materials.

Lithuania

area	65,200 km²
GDP, per capita	$8,400 USD
official languages	Lithuanian, Russian, Polish
population	3.6 million

The Republic of Lithuania (*Lietuva* in Lithuanian) is one of the three Baltic States situated along the Baltic Sea. It shares borders with Latvia to the north, Belarus to the southeast, Poland to the south, and the Kaliningrad Oblast of Russia to the southwest.

Independent between the two world wars, Lithuania was annexed by the U.S.S.R. in 1940. Since 1940 (as well as from 1323 to 1919), its capital city has been Vilnius. Predominantly Christian, this Eastern European country seceded from the Soviet Union in 1991, becoming a parliamentary democratic republic. Subsequently, Lithuania restructured its economy for eventual integration into Western European institutions and was invited to join NATO in 2002. It joined the European Union in 2004. Prior to 1998, Lithuania had conducted most of its trade with Russia, but the 1998 Russian financial crisis forced the country to orient toward the West. In 2003, Lithuania had the highest economic growth ratio among all European Union candidates, and 2004's GDP growth rate reflects further impressive economic development.

 = 1 million

design firm   Gedimino Lašo Design Studio
art director   Gediminas Lašas
designer   Gediminas Lašas

client   **Kreisel Vilnius UAB**
The client is a newly formed company producing adhesives, plaster coatings, leveling mixtures, and insulation systems for the building industry. In Lithuania, the word *Limpa* means "stick" or "sticky." A new brand name and logo was needed that would "provide differentiation from competitors, be 'shiny,' and apply easily with flexo printing to paper sacks and various substrates." The solution uses the Cooper font, because, as the designer states, "it has a sticky character." The background rectangle is the traditional shape of a ceramic tile. The red color provides a strong contrast with the black text, and a red line with a soft shape surrounds the logo, which helps reinforce the mark's "stickyness" and describes the edge of the logo, making application to various surfaces easier.

design firm   Aušra Lisauskiene
designer   Aušra Lisauskiene

client   **"Zonta" International Vilnius**
This identity was designed for the International Women's Art Works Exhibition "Flying Carpet," creating a "low-budget, original, and elegant identity that symbolizes women's dreams and ideas." The calligraphic solution possesses an expressive, spontaneous, and feminine feel.

design firm   Gedimino Lašo Design Studio
art director   Gediminas Lašas
designer   Gediminas Lašas

client   **Association of Lithuanian Guides**
The client is a nonprofit organization of guides working in the tourism field. The task was to create for this "union of guides" a logo with a Lithuanian character that also represented various kinds of people. The basis of the logo comprises the colors of the Lithuanian flag. The differently colored triangles represent various individuals in the association who together form a union, in organized circles at different levels.

design firm   Gedimino Lašo Design Studio
art director   Gediminas Lašas
designer   Gediminas Lašas

client   *Ekstra* **UAB**
This newly formed magazine publishes news from Lithuania and abroad, as well content focused on political, economic, and cultural themes. The challenge was to create a new logo and layout for the magazine that would be expressive and easily recognizable and to provide a suitable introduction into the market. The "red label with yellow color" masthead was chosen because it was unique in the local market. The logotype is set in bold, white Lithos, reversed from the background for excellent contrast. As a special element, the *S* was enlarged and set in yellow. Seen together, these elements create a handsome, recognizable masthead easily distinguished from other magazines on the shelf.

Macau

area	25.4 km²
GDP, per capita	$18,300 USD
official languages	Portuguese, Cantonese
population	469,900

Macau, now the Macau Special Administrative Region of the People's Republic of China, is a small territory on the southern coast of China, 43 miles (70 km) southwest of Hong Kong, and 91 miles (145 km) from Guangzhou. Colonized by the Portuguese in the sixteenth century, Macau was the earliest European settlement in the Far East. Pursuant to a prior agreement between China and Portugal, Macau reverted to Chinese control in 1999. As with Hong Kong, Macau falls under the "one country, two systems" formula whereby the country continues to enjoy a high degree of autonomy for the next fifty years.

Native residents of Macau mostly speak Cantonese and Portuguese, though Mandarin and English are also spoken. Broadly, *Macanese* refers to all permanent inhabitants of Macau, but narrowly, it refers to the ethnic group in Macau originating from Portuguese descent, usually mixed with Chinese blood.

Aside from its historical colonial relics, the biggest attractions in Macau for outsiders are the casinos. Though many forms of gambling are legal, the most popular game is Pai Gow, a game played with Chinese dominoes. Gamblers from Hong Kong often take a one-day excursion to the city; ferry service by hydrofoil between Hong Kong and Macau is available twenty-four hours a day, seven days a week.

Macau's economy is based largely on tourism, as well as the manufacturing of textiles and fireworks. Efforts to diversify have spawned other small industries, such as the production of toys, artificial flowers, and electronics. The clothing industry provides about three-fourths of export earnings, and the gambling industry is estimated to contribute more than 40 percent of GDP.

= 1 million

designers : Filipa Simões
Nuno Soares

client

Conselho das Comunidades Macaenses (CCM)

The Macanese Communities Council (CCM) is a private institution whose main aim is "to incorporate the interests and wishes of the Macanese community in the diaspora (ex-patriot community) and its articulation with their counterparts in Macau." The challenge was to create a logo representing this spirit for use in correspondence and activities of the council. The solution, as explained by the designer, "is based on the iconography of the Chinese carved seals, ratifying the union among the Western communities that form the Macanese diaspora. Western and Eastern calligraphy meets when the abbreviated *CCM* fuses with the Chinese character for *door*, part of Macau's Cantonese designation, symbolizing the melting pot of cultures that defines the Macanese people. The color chosen resembles red sealing wax, and the characteristics of the logo—elegant and institutional—are intrinsically connected to Macau."

CONSELHO DAS
COMUNIDADES
MACAENSES
澳門土生國際聯誼會

design firm : Rita O. Paulo

client

Portugal Telecom

The designer was given six days to design an event identity, an innovative "mooncake" box, and collateral for a special dinner. The result, as explained by the designer, "uses a shadowed outline and a large gradient moon in the background—the image is magical. The design was intended to be a hexagonal box, but there was not enough time to produce such a difficult shape in so short a time." The accompanying leaflet extends the graphic identity and explains the legend of the Chinese Mooncake festival—which takes place every autumn—in three languages: Chinese, English, and Portuguese.

Mexico is a charming nation and an enduring enigma—from the echoed splendor of Mayan civilization, to the choked streets of Mexico City's 20+ million; from Zapatista revolutionaries in the remote mountains, to world-class beach resorts sporting their own airports, and all things Mexican that the world loves—deliciously spicy cuisine; tequila; and the requisite song, dance, and festivals.

Mexico

area	1,972,600 km²
GDP, per capita	$8,800 USD
official language	Spanish
population	105 million

Mexico (Estados Unidos Mexicanos in Spanish) is the most northerly and westerly country in Latin America and the most populous Spanish-speaking country in the world. A federal presidential democratic republic, it is bordered to the north by the United States, to the southeast by Guatemala and Belize, to the west by the Pacific Ocean, and to the east by the Gulf of Mexico and the Caribbean Sea.

Home to advanced Amerindian civilizations, Mexico came under Spanish rule for three centuries before achieving independence early in 1821, though much of the country remains staunchly Catholic. The culture of Mexico reflects the complexity of Mexico's history through the blending of pre-Hispanic Mesoamerican civilizations and the culture of Spain, imparted during its period of colonization. More recently, influences from the United States, and to a lesser extent, influences from Europe, Africa, and Asia, have shaped Mexican culture.

Elections held in July 2000 marked the first time since the 1910 Mexican Revolution that the opposition defeated the party in government. Mexico has a free-market economy with a mixture of modern and outmoded industry and agriculture, increasingly dominated by the private sector. The number of state-owned enterprises has steadily decreased in the past two decades under a policy of privatizing and expanding competition in seaports, railroads, telecommunications, electricity, natural gas distribution, and airports.

A strong manufacturing and export sector have bolstered the Mexican economy, and private consumption has become the leading driver of growth, accompanied by increased employment and higher wages. Trade with the United States and Canada has tripled since NAFTA was implemented in 1994, and Mexico is pursuing additional trade agreements with most countries in Latin America. It has signed free trade deals with the European Union and Japan, putting more than 90 percent of trade under free-trade agreements and lessening its dependence on the United States.

= 1 million

MUSEO DE LA REVOLUCIÓN

design firm — Modulo
art director — Julio Muñoz Del Bosque
designer — Julio Muñoz Del Bosque

client — **Museo De La Revolución**

The Museum of the Revolution is a year-round exhibition of the Mexican way of life, government, weapons, and historical artifacts during the 1910 revolution. The identity for the museum had to be attractive to secondary-school students and their parents. The solution is a stylized perspective of the museum's façade—this is one of Mexico City's best-known historic buildings and is widely recognized.

PRODUCT OF MEXICO

design firm — Burgeff Co.
art director — Patrick Burgeff
designer — Patrick Burgeff

client — **Sabormex/La Sierra**

La Sierra, a Mexican food brand, called for an identity to promote Mexican food for export. The logo needed to "have a Mexican flavor, both visually and literally." The solution combines Mexico's three staple ingredients—beans, corn, and peppers—along with a clay pot to form the logo.

mini

design firm — Modulo
art director — Julio Muñoz Del Bosque
designer — Julio Muñoz Del Bosque

client — **Mini**

Mini is a new grocery store chain in Mexico. The designer was commissioned to design a unique identity. The symbol is an abstracted combination of a circle with the left side of the letter *m*. It creates a simple figure that is recognized easily.

CAFE ARGOVIA

design firm — Burgeff Co.
art director — Patrick Burgeff
designer — Patrick Burgeff

client — **Argovia**

Argovia is a brand of Mexican roasted coffee, which is sold by the bag. The designer was requested to create an identity to represent this good-quality Mexican coffee. The solution uses "a soft, curved form that denotes taste and smell. Black was chosen for elegance, the type for tradition."

*Malaysia represents incredible contrasts—
from the ultramodern skyscrapers of high-tech
Kuala Lumpur (the country's capital), to the
indigenous Iban who still live in traditional
longhouses in jungle villages, to the aboriginal
hunter-gatherer Orang Asli peoples.*

Malaysia

area	329,800 km²
GDP, per capita	$8,600 USD
official languages	Malay, Chinese
population	23 million

The Federation of Malaysia is a Southeast Asian country consisting of two geographical regions divided by the South China Sea: West Malaysia, commonly known as the Malay Peninsula, shares a land frontier on the north with Thailand and is connected by a causeway and a bridge on the south with the island state of Singapore; East Malaysia, the northern part of the island of Borneo, is bordered to the south by Indonesia and shares a frontier with the Sultanate of Brunei on the east, south, and west.

Malaysia was formed in 1963, through a federation of the former British colonies of Malaya and Singapore, including the East Malaysian states of Sabah and Sarawak on the northern coast of Borneo. The first several years of the country's history were marred by Indonesian efforts to control Malaysia, Philippine claims to Sabah, and Singapore's secession from the federation in 1965. In the following decades, Malaysia transformed itself from a producer of raw materials into an emerging multisector economy. Growth has been driven almost exclusively by exports, particularly of electronics.

Malaysia is a uniquely multicultural society, with Malays, Chinese, and Indians living side by side. The Malays are the largest community, numbering 60 percent of the population. They are Muslims, speak Malay, and are largely responsible for the country's political fortunes. The Chinese comprise a quarter of the population; are mostly Buddhists, Taoists, or Christians; speak the Hokkien, Cantonese, Hakka, and Teochew dialects; and have historically been dominant in the business community. The Indians (mainly Hindu Tamils from southern India) account for 10 percent of the population; speak Tamil, Malayalam, and some Hindi; and live mainly in the larger towns on the west coast of the peninsula. There is also a sizeable Sikh community, and Eurasians, Kampucheans, Vietnamese, and indigenous tribes make up the remaining population. Most Eurasians are Christians, and those of mixed Portuguese and Malay descent speak a Portuguese Creole, called Papia Kristang. Other Eurasians of mixed Malay and Spanish descent (descendants of immigrants from the Philippines, mostly in Sabah) speak the only Asian-Spanish Creole, Chavacano. Cambodians and Vietnamese are mostly Buddhists (Cambodians of the Theravada sect, and Vietnamese the Mahayana sect).

= 1 million

art director   Liza Low
designer   Lai Yen Yee

client   **Identity Matters**

Design Matters

Established in 2003, Identity Matters specializes in corporate and brand identity consultancy, "providing 360-degree strategic and visual communications solutions to companies of different sizes across all industries."

the brief   The challenge was to design a distinctive corporate logotype for the new company. The designer states, "Identity is the bedrock for any enterprise to gain recognition. The importance of "Identity Matters" is defined in the self-explanatory name. This mark must be unique, to distinguish itself to target audiences before it can even begin to shape the identity. Thus, a clear and powerful mark was needed to encapsulate the concept of identity."

the solution   The corporate name was abbreviated to "I'M." "The idea is it answers the question, 'Who am I?' prompting the need for a clear and well-defined identity. The logotype uses Frutiger Roman, with the dot and apostrophe modified. The colors are black and Cool Gray 4, delivering a sense of business seriousness with simplicity."

▲ A presentation folder uses the identity and the modified "dot" and "apostrophe" symbols as a background pattern.

▼ Shown here, the identity applied to business cards. The card is two sided, with the color scheme reversed on the opposite side.

UK office Readings, Blackmore End Braintree
Essex CM7 4DH United Kingdom. Tel ++44(0)1787 463206
Fax ++44(0)1787 462122

identity matters sdn bhd 4 Lorong Riong, Bangsar
59100 Kuala Lumpur, Malaysia. Email llow@pc.jaring.my
Mobile +6012 2112 699 Fax +603 2284 4880

Liza Low Managing Director

design firm	Octagon Creative
art directors	Teh Lee See
	Melisa Wong
designers	Melisa Wong
	Teh Lee See
client	**IOI Corporation**

A Distinct Palette

IOI Corporation specializes in property plantations and oleo-chemicals.

the brief — The designers were asked to design a visual palette for annual report covers for the entire corporate group, a scheme that would be used consistently for five years. The designs needed to convey a strong, collective corporate identity.

the solution — The solution uses concise, clear placement of the company's name and logo and a distinctive style based on a refined palette of type, graphic elements, diagrammatic illustrations, and macro photography. Each report is effective on its own, yet shares a distinct corporate personality with the reports of other divisions.

Annual reports signal the corporate divisions they represent starting with a single glance at the cover and carrying a thematic color through the entire report. The reports are effective individually and also project a strong corporate identity collectively.

design firm	Octagon Creative
art director	Melisa Wong
designers	Melisa Wong
	Chuckie Yau
client	**Hilton Kuala Lumpur**

An Old Name Gets an Update

the brief
An international hotel chain opens a new location in Malaysia's capital city. The designers explain the challenge: "Hilton International approached Octagon Creative to create a collection of sales and promotional materials for the opening of their new hotel in Kuala Lumpur. The aim was to create a look that is contemporary and different from the 'old' Hilton, which was getting stale in the market, locally and internationally."

the solution
"We embarked on designing a range of sales and marketing collaterals incorporating the 'Are You Ready' message that was mandatory worldwide," explains the designer. "These printed materials were used during their pre-opening activities. After the official opening, posters for Hilton took a different message—'Live It to the Hilt,' became the tag line. Octagon's solution is to create marketing solutions that are contemporary, funky, arty, and colorful."

▼ A versatile color palette, a distinctive typographic "voice," stylish photography, and special printing techniques (including die-cuts, embossing, foil stamping, and varnishes) tie together an appealing image for the Hilton's opening launch in Kuala Lumpur, as seen here in this sampling of collateral applications.

The Netherlands concocts colorful recall—painterly landscapes, endless fields of tulips, scenic canals, wooden shoes, windmills, fragrant cheeses, Dutch Masters, Amsterdam's red light district, and The Diary of Anne Frank.

Netherlands

area	41,600 km²
GDP, per capita	$27,100 USD
official language	Dutch
population	16 million

The Netherlands is a parliamentary democracy under a constitutional monarch. The Netherlands seceded from Spanish rule in 1581, and the Kingdom of the Netherlands was formed in 1815. In 1830, Belgium seceded and formed a separate kingdom. The Netherlands remained neutral in World War I but suffered invasion and occupation by Germany in World War II. Situated in northwestern Europe, it borders the North Sea, Belgium, and Germany. The country is often referred to by the name Holland, although this is technically incorrect—Holland was the economic powerhouse during the time of the United Provinces (1581–1795), before the Napoleonic era split the nation into North and South Holland.

The Netherlands (its name means "the Low Countries") is one of the most densely populated and geographically low-lying countries in the world, famous for its dikes, dams, canals, and windmills. A modern, industrialized nation, it is a major exporter of agricultural products and enjoys a prosperous and open economy. The country was a founding member of NATO and the E.E.C. (now the E.U.) and introduced the euro in 1999. Industrial activity is predominantly in food processing, chemicals, petroleum refining, and electrical machinery. The Dutch rank third worldwide in value of agricultural exports, behind the United States and France, and ranked fifth on the 2004 list of nations with the highest standard of life, behind Norway, Sweden, Australia, and Canada.

Amsterdam is the official capital as stated by the constitution, whereas the Hague is the administrative capital (the seat of government), the home of the queen, the location for most foreign embassies, and the seat of the International Court of Justice. A predominantly Christian nation, the Netherlands has long been known for social tolerance and its liberal policies (such as those regarding gay marriage, euthanasia, and recreational drug use) are often mentioned abroad.

The Netherlands has a history intertwined with great painters (Rembrandt van Rijn, Johannes Vermeer, Vincent van Gogh, and Piet Mondrian), writers, philosophers (Erasmus of Rotterdam and Spinoza), graphic artists (M. C. Escher), and design movements (such as de Stijl).

♦ = 1 million

design firm	ankerxstrijbos
art director	Hans Strijbos
designer	Hans Strijbos
client	**Stichting CPNB**

Dutch publishers and booksellers have long cooperated in promoting trade books. In 1983, this task was allotted to the Collectieve Propaganda can het Nederlandse Boek (CPNB—Collective Promotion for the Dutch Book), a foundation established in Amsterdam to encourage the habits of book reading and book buying. The designer was asked to create the logo for an annual literary prize, "De Jonge Jury" (the young jury), for the best Dutch youth book chosen by young readers. "The solution is effective because it mingles chaos and diversity in text with order and clearness—just what the jury does by selecting the best books out of a wide range of others." A cluster of Garamond characters in black and bright yellow provides the desired effect.

design firm	ankerxstrijbos
art director	Menno Anker
designer	Frank Stienen
client	**Tracé**

This logo, developed for Tracé (meaning "track" or "route"), a center for physical rehabilitation, depicts a human figure as it extends the boundaries of physical possibilities. The client helps people return to their regular jobs after an injury or illness. The font used is The Sans, and the chosen colors provide "a contemporary, yet trustful, representation."

design firm	ankerxstrijbos
art director	Menno Anker
designer	Menno Anker
client	**CBK Utrecht (Center for Fine Arts Utrecht)**

Centrum voor Beeldende Kunsten Utrecht (CBK) is an art institution in the city of Utrecht. The designer explains, "The mark combines my own handwriting with DIN Mittelschrift (the font) to create a strange sense that represents the personal and very diverse aspects of art. It's effective precisely because it is very atypical for a logo—in trying to read the words it makes you think about why it is formed the way it is, just the way art can trigger your brain. The color was chosen to help create a vivid and modern identity."

design firm	ankerxstrijbos
art director	Menno Anker
designer	Menno Anker
client	**The Dutch Ministry of the Interior and Kingdom Relations**

EVA stands for "Een voor Allen" (One for All), a single nationwide communication system for essential services—the police, the fire brigade, and ambulances. *Eva* is also Dutch for the biblical name Eve. The logo takes a form "distilled from a speech balloon as used in comic books," according to the designer. "It also represents a shield. These forms and the sturdy typography are very appropriate for the services involved. The simplicity of the design makes it easy to use in diverse applications and in various environments, and the logo reinforces the importance of communicating and working together."

design firm   Tarek Atrissi Design
designer   Tarek Atrissi

client   **Qatar Tourism Authority**

Branding a Nation

Qatar is a small but wealthy independent emirate located on the Persian Gulf that wanted to rework its international image. Designing a country's identity is one of the most unique challenges a designer could face. Nation branding is becoming more common as countries consciously position themselves to enhance their images and to compete in the lucrative tourism sector. Shaping exactly the right image with an accurate feel that truly reflects the country is a big task as well as a considerable responsibility. It was no surprise to many that Lebanese designer Tarek Atrissi (whose design studio is based in the Netherlands) was chosen for this exciting project. In the past few years, the twenty-five-year-old designer has become one of the best recognized designers in the Arab world.

Qatar's identity truly makes a unique contribution to the field of nation branding and promises to become an icon in the history of Arabic graphic design as it successfully merges history and modernity—as well as East and West—to position Qatar worldwide as "the Heart of the Arabian Gulf." Atrissi's nation-branding effort reflects the essential characteristics of Qatar with elegance, refinement, and five-star destination quality.

▲ Qatar's efforts to publicize its new identity went well beyond corporate materials.

▲ Arabic calligraphy became a main element of the identity.

► To maintain consistency, a graphic standards manual outlined how the simple, refined, elegant new logo for Qatar could be used.

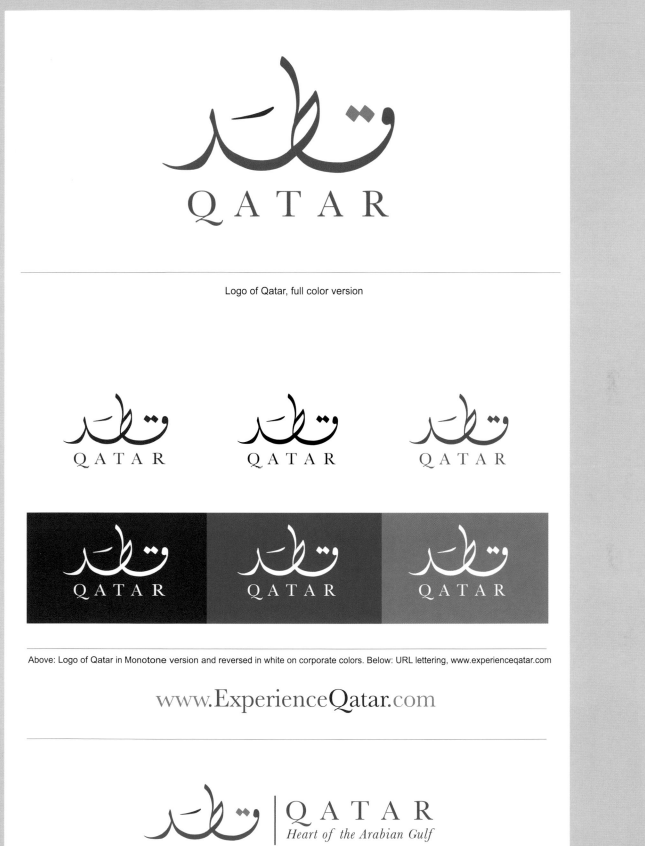

Logo of Qatar, full color version

Above: Logo of Qatar in Monotone version and reversed in white on corporate colors. Below: URL lettering, www.experienceqatar.com

www.ExperienceQatar.com

Logo and strapline

The client's stated objective was to "establish Qatar as one of the world's leading quality destinations for leisure, business, education, and sports" and, thereby, promote Qatar as a significant tourist destination. The desire was to "create a logo and, hence, a complete visual identity of Qatar as a country" and to give the nation's image a visual form that could be applied consistently to all sorts of communication material. The challenge was also "to reflect the modernity of the country, yet to preserve its heritage and its unique position as the heart of the Arabian Gulf—a beautiful meeting point for East and West" through a campaign to inform those who don't know about Qatar. The nation needed "to be seen as a brand, just like an institution, and as a destination packaged in one unified visual language."

The conceptual premise was to simply convey, writ large, what the country is—literally, Qatar—while also highlighting its Arabian flavor. "Simplicity was a main goal, particularly because a simple, clean, refined graphic style is not common in the region," says Atrissi. Therefore, the logo consists of the word *Qatar* written in a calligraphic style of Arabic, with the word *Qatar* in English, set in Baskerville, underneath it. For the Arab reader, the logo communicates through style and a contemporary look. For the non-Arab reader, the abstract forms of the beautiful calligraphy (which carry the essence of Arabic culture) became endless possibilities of shapes that each person saw differently—the dunes of the desert, the waves of the sea, a smile, a boat, a tent, or three big leaps. As the designer states, "In this way the abstract look does not limit the entire country to one visual, one symbol, or one idea but, rather, keeps it open for the viewer's interpretation according to his or her own experience of Qatar."

The new identity extends beyond the calligraphic logo to form a unique visual language that links all graphic and interactive material, promoting Qatar under one strong unified look, with a delicate stress on culture and heritage throughout. Everything that carries the new logo falls under the same color scheme of white, blue, red, and orange. Royal blue is the dominant color, symbolizing hospitality, as well as the sea and the beaches, whereas red and orange are the complementary colors reflecting the warm and welcoming aspect of Qatar and the colors of the Sun and the desert.

An interactive website, www.ExperienceQatar.com, a good example of the high-tech aspect of Qatar, takes users from around the world on a virtual experience of the country using the latest Macromedia Flash technology and user-friendly interaction. The website literally puts Qatar on the map and provides images, music, and sounds chosen to highlight the Arabic culture in a mix of tradition and modernity.

▲ All identity elements and the graphic standards manual were consolidated on a convenient resource image manual disk.

▼ The graphic identity palette dominates print materials, bags, and packaging in a dynamic fashion that is simple yet bold and modern.

Q&A

The official newsletter of Qatar Tourism Authority

Issue 1- November 2003

QATAR
Tourism Authority

Welcome to this special edition of Q&A, the newsletter of Qatar Tourism Authority (QTA). Produced monthly, this newsletter charts the progress of Qatar as a tourist destination and highlights the exciting events and initiatives supported by QTA. This special edition celebrates the World Travel Market and outlines QTA's activities during the show. We invite your comments and encourage you to keep abreast of QTA's initiatives through this newsletter and to share in the growth of Qatar's tourism sector.

10 November 2003

Dear Tourism Industry Colleagues,

I extend a warm welcome to the readers of this special edition of Q&A. We here at Qatar Tourism Authority are delighted to participate in World Travel Market (WTM). This remarkable international travel and tourism industry event provides a wonderful occasion for countries and regions to market their own territories and, perhaps more importantly, to interact with tourism stakeholders throughout the world. With the inclusion of the seminars and workshops offered during the conference, WTM provides a fantastic environment to learn, promote, and network.

This important conference is one of the approaches defined in our new tourism strategy to market Qatar internationally. With the theme of "experience Qatar," over ten Qatari-based companies will be represented at the QTA exhibition stand; a fine example of the collaboration and commitment that QTA and its partners have for further developing the local tourism industry.

We have established ambitious goals for this emerging sector in Qatar and the latest market study of worldwide visitor levels shows tremendous growth in the Middle East region. With the development and construction of new hotels and infrastructure, combined with the preservation of the country's heritage and culture, Qatar is quickly becoming known as a luxury tourist destination. Our new marketing and promotions strategy targets the sports and business sectors, as well as the luxury traveller. With a new Board and management team in place to implement this strategy, QTA is poised to further develop Qatar's emerging luxury tourism industry.

With the continued support of His Highness the Emir Sheikh Hamad bin Khalifa Al-Thani and cooperation from Qatar Airways and other fine companies involved in the tourism industry, each day I look forward to moving closer to the goal of establishing Qatar as a premier tourist and MICE destination. Through partnership with Qatar Foundation, QTA is able to work alongside community programmes to highlight and promote social and cultural activities within Qatar. Lead by Her Highness Sheikha

Mozah bint Nasser Al-Missned, Qatar Foundation has a vision to ensure that current and future generations of Qataris reach their full potential through education, state-of-the-art technology, and community programmes.

Qatar is a welcoming Gulf country rich in values, culture, nature, and heritage offering an inspiring experience to the discerning business and leisure traveller and to the national and expatriate communities. Its modern and vibrant capital, Doha, is a unique blend of state-of-the-art facilities, quality entertainment, the highest standards, timeless hospitality, and a strong sense of tradition. With this in mind, I will continue to work with all stakeholders to ensure the success of QTA's vision and invite you to assist in the international recognition of Qatar as "the heart of the Arabian Gulf." We hope to see you at the show.

FRED VAN EIJK - CEO, QATAR TOURISM AUTHORITY

Norway

area	385,200 km²
GDP, per capita	$37,100 USD
official languages	Norwegian, Sami
population	4.6 million

Norway is a rugged, mountainous land in northern Europe, featuring a coastline nearly 520,195 miles (84,000 km) in length punctuated by numerous fjords, islands, and islets. Known as The Land of Midnight Sun for its northerly location (part of the country lies above the Arctic Circle and has subarctic conditions), Norway is surrounded by the Atlantic Ocean, the Norwegian Sea, the Barents Sea, and the North Sea, and shares frontiers with Sweden, Finland, and Russia.

Centuries of Viking raids into Europe ended shortly after King Olav Tryggvason's adoption of Christianity in A.D. 994 and the subsequent conversion of the Norwegian kingdom. Norway was absorbed into a union with Denmark in 1397 that lasted for more than 400 years. Then in 1814, Norwegians resisted the secession to Sweden and adopted a new constitution, triggering a Swedish invasion and unification under a Swedish king. Following a rise in nationalism throughout the ninteenth century, a referendum granting Norway independence was held in 1905. Norway remained neutral in World War I but was occupied by Nazi Germany for five years during World War II. Norway became a signatory member of NATO in 1949, and a founding member of the United Nations—the U.N.'s first secretary general was Norwegian Trygve Lie.

This prosperous democratic parliamentary monarchy is known for the world's highest quality of life—it the ranks first on the Human Development Index and second in GDP per capita. The country is richly endowed with natural resources—petroleum, hydropower, forests, fish, and minerals. Only Saudi Arabia and Russia export more oil than Norway. Although not formally part of the E.U., Norway has extensive trade relationships within Europe and the rest of the world. Dominantly Evangelic Lutheran (Christian), Norway has opened up to immigration in recent decades, a significant factor in its becoming more multicultural. Several Sami languages are spoken and written in the northern regions by the indigenous Sami people.

= 1 million

ANAGADIRRI

designer | Kjetil Vatne

client | **Anagadirri Productions**

The client is a small theater group with children as its main audience. The brief was to create a playful logo that could be used over time as the group developed. The solution, as explained by the designer, "started out with characters in different shapes and forms. The forms melted into the shape of a rubber duck in the process, something children can easily relate to. The red nose puts something unexpected into the equation, with its references to clowns and fun."

design firm | Tank Design
art directors | Bernt Ottem
| Bjørn Ottem
designers | Bernt Ottem
| Bjørn Ottem

client | **Macks Ølbryggeri AS**

SMS: "time for a beer"

Macks Ølbryggeri AS is the world's northernmost brewery, situated in Tromsø, Norway. The brewery is one of the country's oldest, established in 1877. Advertisements for alcoholic beverages are not permitted in Norway, so guerilla marketing and shelf impact of products are essential. Each year, every national brewery launches "summer-beers," and these dominate sales in the summer months. The client wanted to target their summer-beer to active individuals, in the most active of seasons. The designers were tasked with designing a unique product identity and packaging system that challenges the (boring) summer-beer category (represented by relaxation-oriented imagery of sunny beaches, cozy boat trips, sunset barbeques, and so forth) and addresses "young people of all ages" who use the summer season actively. The unique name, "smrprty™," is "summer party" in SMS parlance (SMS, or short message service, is the latest promotional medium, allowing wireless phone users to send/receive brief alphanumeric messages). The design needed to be distinctly different from products offered by other breweries, and should have "massive shelf impact."

the brief

the solution

"The design is a bright orange floral pattern with a banner at the top of the can for the product name and additional information," explain the designers. "The floral pattern is based on traditional Norwegian 'rosepainting.' The pattern includes so-called 'tribals,' decorative symbols from tattooing. This pattern is applied to the aluminum can in two colors, with the can color used as an active element in the design. The banner at the top features the product's name spelled in SMS. The product was rated as Norway's best tasting summer-beer, got immediate and complete listing in Norway, and was sold out in the beginning of July, requiring production to be increased." The brewery experienced a 30 percent sales growth over the previous year, and the product has been described as "the most daring and innovative project in the Norwegian brewery industry."

The aluminum can and bottle design with its unique "SMS-influenced" name and strident product graphics.

Often "left off the map" by Eurocentric cartographers in the past, New Zealand has been steadily making a mark for itself—think Sir Edmund Hillary (first successful Everest summiteer), the All-Blacks (its champion rugby team), the origins of bungee jumping, and home of the the kiwi bird and ubiquitous fruit by the same name.

New Zealand

area	268,700 km²
GDP, per capita	$19,800 USD
official languages	English, Maori
population	4 million

New Zealand is a parliamentary democratic state in the South Pacific, a country formed of two major islands and a number of Pacific Ocean dependencies (Cook Islands, Niue, and Tokelau). A common Maori name for New Zealand is Aotearoa, popularly translated as "Land of the Long White Cloud." New Zealand has an aboriginal Maori minority.

The Polynesian Maori reached New Zealand in about A.D. 800. In 1840, their chieftains entered into a compact with Britain—the Treaty of Waitangi—in which they ceded sovereignty to Queen Victoria while retaining territorial rights. In that same year, the British began the first organized colonial settlement, and a series of land wars between 1843 and 1872 ended with the defeat of the native peoples. The British colony of New Zealand became an independent dominion in 1907, and later provided military support to the United Kingdom in both world wars.

In recent years, the government has sought to address longstanding Maori grievances. During the late 1980s, the New Zealand government sold a number of major trading enterprises, including its telecommunications company, railway network, a number of radio stations, and two financial institutions in a series of asset sales. Although the New Zealand government continues to own a number of significant businesses, collectively known as State-Owned Enterprises (SOEs), they are operated through arms-length shareholding arrangements as stand-alone businesses that are required to operate profitably, just like any privately owned enterprise. Postal services, electricity companies, and radio and television broadcasters, as well as hospitals and other trading enterprises are established in this way. The core state service consists of government departments and ministries that primarily provide government administration, policy advice, law enforcement, and social services.

Modern New Zealand has a liberalized, well-developed economy. Its primary export industries are agriculture, horticulture, fishing, forestry, and information technology, the latter in keeping with a concentrated effort of the government to build a "knowledge economy." There is also a substantial tourism industry, and both the film and wine industries are considered to be up-and-coming. In 2004, New Zealand began discussing free trade with China, one of the first countries to do so.

= 1 million

design firm Clemenger Design
art director Rod Schofield
designer Tim Christie

client **Interislander**

Travel by Dolfern

Interislander is New Zealand's oldest and foremost ferry company operating a fleet of ships that connects the north and south islands, providing travelers with one of the world's most scenic journeys.

the brief The challenged was to design a new identity for Interislander that acknowledges aspects of the existing brand but also promotes the service as a truly New Zealand travel experience.

the solution The logo redesign retains "Pelorous Jack," the historic dolphin that guided earlier vessels across Cook Strait, restylized and incorporated with the "silver fern," an icon rich with New Zealand symbolism and national pride. The result is the Dolfern, which depicts the dolphin leaping from the water and leaving a wake pattern that doubles as a silver fern.

Shown here, the Dolfern logo and its high-visibility application to the Interislander ferry.

design firm   Niche Design
art director   Lindsay Collins
designer   Lindsay Collins

client

The Postmaster's House

The client is a new, up-market Pacific Rim–styled restaurant situated in a picturesque village. The client requested that the designer create an identity that would present an exclusive image that promised a unique dining experience. The building housing the restaurant is a former Royal Post Office in a town with an illustrious gold-mining history. The solution is a leaf icon, borrowed from the magnificent tree-lined streets of the Arrowtown location, treated in two textures to reflect the fresh "green" influence on the cuisine and the rolling golden valleys of the region. The icon is encompassed by a pseudo postmark to signal the heritage of the venue.

design firm   Niche Design
art director   Nik Sweeney
designer   Nik Sweeney

client

The Loose Box

The Loose Box is an exclusive accommodation venue located in a sumptuously refurbished historic family estate, housing one to four guests at any given time. The Loose Box name is derived from the restored horse boxes, which now form part of the guest house, but this name also has some colorful meanings in local vernacular. The client's key objective was to diffuse all jokes and create an impression of relaxed sophistication for the discerning. The solution is a horse, relaxing in an Edwardian wingback chair, cognac in hand, with the sleeping family Labrador for company—immediately setting a context for the evocative name. The luxurious color treatment is reflective of the rooms' interiors, whereas the quirky typography suggests the juxtaposition of old and new.

design firm	Clemenger Design
art directors	Dianne Fuller
	Rod Schofield
designer	Dianne Fuller
client	**Duty Free Stores New Zealand**

Something to Declare

the brief   The client sells tax-free luxury goods to international travelers. The designer was challenged to create a new downtown (out-of-airport) duty-free shopping brand for use in Wellington that capitalized on the essence of duty-free shopping as an extension of the travel experience and repositioned the competitors as "just purveyors of luxury goods."

the solution   "The idea was to bring the international-airport experience into the inner city," explained the designers. "We used the language of the airport, customs, and the duty-free shopping experience to create a new name: Red Lane—the path you take when you have purchased something to declare. This new name was supported visually by imagery of luxury and fashion goods shown as x-rays. We used the shopping bag as a 'branded badge' that customers wear with pride long beyond their journey." An instant success, in the first quarter of reopening, sales were up 98 percent over the same period the previous year.

The Red Lane "collection wallet" is reminiscent of airline travel documents.

► Even a glimpse of these shopping bags leaves no doubt as to their origin or context. They successfully communicate Red Lane's unique positioning as a tax-free shopping outlet.

► The highly successful concept of using "the language of the airport" as a distinct brand identity is shown here through the effective use of signage and storefront display in downtown Wellington.

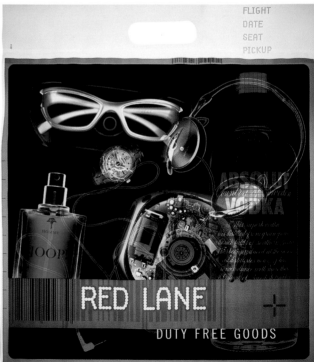

Russia is famous in the design world for Constructivism and the heroic styling of later propaganda art. The rest of the world knows Russia for its great authors, the legacy of Marx and Lenin, Moscow's Kremlin collections and Cold War infamy, St. Petersburg's Hermitage, the Bolshoi, Olympic dominance, and, of course, borscht, vodka, and caviar.

Russian Federation

area	17 million km²
GDP, per capita	$9,800 USD
official language	Russian
population	144.5 million

The Russian Federation, or Russia, is by far the largest country in the world, stretching across a vast expanse of Eastern Europe and northern Asia. It ranks as the world's seventh-most populous nation and until 1991 was the preeminent republic of the Union of Soviet Socialist Republics (U.S.S.R. or Soviet Union) until becoming an independent country through the union's dissolution. The Russian Federation still includes the autonomous republics of Adygeya, Altai, Bashkortostan, Burjatia, Chakasia, Chechnia, Chuvasia, Dagestan, Ingushetia, Kabardino-Balkaria, Kalmukia, Karacha-Cherkesia, Karelia, Komi, Mari El, Mordovia, North-Ossetia, Sacha (Jakutia), Tatarstan, Tuva, and Udmurtia. Russia's influence on the world stage is still notable but has diminished dramatically from the former role it played as one of the world's superpowers.

The Russian state was originally formed in 1521, becoming the dominant constituent of the Soviet Union in 1922. Devastating defeats of the Russian army in World War I led to widespread rioting in the major cities of the Russian Empire and to the 1917 overthrow of the 300-year-old Romanov Dynasty. The Communists under Vladimir Lenin seized power soon after and formed the U.S.S.R. The brutal rule of Josef Stalin (1928–1953) strengthened Russian dominance of the Soviet Union at a cost of millions of lives. The Soviet economy and society stagnated in the following decades until General Secretary Mikhail Gorbachev (1985–1991) introduced *glasnost* (openness) and *perestroika* (restructuring) in an attempt to modernize Communism.

Today, the country is a federal presidential democratic republic, though still with authoritarian tendencies. More than a decade after the collapse of the Soviet Union, Russia is still struggling to establish a modern market economy and achieve strong economic growth. Russia remains heavily dependent on exports of commodities, particularly oil, natural gas, metals, and timber, which account for more than 80 percent of exports. The greatest challenge facing the Russian economy is how to encourage the development of SMEs (small and medium-sized enterprises) in a business climate dominated by Russian oligarchs and a large, dysfunctional banking system.

Russia has a rich cultural heritage, embodied in the cities of Moscow and Saint Petersburg. Many other cities hold their own rich traditions, and the Russian countryside has many little towns with old cloisters and castles. Famous tourist trips include the river Volga, the Trans-Siberian railway to Vladivostok on the Pacific Ocean, and visits to coastal resorts on the Black Sea and Caspian Sea.

👤 = 1 million

design firm | 105 red
art director | Valentina Korobeinikova
designer | Valentina Korobeinikova

client | **GSL Law & Consulting**
The client, a financial auditing and consulting firm, required a logo that would suit their image, catch the attention of clients, and signify "three levels of difference in taxation levels of different countries," as the designer explains. "The logo depicts three individuals carrying different weights."

design firm | 105 red
art director | Valentina Korobeinikova
designer | Valentina Korobeinikova

client | **Roff Technologis**
The client is a record company who approached the designer to design a logo for the folk rock group Kitti Louis to be used on their new album. The solution, as described by the designer: "The horse is a talisman of musicians. The calligraphic logotype appears as a signature. The green background symbolizes sound harmony with nature."

design firm | O.P. Design
art director | Oleg Pudov
designer | Oleg Pudov

client | **Oleg Pudov**
The designer specializes in graphic arts and applied design. For his own logo, he wanted something that would represent him and his activities well. The solution is a graphic interpretation of the designer's initials, and, as he states, "the circle and square are the symbols of graphic order."

design firm | 105 red
art director | Valentina Korobeinikova
designer | Valentina Korobeinikova

client | **World Wildlife Fund (WWF)**
WWF is a social organization involved in ecological advocacy and protection of Earth's natural and human environment. WWF required two identifiers—one for its Russia Marine program, and another for its "Rescue the Russian Leopard and Amur Tiger" initiative—both logos needed to be creative, colorful, fun, and attractive to children. The identities needed to reproduce well on T-shirts and other souvenirs. As the designer explains, "The [Russia Marine program] solution shows animals in an ancient and primitive style, bringing to mind the many animals that are about to become extinct." The second solution depicts the leopard and tiger in an intimate, compelling style.

design firm   Direct Design Studio
art director   Peryshkov & Feigin
designer   Busygin

client   *Izvestia* Newspaper

Izvestia Reborn

the brief   The client is Russia's prominent national newspaper, published since 1917. The designer was given the task of designing a new identity for the paper that would pay tribute to the paper's longstanding history.

the solution   The solution uses old, bold typefaces "in a style generated according to technologies evident in a time-capsule view of the newspaper's first issue."

▲ Shown here, the new identity for *Izvestia* applied to stationery in a restrained color palette appropriate to the nostalgic recall of the retro-styled logotype.

◄ Shown here, the "new" *Izvestia* identity as promoted at the turn of the millennium, with clear links to its origins some eighty years earlier.

► The *Izvestia* identity has been applied to various print and promotional materials.

design firm · Zebra Design
art director · Andrey Mitin
designers · Andrey Mitin
Alexandr Shpagin

client · **AVTOVAZ, TorgMash**

Auto-Revolution

The client is the Volga automobile factory. Lada Revolution is a sports car aimed at a young market, aged 16 to 45 years, automobile sports enthusiasts, and automotive journalists.

the brief

The challenge was to develop a trademark, corporate style, and presentation materials to help launch the new sports prototype Lada Revolution to a worldwide community. The brief called for an identity that would position the brand as active and dynamic and would also lend itself to a new racing series.

the solution

The symbol uses a hammer and sickle (elements of the former Soviet Union's iconography) combined to form the letter *R*. The red-and-black color scheme is also reminiscent of the Russian Revolution. For the catalog presentation, a 3-D model was created, because the race car was not yet ready to photograph.

Shown here, the dynamic Lada Revolution mark and a catalog developed for the launch of the new sports car brand.

design firm	Zebra Design
art director	Andrey Mitin
designers	Andrey Mitin
	Evgeny Mitin
client	**IVS Company**

Play. Learn. Think. Work. WIN!

The client is involved in the assembly and sale of computers under the regional trademark Froggy.

the brief — The designers were approached to rebrand this regional trademark so that it would exude the characteristics of a computer company—"modern, up-to-date, self-improving, logical, adaptable to manufacture." There was also the necessity to reflect a new slogan: "Play. Learn. Think. Work. WIN!"

the solution — The designer explains, "At the first level of recognition, the trademark resembles the foot of a frog. Besides that, the graphic symbol schematically reflects the four directions of activity—play, learn, think, work—which are distilled in the main principle of the trademark—WIN!"

The Froggy trademark is shown here in several variants, along with applications for packaging, stationery, a manual cover, disk graphics, a Froggy card, and an effective two-color mouse pad that creates an engaging pattern out of repeated footprint symbols.

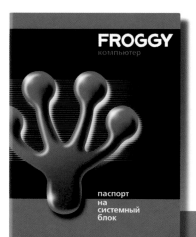

art director Adelina Abdurakhmanova
designer Adelina Abdurakhmanova

client **Montessori**
Montessori is a chain of kindergartens in which children
learn from hands-on experience and working with crafts. The
energetic, youthful logo appears to be hand-made, reinforcing
the teaching basis of the school.

art director Adelina Abdurakhmanova
designer Adelina Abdurakhmanova

client **Homeopatia**
The client is a website on homeopathic medicine. The central
idea of Homeopathic medicine is the preparation of herbal
remedies. The logo reflects the natural, holistic, and humane
characteristics of homeopathic cures.

art director Adelina Abdurakhmanova
designer Adelina Abdurakhmanova

client **Pepper Publishing House**
Pepper is a publisher of witty and spicy books. The concept
of the logo was to use a pepper to replace one letter of the
name—the choice of the red color is obvious.

art director Adelina Abdurakhmanova
designer Adelina Abdurakhmanova

client **Tair Tairov's Art Gallery**
The client is an art gallery that features Asian art. The
solution uses calligraphic brush strokes to create an
expressive monogram of the client's initials, in a style
reminiscent of Asian calligraphy.

art director Ekaterina Gonchar
designer Ekaterina Gonchar

client **Moonsun Green Tea**
Moonsun is a naturally pure green tea, ready to use and
packed in bottles. The logo for the package refers to purity and
natural ecological quality. The conceptual core of the logo is
the letter *U* as a cup that contains green tea.

design firm   Direct Design Studio
art director   Peryshkov & Feigin
designer   Rapota

client   **Moscow International Festival of Advertising**

The Golden Apple

the brief   The client required a visual identity for the 11th
Moscow International Festival of Advertising.
A stated requirement was to incorporate the
festival's symbol—a golden apple.

the solution   The solution for the festival's identity merges
anime-style illustration with recognizable symbols
and scenes of the city of Moscow.

► The festival identity was applied to
various print materials.

▼ The designer created a palette of
anime-style illustrations of a provocative
mascot to promote the festival. All
images incorporate the festival's
symbol, the golden apple.

art director | Michael Gubergritz
designer | Michael Gubergritz

client | **Moscow Cultural Center "Dom"**
The client is a music and exhibition center in an old section of
Moscow. The designers were tasked with creating an identity
for a photo exhibition inspired by "eight bright and unforgettable
days in India experienced by two Moscow designers and
photographers." The logo was to be bright, authentic, unusual,
and colorful, reflecting India's culture and people. The exhibition
was named *Dni Indii* (Days of India), and the eight letters of
the logo were made of authentic colored Indian cotton paper.
In Russian, the correct spelling of the name is *DNI INDII*, but
the designer shifted the first letter of the second word to the
first word and created two new words: *DNII* and *NDII*. After the
words were placed one on top of the other, the result was an
interesting and attractive play of letters: *D-N-N-D* on the left,
and *I-I-I-I* on the right makes this logo unusual and memorable.

design firm | Linia Grafic design studio
art director | Maksim Gourbatoff
designers | Mariya Petrova
Maksim Gourbatoff

client | **ArtLinkInter**
ArtLinkInter (International Foundation for the Arts) needed
an identifier that would exude Russian national culture and
authenticity. For the solution, the designers created a new,
modern typographic logotype imitating *"vyaz"*—Russian
medieval title letters in handwriting.

art director | Ekaterina Seretchenko
designer | Ekaterina Seretchenko

client | **Identity Center**
The client, who specializes in Web security, wanted to create
an electronic signature for use in ecommerce and other Web
operations. "The client asked for a remarkable and meaningful
sign," explains the designer. "The solution comprises two
significant elements: @ and sunglasses. The @ symbolizes
the Web audience, and sunglasses symbolize security and
protection."

design firm | Linia Grafic design studio
art director | Maksim Gourbatoff
designer | Mariya Petrova

client | **ApixPharm**
The client, a pharmaceutical company, asked the designer to
create a logo that would represent its activities and express
the name's semantics. The designer explains, "*Apix* is a bull.
The letter *A* first appeared in ancient Babylonian writing as a
pictographic bull's head (the origin of our modern A, turned
upside down)."

art director | Michael Gubergritz
designer | Michael Gubergritz

client | **Oxygen Model Management—Paradox**
Paradox is a women's fashion trademark. The target audience
is active women aged 25 to 40. The client wanted a logo that
would "work well in both small and large formats; use only one
color; and be spectacular, stylish, glamorous, fashionable,
and feminine." The designer explains, "Women are always
paradoxical! And Paradox is for women. So, I used a female
symbol as a ligature between the *O* and *X*. Reversed type and
capital letters with rounded contours provided the desired effect."

art directors   Alexander Petrakov
designer   Alexander Petrakov

Cinema Center Luch

Luch (meaning "ray") is a family-owned movie theater showing classic, modern, and documentary films. The challenge was to design a logo that would correspond to the constructivist style of the movie theater's architecture. A ray of light takes on a negative form in a simple, stylized, triangular shape that acts as a spotlight to "lead the audience boldly to the clean quality of the logotype."

art director   Anatol Kuzmin
designer   Anatol Kuzmin

Career Development Center

The client is an employment agency that renders job placement services to both the jobless and employed people looking for better jobs. As described by the designers, "The challenge was to create a sign that would unambiguously attract the attention of people looking for a job. The solution was to portray the emotions of the jobless and the employed. The symbol shows the shifts of emotion from sadness and uncertainty when one is jobless toward happiness and confidence when one is engaged in well-paid work."

АрхАгроПромБанк

design firm   White&Black Advertising Agency
art director   Maksim Gourbatoff
designer   Maksim Gourbatoff

ArkhAgroPromBank

ArkhAgroPromBank (Agrarian and Industrial Bank of Arkhangelsk) works with Russian agricultural enterprises. The logo reflects the ideas of the bank: The earth represents the country's riches, and the plowed field extending to the horizon is set in a square, representing the material world.

art director   Anatol Kuzmin
designer   Anatol Kuzmin

The "Velvet School" of calligraphy of Evgeny Dobrovinsky

The designer explains, "The 'Velvet School' of calligraphy of Evgeny Dobrovinsky is carried out annually in Crimea, at the end of summer. About twenty students from Russia, Ukraine, Belorus, and other countries spend two weeks drawing calligraphy with Evgeny Dobrovinsky. The brief was to create a sign that would capture the spirit of freestyle calligraphy. The solution was simple—I used india ink and a bamboo stick to quickly create a handmade sign, with a water blur symbolizing freestyle calligraphy, the sea, and the fast pace of the course."

МАРШАЛ

design firm   White&Black Advertising Agency
art director   Maksim Gourbatoff
designer   Maksim Gourbatoff

The Marshal Company

The client, a manufacturer of jeans and denim clothing, commissioned the designer to design a logo to reflect appropriately the client's national identity. The designer explains, "The new logo reflects the semantics of the Marshal name. The military rank of marshal first appeared in Russia's Civil War at the beginning of the twentieth century. So, through semantic association: Moscow, Russia, a victory—a solemn and celebratory character." And, can you see the jeans?

Sweden

area	450,000 km²
GDP, per capita	$33,600 USD
official language	Swedish
population	9 million

Sweden (*Sverige* in Swedish) is a peaceful, neutral country situated in North Europe, sharing borders with Norway on the west and Finland on the northeast. A member of the European Union since 1995, this wealthy parliamentary democratic monarchy has one of the world's highest life expectancies (and one of the lowest birth rates).

Archaeological evidence indicates that Sweden was first settled during the Stone Age, as the inland glaciers of the last ice age receded. Remains of large trading communities in southern Sweden indicate that by the Bronze Age, a dense population had already developed. Hundreds of years of Scandinavian Viking culture ended with Christianization in the twelfth century, along with the consolidation of the Swedish state. In 1389, the three countries of Norway, Denmark, and Sweden were united under a single monarch—Sweden eventually broke away in 1521, with King Gustav I of Sweden reestablishing separation of the Swedish crown. A military power during the seventeenth century, Sweden has not participated in any war since its campaign to dominate Norway in 1814. Its success in remaining armed but neutral through World War I and World War II provided it with a significant advantage as the rest of Europe rebuilt itself, helping lend the country a particularly high standard of living. Sweden continues to stay militarily nonaligned.

Sweden's long-successful economic formula and enviable standard of living result from a mix of high-tech capitalism and substantial welfare benefits. Modern Sweden has a skilled labor force, modern distribution and transportation systems, and excellent internal and external communications. Timber, hydroelectric power, and iron ore form the base for a trade-oriented economy. Approximately 90 percent of industrial output is due to privately owned firms, and engineering accounts for nearly 50 percent of output and exports.

= 1 million

design firm	WE RECOMMEND
art directors	Martin Fredricson
	Nikolaj Knop
designers	Martin Fredricson
	Nikolaj Knop
client	**Kapacitet AB (www.kapacitet.com)**

Taking the Leap

Leap, a Web-content management product developed by the Swedish I.T. company Kapacitet AB, is simple, transparent, open, and easy to use compared to similar products. It is targeted to companies and organizations who want to maintain and update their websites on a regular basis.

the brief The designers were tasked with creating a name and product identity that "visualizes the core values of leap and enables the building of a strong brand in the Web-content management market."

the solution As explained by the designers, "Because the product's core values are unique compared to its competitors, we developed a simple, transparent, and open name and product identity—different from anything else on the market."

leap

▲ The leap logo is simple and strong.

▼ In keeping with the clean, bold graphic approach of the logo, a visual palette of red and white, sans serif typography, and bright sun-soaked photography round out the graphic vocabulary of the leap visual presence.

Singapore's cultural diversity reflects its rich colonial history and Malay, Chinese, Arab, and Indian ethnicities—its main religions are Buddhism, Islam, and Christianity.

Singapore

area	693 km²
GDP, per capita	$24,400 USD
official languages	Chinese, Malay, English, Tamil
population	4.6 million

The Republic of Singapore is an island city-state in Southeast Asia, situated on the southern tip of Malay Peninsula, south of Peninsular Malaysia, and north of the Indonesian islands of Riau. Established as a trading port by the British in 1819, Singapore became a center of British influence in Southeast Asia. It joined the Malaysian Federation in 1963; then claimed independence in 1965. Since then, the country has rapidly advanced from a Third-World to First-World nation. Singapore has one of the world's busiest ports and strong international trading links and is known today as one of the East Asian Tigers.

For many years considered to be the business hub of Southeast Asia, Singapore's economy has depended heavily on exports, particularly in electronics and manufacturing. Singapore is also a popular tourist and shopping destination. Its aims to become Southeast Asia's financial and high-tech hub are supported by government efforts to remake Singapore into a key node in the globalized network—linked to all the major economies and with a diversified economy of its own powered by the twin engines of manufacturing and services.

Singapore is a parliamentary republic and a member of the Non-Aligned Movement, the United Nations, and the Commonwealth of Nations. Singapore supports the concept of Southeast Asian regionalism and plays an active role in the Association of Southeast Asian Nations (ASEAN) and the Asia Pacific Economic Cooperation (APEC) forum.

= 1 million

AUXIGEN™

design firm · sinkid pte ltd.
art director · Way Tay
designers · Way Tay
· Elaine Loo
· Karin Koh

client · **Carsonic**
Auxigen is part of the Carsonic group of companies. The designers were commissioned to develop a brand identity, logo, and packaging. As they explain, "The solution is a take on 'accessories' and 'oxygen,' two key components of the business."

design firm · sinkid pte ltd.
art director · Way Tay
designers · Way Tay
· Elaine Loo
· Karin Koh

client · **Dorian Ho**
The client is an eveningwear designer from Hong Kong. The challenge was to create a logo for his new D'Orient clothing line. The solution reflects luxury, femininity, elegance, and a touch of the Orient.

design firm · Interbrand Singapore
art director · Stuart Green
designer · Rofizano Zaino

client · **Entellium**
The client is an Asia-wide application service provider (ASP) that provides small and medium-sized companies with key ebusiness tools. The challenge was to create a brand that broke the category norms of high tech and business-to-business brands. The designers explain, "Working closely with the client, we created a brand strategy based around 'changing the way business software is designed, supplied, and implemented.' We also designed an identity that uses the metaphor of an ant—a creature that is able to carry several times its own body weight—to create a brand image that is personable, charming, and most of all, accessible."

design firm · Interbrand Singapore
art director · Stuart Green
designers · Tim Arrowsmith
· Rachel Terkelsen

client · **Addvalue Technologies**
Addvalue Technologies is the parent company of Wideye, which designs and manufactures high-quality communications devices in the field of wireless and broadband technology. The designers were asked to develop a brand identity to encompass a range of communications devices in the areas of broadband and wireless, voice and telephony, gaming and entertainment, and mobile computing. The designers explain their solution: "The Wideye name captures the excitement and sense of wonder that the company's founders wanted to instill in all their future products. The ever-changing form of the identity expressed the dynamic quality of the brand and its continuing effort to adapt itself to its customers' changing lifestyle."

design firm   sinkid pte ltd.
art director   Way Tay
designers   Way Tay
   Katey Ouyang

client   **Levi's**

Levi's for Girls

the brief   The Levi's company approached the designers with the challenge of creating a concept for a Levi's Girls store design. They were asked to reinterpret inspiration from the popular psychedelics of the late 1960s in a new, contemporary way, while keeping the image of the Levi's girl intact.

the solution   The designers explained, "Our creative concept was rendered for application in the following styles: Singal Motif: an original artwork created in a groovy, fluid pattern with an emphasis on psychedelic, to achieve an optical illusion while creating space and depth in the store. Singal Silhouette: an original design created to represent the modern Levi's girl who is a bold, sexy, and confident individual. Singal Lipstick Font: an original, expressive, unique, and feminine typeface hand-written in lipstick. Levi's Girls Logo: an original artwork that reinterprets the classic Levi's heritage with a modern flair to project the special qualities of the Levi's girl."

The identity developed by sinkid for the Levi's Girls store consists of a visual system of unique elements that are combined for great effect, as shown here. The consistent use of the red/violet color palette contributes to the strength of this strong, unmistakable identity.

Turkey is famous for its bellicose sailors, belly dancers, Turkish baths, Istanbul's Blue Mosque, textiles, olives, dates, tobacco, finely ground coffee, and, of course, Turkish delight.

Turkey

area	780,600 km²
GDP, per capita	$7,200 USD
official languages	Turkish, Kurdish
population	68.1 million

The Republic of Turkey is located on two continents—a portion of its capital Istanbul (formerly named Constantinople) is in Europe, whereas the rest of the city of seventeen million lies across the Bosporus in Southwest Asia. Turkey is bordered to the east by Georgia, Armenia, Azerbaijan, and Iran; to the south by Iraq and Syria; and to the west by Greece and Bulgaria. The strategically positioned Anatolian peninsula lying between the Black Sea and the Mediterranean Sea forms the country's core.

Turkey (formerly known as the Ottoman Empire) became an independent state in 1327. Present-day Turkey is a parliamentary democratic republic, created in 1923 from the empire's Turkish remnants. Soon afterward, the country instituted secular laws to replace traditional religious fiats. Turkey joined the U.N. in 1945, and in 1952 became a member of NATO.

Turkey's economy is a complex mix of modern industry and commerce along with a traditional agriculture sector that accounts for a significant portion of the country's employment. Turkey has a strong and rapidly growing private sector, yet the state still plays a major role in basic industry, banking, transport, and communication. The most important industry and largest export is textiles and clothing, a sector almost entirely in private hands.

The culture of Turkey draws customs from the Ottoman Empire and Islamic traditions, modernized primarily by Kemal Ataturk and his "Young Turks" movement. The country's main religion is Islam, though the Kurdish, Greek, Armenian, and other non-Turk populations in the country follow different customs.

= 1 million

art director   Umut Südüak
designer   Umut Südüak

client   **Grafist Organization Committee, Graphic Design Department, Mimar Sinan Fine Arts University**
Grafist is an annual graphic design exhibition and event in Turkey. Its logo design needed to be visually engaging for a design audience but kept as simple as possible without losing its effectiveness and be produced on a limited budget.

GRAFiST

art director   Umut Südüak
designer   Umut Südüak

client   **Marmarabirlik**
Marbir is a new product from one of Turkey's largest producers of olives and olive oil. The designer describes the client's requirements as, "a new and younger design for the new product, mostly for international markets. Our approach was to make the logo understandable in any language and effective by using one color."

Taiwan is known for its resilience, hard-working people, and ingenious and rigorous manufacturing sector—the words Made in Taiwan are recognized worldwide.

Taiwan

area	36,000 km²
GDP, per capita	$18,000 USD
official language	Chinese (Mandarin)
population	22.6 million

The island of Taiwan is located in the Pacific Ocean off the coast of mainland China. It is also known by its Portuguese name, *Ilha Formosa*, meaning "beautiful island," and as the Republic of Taiwan (ROC). Following military defeat in 1895, China was forced to cede Taiwan to Japan. The island reverted to Chinese control after World War II, and following the Communist victory on the mainland in 1949, two million Chinese Nationalists led by Chiang Kai-shek fled to Taiwan to establish a government in exile. Over the next five decades, Taiwan's ruling authorities gradually democratized and incorporated the native population within the governing structure. During this time, the presidential democratic republic prospered and became one of East Asia's economic successes. The dominant political issue today continues to be the relationship between Taiwan and China—specifically the question of eventual unification.

Taiwan's culture is a blend of traditional Chinese with significant Japanese and Western influences, including Dutch, Spanish, and American. The Taiwanese aboriginals also have a distinct culture. Fine arts, folk traditions, and popular culture embody traditional and modern, as well as Asian and Western motifs. One of Taiwan's greatest attractions is the National Palace Museum, housing more than 650,000 pieces of Chinese bronze, jade, calligraphy, painting, and porcelain. (This collection, estimated to represent one-tenth of all Chinese cultural treasures, was moved from the mainland in 1949 when the Nationalist Party fled to Taiwan.)

Most people in Taiwan speak Mandarin, the language of instruction in schools for more than four decades. About 70 percent of the people in Taiwan also speak Taiwanese, a variety of Min-nan; the Hakka, who constitute 10 percent of the population, have their own distinct language. Between 1895 and 1945, under Japanese rule, the official language on Taiwan was Japanese, so many older residents still speak that language more fluently than Mandarin. The aboriginal minority groups still speak their native languages, but most can also speak Mandarin and Taiwanese. The island's main religions are Buddhism and Taoism, though there is also a strong belief in folk religion, and Christian churches have also been active for many years.

♦ = 1 million

<table>
<tr><td>design firm</td><td>Up Creative Design & Advertising Corporation</td></tr>
<tr><td>art director</td><td>Ben Wang</td></tr>
<tr><td>designer</td><td>Ben Wang</td></tr>
</table>

client

Up Creative Design & Advertising Corporation
This design firm, with offices in Taipei and Beijing, needed a simple, memorable identity that could be applied consistently across a wide range of media. A symbol consisting of an upward-pointing triangle inside a circle creates a geometric form reminiscent of both a directional arrow and a pencil tip. As stated by the designer, the selection of a happy, bright orange as the corporate color "symbolizes our enthusiasm for design." Strong use of a single corporate color makes a lasting visual impression.

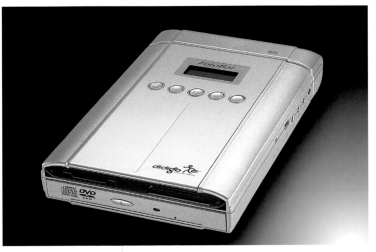

design firm | Venus Design Inc.
art directors | Tong Wai Hang
| Frank Jiang
designer | Tong Wai Hang

client

Carry Computer Eng. Co., Ltd.
This identity for Carry Computer's didigo consists of a literal representation of the computer manufacturer's product—portable digital devices—rendered in a geometric stick-man vernacular appropriate to the accompanying tag line, *carry on digital*. Shown here are two-sided business cards and the firm's portable FotoBar.

United Kingdom—think rolling countryside,
Hadrian's Wall, the Magna Carta, the Thames,
London Bridge and Big Ben, the royal family,
British racing green, Wimbledon, Liverpudlian
rockers, the Bard, Robin Hood, fox hunts,
Beefeaters, high tea, fish & chips, fine ales…
the list goes on and on.

United Kingdom

area	241,600 km²
GDP, per capita	$25,400 USD
official language	English
population	60 million

The United Kingdom of Great Britain and Northern Ireland, or simply the United Kingdom (UK), was formed by a series of Acts of Union that united the countries or territories of England, Wales, Scotland, and Ireland (the island) under a single government in London. The greater part of Ireland left the United Kingdom in 1922, and is today the Republic of Ireland. The United Kingdom is situated off the northwestern coast of continental Europe, sharing a land border with the Republic of Ireland, but otherwise surrounded by the North Sea, the English Channel, the Irish Sea, and the Atlantic Ocean.

Great Britain, the dominant industrial and maritime power of the nineteenth century, played a leading role in developing parliamentary democracy and in advancing literature and science. At its zenith, the British Empire stretched over one-fourth of the earth's surface. The first half of the twentieth century saw the United Kingdom's strength seriously depleted in two world wars. The second half witnessed the dismantling of the empire and the United Kingdom rebuilding itself into a modern and prosperous European nation. As one of five permanent members of the U.N. Security Council, a founding member of NATO, and of the Commonwealth, the United Kingdom pursues a global approach to foreign policy. A member of the E.U., it has chosen to remain outside the European Monetary Union for the time being.

The United Kingdom is a leading trading power and financial center, with one of the largest capitalist economies of Western Europe. Agriculture is intensive, highly mechanized, and efficient by European standards. The country has large coal, natural gas, and oil reserves; primary energy production accounts for 10 percent of GDP, one of the highest shares of any industrial state. Services, particularly banking, insurance, and business services, account for by far the largest proportion of GDP. With more than 23 million tourists a year, the United Kingdom is ranked as the world's sixth major tourist destination.

The United Kingdom can boast some of the world's most famous universities (Cambridge and Oxford), great scientists and engineers (Isaac Newton, Charles Darwin, and Michael Faraday), renowned writers (Shakespeare, the Brontë sisters, Jane Austen, Agatha Christie, Tolkien, and Dickens), important poets (Lord Byron, Robert Burns, Thomas Hardy, and Dylan Thomas), as well as notable composers, artists, architects, and designers. It can also claim the origin of many sports (soccer, golf, cricket, rugby, lawn tennis, and billiards) and, along with the United States, the development of rock and roll with famous bands including the Beatles, the Rolling Stones, Led Zeppelin, Pink Floyd, and many others—this followed by the forefront of punk with the Sex Pistols and the Clash, and the subsequent rebirth of heavy metal with bands such as Motorhead and Iron Maiden.

= 1 million

design firm	Heath Kane Design
art director	Heath Kane
designer	Heath Kane
client	**Mobaitec**

2-D/3-D I.T.

Mobaitec is a start-up business founded in 2004 by a leading team of international I.T. professionals. They provide tools that allow business customers to manage complexity in Web-service development.

the brief
Like any start-up business, Mobaitec wanted to make its presence known. The brief was simple—create a brand that defines and positions Mobaitec as a clear leader in this fast-growing field. Because the competitive market includes "behemoth companies like IBM, Collaxa, and Sun," something unique was needed to grab customers' interests.

the solution
As described by the designer, "The Mobaitec cube is seen as both a two-dimensional and three-dimensional element. As a two-dimensional element it conveys the concept of an environment where the center controls the relationship it has with the outside junctions. As a three-dimensional element it lends itself to the metaphor of a box—in this case a transparent box. In both cases, this design illustrates some of Mobaitec's key features and customer benefits in a simple, distinct way."

► The Mobaitec brand features a distinctive cube symbol that comes to life in its applications, and, as described by the designer, "reminds us that, after all, 'technology is human serving.' As such, Mobaitec is both host and hero, extending itself beyond the 'faceless entities' of its competitors and paving a direction for the brand that conveys empathy and clarity into what it provides both as a product and as a service-oriented company."

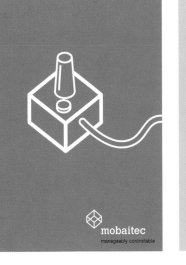

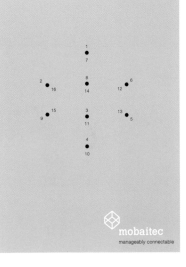

design firm   MetaDesign
art director   Steve Rigley (GSA)
designer   Tarek Atrissi

client   **The Glasgow School of Art**

**SCHOOL:
OF FINE ART
THE GLASGOW
SCHOOL: OF ART**

Mackintosh
and Beyond

The Glasgow School of Art (GSA) is one of the last
remaining independent art schools in the United Kingdom.
A higher education institution, the GSA specializes in fine
art, design and architecture teaching, and research. It has
more than 1,600 students, of which 15 percent are from
outside the United Kingdom; in addition, the school has
an impressive international reputation for the quality of
its staff, students, and alumni. Among GSA's high-profile
alumni is Charles Rennie Mackintosh, one of the twentieth
century's most influential architects, designers, and artists.
Mackintosh designed the GSA's main school building, a
structure that attracts in excess of 25,000 visitors a year.

► The GSA's magazine, *Flow*, is an effective information piece
as well as a corporate communication tool that furthers the
School's brand presence. Design is by Third Eye Design,
Glasgow.

▼ As seen here, the GSA's individual academic schools, research
centers, and subentities all share the characteristic Hothouse
face and common building brown, but each is differentiated
with its own logo in a unique second color.

**SCHOOL:
OF DESIGN
THE GLASGOW
SCHOOL: OF ART**

**MACKINTOSH SCHOOL:
OF ARCHITECTURE
THE GLASGOW
SCHOOL: OF ART**

**DIGITAL
DESIGN STUDIO
THE GLASGOW
SCHOOL: OF ART**

**CENTRE FOR
ADVANCED TEXTILES
THE GLASGOW
SCHOOL: OF ART**

**THE GLASGOW
SCHOOL: OF ART
ENTERPRISES
LTD**

**THE GLASGOW
SCHOOL: OF ART
TRUST**

the brief

"The GSA did not have a formal corporate identity or brand hierarchy, although the Mackintosh typeface (designed in the late 1970s from lettering used by Mackintosh in architectural drawings) and iconic Mackintosh symbols were omnipresent," explains the school. "Not only was this not suitable for all departments (research indicated that although Mackintosh was an important part of the school's heritage, it was only one part of what is a successful fine art, design, and architecture school), it was no longer unique to the GSA. In fact, the Mackintosh style had been so widely imitated and used by other organizations in Glasgow and Scotland that it had been devalued and was known locally as 'Mockintosh.' In 2001, the GSA invited Berlin-based MetaDesign to create a new visual identity for the GSA. The new identity had to reflect the GSA now and in the future, while being sympathetic to its past, in particular regarding the Mackintosh connection for which the School was internationally known."

the solution

"MetaDesign proposals comprised two key elements," explains the school. "Hothouse, the new font, has been developed in a way that allows it to be used flexibly as a headline font on all media—it draws on stylistic elements employed by Mackintosh. The brand hierarchy allows the individual academic schools and research centers prominence, bound together by the typeface and a color environment centered around what MetaDesign termed 'building brown.' Every brand (academic schools and research centers) uses the building brown plus its own specific color. The overall approach to finding the brand colors was to represent the GSA as a creative hothouse, so the colors chosen are fairly bright rather than dark.

Binding together the colors is a design principle in the form of a segment. This graphic element is used in all GSA media (print and electronic) and aims to present the school as a creative, flexible organization.

The chosen design solved a number of issues. First, the Mackintosh heritage is preserved in a modern, sensible way. The brand hierarchy was resolved, allowing academic schools and research centers to have their own identities in the GSA family, and it allows all media to be individual and contemporary while still retaining a corporate feel, which while not overbearing, clearly reminds the audience that the publication or website is from the GSA."

This *05:06 Prospectus* illustrates the effectiveness of the GSA's new identity when it is applied to print materials. The richly illustrated prospectus was designed by Pure Design of Edinburgh, following the brand guidelines developed earlier by MetaDesign. Spreads from the prospectus are shown on the opposite page.

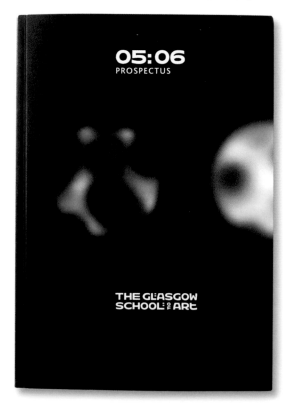

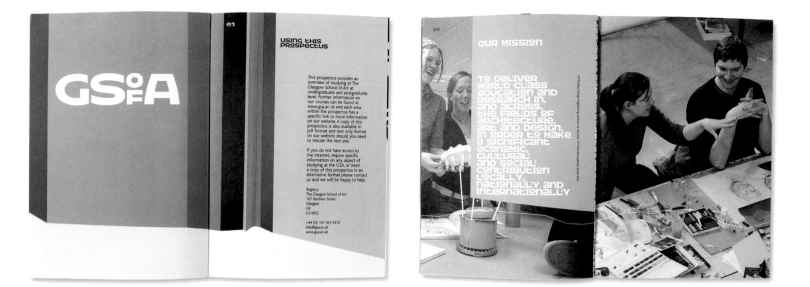

Yugoslavia

area	102,400 km²
GDP, per capita	$2,200 USD
official language	Serbian
population	10.7 million

Serbia (Republika Srbije) is united with Montenegro (Republika Crna Gora) in a loose confederation known as the State Union of Serbia and Montenegro—the two constituent republics reconstituted as Yugoslavia between 1992 and 2003, following the earlier secession (in 1991) of Slovenia, Croatia, Bosnia & Herzegovina, and Macedonia from the wartorn and disintegrating former Federal Republic of Yugoslavia situated in southeastern Europe.

The roots of the Serbian state reach back to the early ninth century—the Kingdom of Serbia was established in the eleventh century, and in the thirteenth century, the Serbian Empire was formed. The Kingdom of Serbs, Croats, and Slovenes was formed in 1918, following World War I—its name was changed to Yugoslavia in 1929. The 1941 Nazi occupation of Yugoslavia was resisted by various paramilitary bands, with a group headed by Marshal Tito taking full control after German expulsion in 1945. Although Communist, Tito's new government successfully steered its own path between the Warsaw Pact nations and the West for the next four and a half decades. In the early 1990s, post-Tito Yugoslavia began to unravel along ethnic lines.

Since 1992, Serbia led various military and paramilitary intervention efforts to unite Serbs in neighboring republics into a "Greater Serbia"—all of these efforts were ultimately unsuccessful. In 1999, massive expulsions of ethnic Albanians living in Kosovo provoked an international response, including the NATO bombing of Serbia and the stationing of NATO, Russian, and other peacekeepers in Kosovo.

Federal elections in 2000 brought about the ouster of Slobodan Milosevic. His arrest for crimes against humanity and subsequent transfer to the International Criminal Tribunal for the former Yugoslavia in the Hague in 2001 led to the country's suspension being lifted and its reacceptance into U.N. organizations under the name of Yugoslavia.

= 1 million

designer Jelena Drobac

client **Ladybug Handmade**

The client, who designs authentic, handmade textiles and artifacts using old-fashioned methods and materials, wanted a clean, simple approach to a symbol with a feminine touch that would be easily recognized when applied to small print applications such as hang tags. The solution is the Ladybug, a simple mark with heart-shaped wings "to give it a girly feel."

art director Aleksandra Prhal
designer Aleksandra Prhal

client **Nadezda Milenkovic—writer**

The designer was approached by the writer of the best-selling book, *How to Devastate Your Own Child*, a humorous view of the relationship between parents and their children, to create a symbol for a chapter in the book's reprinted edition entitled "To Beat or Not to Beat." The effective visual pun makes a connection between the belt (the most common symbol of beating and violence) and a question mark. The symbol will also be used in a media campaign to counter what the designer describes as "a huge number of scenes of domestic violence against children in Yugoslavia/Serbia and Montenegro."

designer Jelena Drobac

client **Jelena Drobac**

The designer states, "For a graphic designer, a personal identity is key to future projects, especially when launching a career. I wanted not a mere game of my initials (JD) but something with more depth. I was looking for something with an almost heraldic meaning. In heraldry, a foot stands for strength, but in everyday life it represents movement, dance, progress. In this position, it resembles the letter *J*, and I added a dot above the foot."

design firm Synergy Leo Burnett, Belgrade
art director Aleksandra Prhal
designer Aleksandra Prhal

client **Djordje Kolundžija—fitness trainer**

The client's "excellence in fitness and wellness, strong body, and training skills allowed us to position him as a brand," explains the designer. "He will be the lovemark." The designer created an identity that would signal the client's knowledge of fitness programs, bodybuilding skills, and health exercise training. "The mark includes a mixture of three key points: a visual of a well-shaped bodybuilder/sportsman in top condition, a *Strong as a bull* tag line (a local expression for well-shaped, strong people), and the all-seeing eye of a professional who takes care of every detail important to your condition and health."

design firm	McCann Erickson, Belgrade
art director	Aleksandra Prhal
designer	Aleksandra Prhal
client	**Raiffeisen Bank, Yugoslavia**

Raiffeisen Bank, one of the most successful foreign banks in the domestic market, was on the verge of launching a new service: online eshopping. The designer was asked to create a symbol for the campaign, in line with the existing Raiffeisen Bank logotype (a well-known black and yellow scheme). The solution takes into account that the target audience is familiar with the language of pictograms—the symbol makes an obvious connection between the Internet, shopping, and banking.

design firm	Synergy Leo Burnett, Belgrade
art director	Djordje Stanojevic
designer	Djordje Stanojevic
client	**Topiko—chicken meat industry**

Topiko is in the chicken meat industry in Backa Topola (Serbia and Montenegro). The designer was commissioned to develop a visual identity "that would communicate strength and stability, does not diminish its elegance and simplicity, and is remembered after the first look."

design firm	Studio Maksimov
designer	Ljubomir Maksimov
client	**Execom Company SCG**

Execom is an international firm that provides I.T. business solutions. The designer was asked to create an identifier that was "something contemporary but stylish." The result speaks for itself.

design firm	Studio Maksimov
designer	Ljubomir Maksimov
client	**Golden Eye (Center for Visual Arts)**

The designer was approached to create the identity for a contemporary art exhibition—the Third International Triennial of Contemporary Art, Novi Sad, Yugoslavia. The solution is an effective and visually engaging two-color logotype.

3. internacionalni trijenale savremene umetnosti
3rd internacional trienial of contemporary art
Novi Sad, Yugoslavia 2002.

voodoo

design firm   Synergy Leo Burnett, Belgrade
art director   Aleksandra Prhal
designer   Aleksandra Prhal

client   **Čoka Winery**

Trying New Things

Vinarija Čoka (Čoka Winery) is a well-known local producer of tasty wines as well as nonalcoholic and alcoholic drinks, such as sangria. Their target market for this new beverage is 18- to 25-year-old urban males and females who are ready to try something new—"a little bit dirty, provocative, and trendy."

the brief   After the first wave of foreign alcopop drinks (Bacardi Breezer, Smirnoff Ice, and so on), the client decided to launch their own, locally produced alcopop beverage named Voodoo—a mixture of fruit juice and alcohol. The designer was engaged to create a logotype/label for the new drink that would position it as a unisex beverage.

the solution   The designer developed a product identity that used tribal/tattoo art, a visual vernacular popular with the target audience. The use of tribal/tattoo art as a brand signature introduces Voodoo as part of the original iconography to pique the interest of the target audience.

▲ Individual numerals from the Bodoni typeface combine to create the logotype.

▼ Application of the logotype to a reception window makes the numeric construct obvious in an engaging and memorable fashion.

South Africa is infamous for apartheid, the Sharpeville Massacre, the Soweto riots, and the international boycott against white racial domination. It's famous for its former president and Nobel Peace Prize winner Nelson Mandela, the DeBeers diamond cartel, its rugby and cricket teams, safari tourism, and fine wines.

South Africa

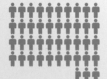

area	1.2 million km²
GDP, per capita	$10,000 USD
official languages	Afrikaans, English, Zulu, Xhosa, Swazi, Nguni, Sindebele, Ndebele, Southern Sotho, Northern Sotho, Tsonga, Tswana, Venda
population	42.8 million

South Africa, a parliamentary democratic republic, lies at the southern tip of the African continent. Bordered to the north by Namibia, Botswana, and Zimbabwe and to the northeast by Mozambique and Swaziland, it entirely encircles Lesotho. One of Africa's most ethnically diverse countries, South Africa has the largest white population on the continent, as well as the largest Indian population outside Asia. Racial and ethnic strife have played a large part in the Rainbow Nation's history and politics—South Africa is so ethnically diverse that no single culture exists.

Fossil remains suggest that various ape-men existed in South Africa as far back as three million years ago, and archeologists have dated rock paintings in the Ukhahlamba-Drakensberg area to approximately 3,000 years ago. Iron Age populations moved south and displaced earlier hunter-gatherer peoples as they migrated. Dutch settlers (Boers) first arrived in South Africa in 1652 to find various tribal habitations, including the Khoi, San, Xhosa, and Zulu. After the British seized the Cape of Good Hope area in 1806, many of the Boers trekked north to form their own republics. The discovery of diamonds and gold in the late 1800s spurred wealth and immigration, and the Boers resisted British encroachments until defeat in the Boer War of 1899 to 1902. The resulting Union of South Africa operated under an official policy of apartheid (the separate development of the races), and even though South Africa gained independence from the United Kingdom in 1960, apartheid would carry on until the early 1990s.

Apartheid imposed a heavy burden on the majority of South Africans. The economic gap between the wealthy white population (well fed, housed, and cared for) and the poor masses, virtually all of whom were African, colored, or Indian (and who suffered widespread poverty, malnutrition, and disease) was larger than in any other country. In its opposition, the African National Congress (ANC) and other organizations made steady gains over several decades in the fight to end apartheid. Following the Soweto riots of 1976, most of the countries in the world (with the notable exceptions of the United Kingdom and the United States) imposed economic sanctions on South Africa. One of the chief antiapartheid activists (who had spent much of his life imprisoned for his ANC activities), Nelson Mandela became the nation's first black head of state following the end of apartheid, the beginning of majority rule, and the nation's adoption of a new constitution. Beginning in 1994, Mandela presided over South Africa's transformation, winning international respect for his advocacy of national and international reconciliation.

Modern South Africa is a developed country with an abundant supply of resources; well-developed financial, legal, communications, energy, and transport sectors; and modern infrastructure supporting an efficient distribution of goods. It's estimated that South Africa accounts for up to 25 percent of the African continent's GDP and that it produces two-thirds of the continent's electricity.

= 1 million

design firm	Roy Clucas Design Process
art director	Roy Clucas
designer	Roy Clucas
client	**Pikitup**

Picking up the Trash

the brief — Pikitup, Johannesburg's aptly named waste-management utility, needed an engaging visual identity that would be readily understood and accepted by the city's citizens.

the solution — The designer created a powerful, colorful identity that incorporates a playful visual attitude. A unique sans serif logotype appears on two lines, broken in accordance with the local expression of the name—"piki-tup"—and the letter *U* sports an upward arrow that reinforces the name's admonition. Successfully implemented in numerous landfill sites, livery, and public-awareness promotions, the memorable identity is supported by an encouraging tag line: *It's a collective effort.*

◄ The Pikitup logo—bold, colorful, and to the point—functions as a call to action. Landfill site signage extends the logo's diamond-form visual arrangement as seen on this pylon sign.

▼ The color scheme for Pikitup vehicles and trash containers reinforces the "clean, green" environmental management message.

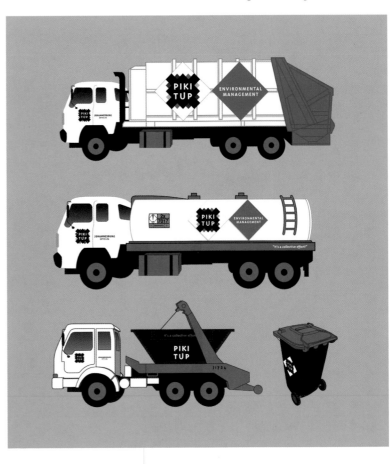

design firm   Orange Juice Design
art director   Garth Walker
designer   Garth Walker

client   **Orange Juice Design—*i-jusi***

i-jusi

Orange Juice Design is a visual communications firm with
offices in Durban and Cape Town, South Africa.

the brief   *I-jusi* (pronounced "ie-juice-ie" and is roughly translated as
"juice" in Zulu) is a magazine published quarterly (or, "now and
then," as some issues state) by Orange Juice Design as part
of an ongoing commitment to excellence in South African
design. The publication has become a widely recognized
identifier for the design firm and its principal, Garth Walker.

the solution   Nothing is sacred for this unique house title. Themed issues
cover the gamut from religion to typography to komix to porn
and well beyond. Each issue is filled with vernacular visual
expression unique to the rapidly changing post apartheid
South Africa of the last decade. Much of the content consists
of ephemeral graphics gathered from the streets or rich and
raw visual explorations by untaught, "natural" designers and
communicators. The large format, exuberantly full-color magazine has, in itself, become an identifier for open and uncen-
sored visual expression in the new and unbiased (on paper at
least, as a recent issue points out) South Africa.

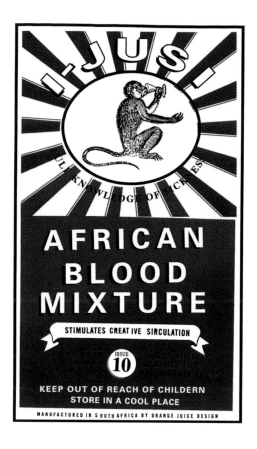

▲ *i-jusi* cover #10. There is no set masthead or visual style,
other than the expressive changeability of each issue—
an ironic and effective identity in itself.

▼ Shown here is the cover and spread from *i-jusi* #14—
the travel issue. The inside spread features the must-know
facts and finer points of sheep's head cuisine.

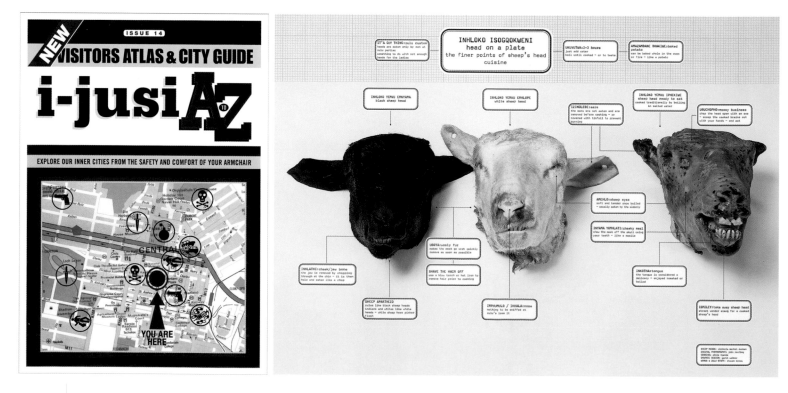

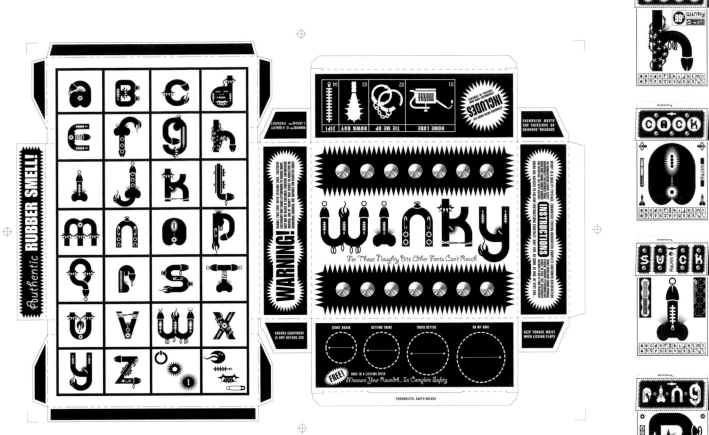

▲ Shown here, a spread from the *i-jusi* porn issue, featuring the font Winky—"for those naughty bits that other fonts can't reach."

◄ Here, front and back covers of *i-jusi* cover #6—"now with V8 power."

design firm | Interbrand Sampson
project leader | Giles Sheperd
designer | Rudo Botha

client | **SASOL Limited**

Reaching New Frontiers

SASOL is an integrated oil and gas company with substantial chemical interests. In South Africa, operations are supported by mining coal and converting it into synthetic fuels and chemicals through SASOL's proprietary Fischer Tropsch technologies. SASOL also has chemical manufacturing and marketing operations in Europe, Asia, and the Americas. The group produces crude oil in offshore Gabon, refines crude oil into liquid fuels in South Africa, and retails liquid fuels and lubricants through a growing network of SASOL retail convenience centers (gas stations). During the first quarter of 2004, the group began to supply Mozambique natural gas both to customers and to its own petrochemical plants in South Africa. They are also developing two gas-to-liquid fuel joint ventures with ChevronTexaco in Qatar and Nigeria. SASOL is listed on both the JSE Securities Exchange Johannesburg and the New York Stock Exchange.

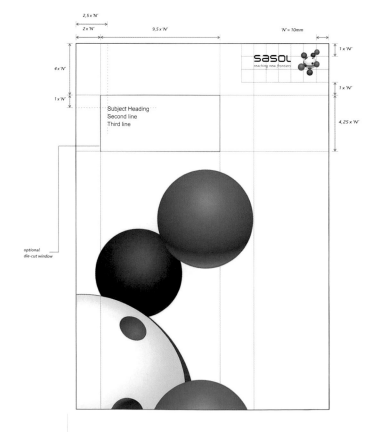

◄ Detailed layout specifications, such as the A4 presentation cover shown here, were provided in convenient "brand principles" guidelines. The next spread shows samplings from the wide range of applications addressed.

► SASOL's "brand box" contains extensive guidelines that outline the identity's proper appearance across the widest imaginable range of applications.

the brief

SASOL wanted to create a strong, monolithic brand identity that would convey the company's dynamic, innovative characteristics globally. They also wanted to underscore their increasing sophistication, as well as their pursuit of world-class standards and a stronger, more instantly recognizable branding. They also wished to introduce a set of values as a part of the process and to integrate its activities. SASOL is committed to the values of the "new South Africa" and its fledgling democracy, so the new brand had to be achieved in the context of an entirely new sociopolitical environment, showing the corporation's commitment to renewal and transformation. The company wanted to streamline its brand architecture and to dispense with myriad subidentities and business-specific logotypes, symbols, and other marks. All of this design change was to be rolled out into some fifty different companies in thirty countries around the world, without losing the goodwill of the company stakeholders and ensuring the buy-in of its own employees.

the solution

A striking monolithic identity was initially developed by a company named Trademark. This design consists of a molecular mark or symbol (representing a molecular structure), the wordmark (the name of the company, now modern and contemporary), and the positioning statement (*reaching new frontiers*). The following brand characteristics were developed: inspiring, dedicated, dynamic, innovative, reliable, and ambitious. The rollout process to the public and employees entailed many activities and tools that are underpinned by the brand guidelines, still under development. The introduction of the shared values was done concurrently, and SASOL continues to communicate the values and brand in an interactive and consultative manner.

For the internal rollout of the brand to be successful, the designer wanted the brand champions to identify fully with the process to ensure their commitment and buy-in. The guidelines, and the box containing them, were designed specifically to convey the dynamic and exciting nature of the brand to colleagues. The guideline box has been distributed widely throughout the SASOL group and is updated and supplemented on a regular basis. The contents are reviewed at regular brand forums, and new additions are discussed and presented in some detail. The brand department is respon-sible for guiding the brand champions, other colleagues, and various suppliers in the intricacies of the brand, and the SASOL group all use the brand box extensively in their brand champion function.

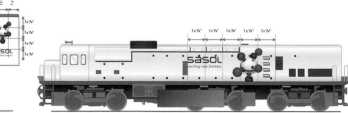

4160 x 1500mm
'N' = 221mm

Welcome to Sasol

These pylons provide
an opportunity to inform
visitors and communicate
any regulatory, legal or
statutory information

The grid provides for
approximately 22
characters per line

should be
selected for
pedestrian areas.

eye level

scale 1:30

2000 x 722mm
'N' = 107mm

cap height
= 0,35 x 'N'

sasol
reaching new frontiers

Sasol Limited
1 Sturdee Avenue

1

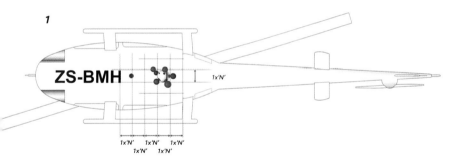

ZS-BMH

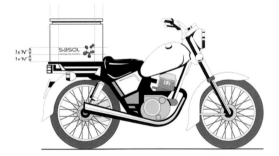

2

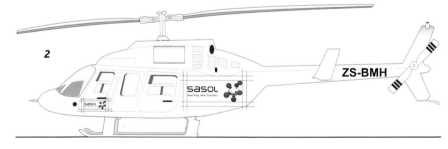

ZS-BMH

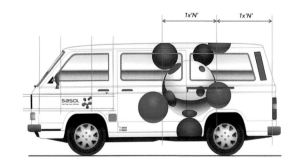

3

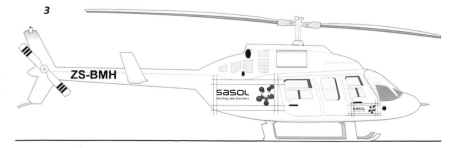

ZS-BMH

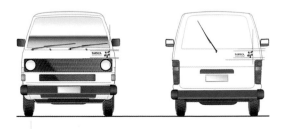

design firm   Orange Juice Design
art director   Garth Walker
designer   Garth Walker

client   **South African Constitutional Court**

A New Voice

the brief

Johannesburg's new Constitutional Court sits on the footprint of the former Awaiting Trial Cell Block. The court commissioned the designer to create a custom typeface for the court's signage—a sign of the progressive outlook evident in South Africa ten years after the end of apartheid (forty-four years of institutionalized racial segregation ended in 1994).

the solution

To shape the typeface, the designer began by roaming the ruined cell block to record political prisoners' graffiti from the abandoned prison's dirty walls and to gather samples of the former captors' writing and signage. He then drew from these "voices" and selected individual letterforms to generate the court's distinctive typeface. The designer states, "The graffiti spoke of people who, despite their surroundings, retained humor and optimism. This [font design] is my contribution to the ideals of a nation of truth, dignity, and freedom, in a place that was once a bastion of incarceration, torture, and repression."

▲ Here, the final, unnamed font for the Constitutional Court.

▼ Samples of the prisoners' graffiti found in the deserted jail cells formed the basis for the letterforms used in the custom font design.

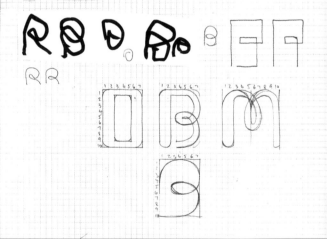

▲ The Constitutional Court font appears in South Africa's eleven official languages over the main entrance of the court complex.

► Here, an interior view of the court chambers and signage details featuring the unique unicase font.

design firm	Martha Bateman Concepts
art director	Martha Bateman
designer	Mona Craven
client	**African Explosives Limited**

The client is one of the world's largest manufacturers and suppliers of commercial explosives and initiating systems, selling mainly to the sub-Saharan African market. The logo speaks for itself.

design firm	Enterprise IG
art directors	Dave Holland
designers	Dave Holland
	Adam Botha
client	**Medihelp**

Medihelp is a medical plan, formerly part of the South African government's medical aid program for its employees. Medihelp's core business is the provision and funding of medical coverage for its members. The target audience is middle- to higher-income groups. The design challenge was to move Medihelp toward becoming the most open, transparent, honest, and simple medical plan in the market, reflecting a "fresh sense of self," and developing a unique style or icon that would become the instantly recognized property of the brand. The solution uses simple, clear, and contemporary typography, complemented by a fresh color palette and an icon that is an abstracted evolution of their original medical cross icon contained in a diamond shape. Although the new icon still contains a medical cross, it can also be interpreted as being two faces, two hearts, or even a pair of lungs—a breath of new life?

design firm	Enterprise IG
art director	Alexis Visser
designer	Alexis Visser
client	**Jumeirah Group**

The client, Madinat Jumeirah, operates a themed resort complex in the Arabian resort of Dubai, with three five-star hotels, a traditional *souk* (market), and conference and banqueting facilities, and is intertwined with 2⅕ miles (3.5 km) of man-made waterways that one can explore by traditional dhows (Arabian boats). This corporate identifier takes the form of a blue and gold medallion, appropriately regal in appearance.

design firm	Enterprise IG
art director	Beverley Field
designer	Beverley Field
client	**South African Premium Wines**

South African Premium Wines is a young, dynamic company that thinks differently. They collaborate with wine-producing experts and partners who give them the infrastructure to penetrate global markets. The challenge was to create an elegant identity that would position South African Premium Wines as a credible, dynamic brand in the minds of U.S. distributors. The solution employs a simple, yet elegant, typographic approach using the packaging symbol and wine glass as the *U* in the word *South*. Colors of berry-wine red and metallic green-gray provide a fresh, yet corporate, combination.

Royal Bafokeng Finance

olives

RESTAURANT

TEEMANE

REFINED SINCE THE BEGINNING OF TIME

Madinat Arena

Madinat Conference Hall

Madinat Theatre

design firm · Enterprise IG
art director · Beverley Field
designer · Beverley Field

client · **Royal Bafokeng**

The designer was approached by the Royal Bafokeng Nation, Investment Finance, to design a division identity to fit with two other identities that had already been created for Royal Bafokeng Resources and the Royal Bafokeng Economic Board. The division identity had to reference the Bafokeng totem, the crocodile, as well as have relevance to and credibility in the community-based investment finance center. The design met the requirements, from color to icon. As described by the designer, "Seeing themselves as the 'silent giant' with real power and money but not being flashy about it, the crocodile half submerged in water was the perfect choice. The ever-increasing circles represent financial growth (coins)."

design firm · Enterprise IG
art director · Alexis Visser
designer · Alexis Visser

client · **The One & Only**

Olives is a relaxed and casual all-day dining room within the Royal Mirage five-star hospitality complex. The restaurant features Mediterranean dining either inside the restaurant or on the beautiful outdoor terrace. The design solution pays tribute to the themed cuisine and the outdoor environment.

design firm · Roy Clucas Design Process
art director · Roy Clucas
designer · Heiko Mittwoch

client · **Teemane**

Teemane is a diamond distribution company (the name means "diamond" in the South Sotho language). The new corporate identity incorporates a stylized cut-diamond symbol in the form of a *T* with a distinctively serifed logotype and the tag line *Refined since the beginning of time*. The silver and black color combination provides an air of restrained elegance.

design firm · Enterprise IG
art director · Alexis Visser
designer · Alexis Visser

client · **Jumeirah Group**

Jumeirah Group operates three five-star venues: the Madinat Conference Hall, Madinat Arena, and Madinat Theatre. The designer was tasked with creating an identity themed in traditional Arabic styles, leaning toward Middle Eastern regality and opulence. All three venues are high-class facilities, often hosting local royalty and VIPs. The solution is a design using traditional Arabic calligraphy and the color gold.

icograda
IDA

**International Council
of Graphic Design Associations**
A Partner of the International
Design Alliance

A Global Design Community

G raphic design is finally coming of age. Born in the last century of mother Art and father Commerce, (and therefore named "Commercial Art" in its infancy) graphic design has developed a sense of its own identity, along with an understanding of its role and responsibilities relative to society. No longer content with being the whipping boy of marketing, graphic design is evolving into a true profession and is adopting all that comes with professionalism—best practice models, codes of ethics, certification standards, and considered criticism. Icograda estimates that there are now more than 1.1 million professional graphic designers practicing around the world.

Icograda was founded in London in 1963—a time of great growth for graphic design and visual communication. That was a time of postwar reconstruction, and a time in which socioeconomic and political boundaries were being redrawn. On one hand, the culture of consumption was growing rapidly, and on another, restrictive spheres of influence and collectivism were being entrenched. Around the world, there was a resolve to find more humane and more equitable solutions—Icograda's founders saw the need for a coming together of the national associations representing the rapidly emerging profession of graphic design—for integrative synergies, the sharing of best practices, and networking.

*There is too much visual and cultural pollution
in the world; against this, the designer's mind, eye,
and heart are the best weapon.*

—Henry Steiner, Hong Kong, *Who's Who in Graphic Design*

*The artist's ability to perceive,
and the designer's innate tendency
to question, place us among the
few guardians of humanity.*

—Erskine Childers, Ireland

A Unified Voice

Icograda is the world body for professional graphic design and visual communication. As the international, nonpolitical, nongovernmental, representative, and advisory organization for graphic design, it unifies the voice of designers worldwide and promotes their dynamic role in society and commerce. Begun as a voluntary coming together of associations concerned with graphic design, design management, design promotion, and design education, Icograda now has seventy-seven member associations on six continents. Headquartered in Brussels since 1999, Icograda moved to Montreal in 2005, where it shares a new secretariat with its sister organization, the International Council of Societies of Industrial Design (ICSID), a cofounder along with Icograda of the International Design Alliance (IDA).

Icograda's Purpose

Icograda serves the worldwide community of graphic designers. In doing so, it and its members aim to

- raise the standards of design, professional practice, and ethics
- raise the professional status of the graphic designer
- further the appreciation of designers' professional achievements
- extend design's contribution to understanding among people
- promote the exchange of information, views, and research
- contribute to design education—theory, practice, and research
- coordinate matters of professional practice and conduct
- establish international standards and procedures
- hold congresses, conferences, seminars, and symposia
- publish and distribute information concerned with graphic design.

Icograda Membership

As an association of independent member associations, Icograda forms a global network representing common concerns, commitments, and standards. Professional design organizations join Icograda as full members, while promotional or technical organizations join as associate members—all with voting rights. Nonvoting members include patron members, who contribute financially; subscriber and education members, engaged in education, the raising of standards, or design research and practice; corresponding members, residing in a country not represented by a member organization; and affiliate members, international organizations concerned with professional practice in fields related to graphic design.

Change is the only constant, technology is the fuel, and designers are the catalysts.

—David Grossman, (Icograda president, 1999–2001)

Member Benefits

Member associations benefit from being connected with other associations and from being part of the worldwide community of graphic designers— through exchange of information, sharing of best professional practices, policy development regarding international issues, and collaboration regarding international advocacy. Individuals within Icograda's member associations benefit from: networking with design organizations and colleagues worldwide; access to members-only resources on Icograda's website; free subscription to *eNews*, Icograda's weekly email newsletter; and reduced fees to select Icograda events.

Icograda's Core Values

Icograda is guided by core values that influence both individual and collective conduct. We strive for continual improvement, and we strive to have our actions reflect these values, demonstrate accountability, and be publicly defensible.

1. We conduct ourselves ethically and with integrity.
2. We show respect for others in our words and actions.
3. We act in the spirit of a global community and cooperation.
4. We respect the diversity of human beings, and their social, ethnic, and cultural differences.
5. We respect the natural environment.

International Affiliations

Icograda has consultative status with UNESCO (the United Nations Educational, Scientific and Cultural Organization); UNIDO (the United Nations Industrial Development Organization); ISO (the International Standards Organization); and WIPO (the World Intellectual Property Organization).

Congresses, General Assemblies, and Events

One of Icograda's most valuable activities is the organization of congresses, meetings, and conferences to further international exchange of information. An international congress is organized every second year in a different location. An Icograda General Assembly is held biennially in conjunction with the international congress. General assemblies are attended by delegates of Icograda member associations, who elect the Icograda executive board from nominees put forward by the member associations. Regional meetings are part of Icograda Design Weeks, held throughout the world to provide a forum for exchange of views and the development of regional strategies and initiatives related to design.

Design has become the most important and powerful tool with which man shapes his tools and environment, and by extension, society itself.

—Viktor Papanek (1925–1988)

Icograda Networks

Friends of Icograda is a worldwide network of individuals and corporations who share a common interest in graphic design and visual communication and support Icograda's aims and values. The Icograda Education Network (IEN) connects the worldwide community of graphic design educational institutions for exchange, sharing, collaboration, and advancement of teaching methods and research opportunities. The Icograda Design Media Network (IDMN) is dedicated to establishing and promoting standards and ethics in design journalism, creating a forum for sharing ideas, and promoting design publishing and the role that design plays in modern society. It brings the world's design media together in a single, convenient, online community.

The Icograda Foundation

The Icograda Foundation was established in 1991 for the advancement of worldwide understanding and education through the effective use of graphic design. The Icograda Foundation is a company limited by guarantee in England and is a charity registered with the Charity Commission for England and Wales. It obtains funds from corporate sponsorships, individual donations, legacies, a tithe from Icograda Education Network participant fees, and various fund-raising activities.

www.icograda.org

The letter at the end of each association's name indicates its status;
(F) full member, (A) associate member
*membership pending ratification by Icograda General Assembly

Icograda Members

Austria AT

DA—Design Austria (F)
Kandlgasse 16
Vienna
Austria (A)-1070
T +43 1 524 49 490
F +43 1 524 49 494
info@designaustria.at

Australia AU

AGDA—Australian Graphic Design
Association (F)
P.O. Box 283
Cammeray, N.S.W.
Australia 2062
T +61 2 9955 3955
F +61 2 9955 0566
secretariat@agda.com.au

DIA—Design Institute of Australia (F)
GPO Box 4352QQ
486 Albert Street
East Melbourne, Victoria
Australia 3002
T +61 3 8662 5490
F +61 3 8662 5358
admin@dia.org.au

Bosnia & Herzegovina BA

ULUPUBIH—The Association of Applied Arts
of Bosnia & Herzegovina (F)
Centar Skenderija, Collegium Artisticum
Terezija b.b.
Sarajevo
Bosnia & Herzegovina 71000
T +387 33 200 723
F +387 33 200 723
apluidbh@bih.net.ba

Belgium BE

UDB—Union des Designers en Belgique (F)
Allee Hof Ter Vleest 5 box 6
Brussels
Belgium B-1070
T +32 2 523 5204
F +32 2 556 2576
info@udb.org

Brazil BR

ADG-BRAZIL—Associacao dos
Designers Graficos (F)
Rua Conego Eugenio Leite, 876 Pinheiros
Saõ Paulo, SP
Brazil 05414-001
T +55 11 3082 9688
F +55 11 3088 1322
adg@adg.org.br

Canada CA

GDC—Society of Graphic Designers
of Canada (F)
Arts Court, 2 Daly Avenue
Ottawa, Ontario
Canada K1N 6E2
T +1 613 567 5400
F +1 613 564 4428
info@gdc.net

IDM—Institut de Design Montreal (A)*
390, rue St-Paul Est, March Bonsecours
(niveau 3)
Montreal, Quebec
Canada H2Y 1H2
T +1 514 866 2436
F +1 514 866 0881
idm@idm.qc.ca

SDGQ—Societe de Designers Graphiques
du Quebec Inc. (F)
55, avenue Mont-Royal Ouest, bureau 1005
Montreal, Quebec
Canada H2J 1X7
T +1 514 842 39 60
F +1 514 842 48 86
infodesign@sdgq.ca

Switzerland CH

SGD—Swiss Graphic Designers (F)
Limmatstrasse 63
Zurich
Switzerland 8005
T +41 1 272 45 55
F +41 1 272 52 82
info@sgd.ch

China CN

BGDA—Beijing Graphic Design Association (F)
Room 208, Tsinghua GongMei Building
No. 34 DongSanHuan Road
Chaoyang District
Beijing
China
T +86 10 65 61 98 68
yli@caadad.com.cn

CCII—Capital Corporate Image Institute (F)
127-408, Wangjing Hua Yuan
Chao Yang District
Beijing
China 100102
T +86 10 64 70 80 82
F +86 10 64 70 80 82
whgao@ccii.com.cn

NJGDA—Nanjing Graphic Designers
Association (F)
Room B, 11th floor, ChangFa digital High-rise
No. 188 Northern Hong Wu Road
JiangSu Province
Nanjing
China 210000
T +86 25 472 09 61
F +86 25 472 09 60
ucking@163.net

SHGDA—Shanghai Graphic Designers
Association (F)
Rm. 2702, Bld. 3 Lane 791, Lingling Road
Shanghai
China 200030
T +86 21 6464 8637
F +86 21 6441 1047
today@shiuol.cn.net

SUGDA—Suzhou Graphic Design Academy (F)
No. 288 East Nanhuan Road
Suzhou
China
T +86 512 65 26 25 01
F +86 512 65 26 24 10
szgg@sz-image.com

SXGDA—Shanxi Graphic Design
Association (F)
Room 605, Bldg B, Shengshijiayuan
No. 98 Jianguo Road, Chaoyang District
Beijing
China
T +86 01 85 80 59 13
F +86 01 85 80 61 78
com@justabc.net

ZhGDA—Zhuhai Graphic Design
Association (F)*
5F, No. 1082, Zhongdian Building
Jiuzhou Avenue
Zhuhai
China
T +86 756 33 24 806
F +86 756 33 24 108
zh-design@126.com

Cuba CU

PROGRAFICA—Comite Prografica Cubana (F)
Calle San Ignacio y Teniente Rey, Plaza Vieja
Havana
Cuba 10100
T +537 861 2779
F +537 204 2744
villaver@cubarte.cult.cu

Czech Republic CZ

AUG—Asociace Uzite Grafiky (F)
Masarykovo Nabrezi 250
Praha
Czech Republic 110 00
T +420 2 292445
F +420 2 292445
augdesign@email.cz

BBA-UVU-CR—Brno Biennale Association (F)
Sdruzeni Bienale Brno c/o Studio Idea
Hrncirska 21
Brno
Czech Republic 602 00
T +420 5 49 25 28 07
F +420 5 49 25 28 07
info@sbb-bienalebrno.cz

DCCR—Design Centrum of the
Czech Republic (A)
Radnicka 2
Brno
Czech Republic CZ-602 00
T +420 5 42 42 59 11
F +420 5 42 21 04 32
design@designcentrum.cz

TDC—Typo Design Club (F)
Kovaku 1077/9
Praha 5
Czech Republic CZ-150 00
T +420 251 56 42 12
F +420 251 56 16 02
petr@typoplus.cz

Germany DE

G—Bund Deutscher Grafik Designer (F)
Flurstrasse 30
Hamburg
Germany D-22549
T +49 40 83 29 30 43
F +49 40 83 29 30 42
info@bdg-deutschland.de

DZNRW—Design Zentrum Nordrhein
Westfalen (A)
Gelsenkirchener Strasse 181
Essen
Germany D-45309
T +49 201 30 10 4 0
F +49 201 30 10 4 44
info@dznrw.com

RFF—Rat fur Formgebung/German
Design Council (A)
Messegel nde/Neue Dependence - Ludwig-
Erhard-Anlage 1
Frankfurt am Main, Frankfurt/Main
Germany D-60327
T +49 69 74 74 86 0
F +49 69 74 74 86 19
info@german-design-council.de

Denmark DK

DD—Association of Danish Designers (F)
Frederiksberggade 26, 4
Kobenhavn K
Denmark DK-1459
T +45 33 13 72 30
F +45 33 32 61 08
design@danishdesigners.com

DDC—Danish Design Centre (A)
H. C. Andersens Boulevard 27
Copenhagen
Denmark DK-1553
T +45 33 69 33 69
F +45 33 69 33 00
design@ddc.dk

Spain ES

ADG-FAD—Art Directors & Graphic
Designers Association (F)
Convent dels Angels, Placa dels Angels 5-6
Barcelona
Spain 8001
T +34 93 443 75 20
F +34 93 329 60 79
info@adg-fad.org

AEPD—Asociacion Espanola de
Profesionales del Diseno (F)
Rafael Calvo 28, Bajo (A)
Madrid
Spain SP-28001
T +349 1 319 5589
F +349 1 310 3065
administracion@aepd.es

Finland FI

GRAFIA—Grafia ry Finnish Association
of Graphic Design (F)
Uudenmaankatu 11 b9
Helsinki
Finland SF-00120
T +358 9 601 942
F +358 9 601 140
grafia@grafia.fi

Greece GR

GGDA—Greek Graphic Design
Association (F)*
16 Drakou Street
Athens
Greece 117 42
T +30 210 36 20 659
F +30 210 36 38 544
info@gda.gr

Hong Kong HK

HKDA—Hong Kong Designers Association
(F)
G.P.O Box 9780
Hong Kong
China
T +852 25 27 39 68
F +852 25 27 54 68
info@hongkongda.com

HKDC—Hong Kong Design Centre (A)
28 Kennedy Road
Hong Kong
China
T +852 2522 8688
F +852 2892 2621
info@hkdesigncentre.org

Croatia HR

ULUPUH—Croatian Association of
Applied Arts Artists (F)
Hrvatska udruga likovnih umjetnika
primijenjenih umjetnosti
Vlaska 72
Zagreb
Croatia HR-10000
T +385 1 455 25 95
F +385 1 455 25 95
ulupuh@zg.htnet.hr

HDD—Croatian Designers Society (F)
Gjure Dezelica 20
Zagreb
Croatia 10000
T +385 98 311 620
F +395 1 38 95 196
info@hdd.com.hr

Hungary HU

MKISZ—Association of Hungarian Fine Artists (F)
Andrassy ut6
Budapest
Hungary 1061
T +36 1 302 22 55
F +36 1 302 22 55
mkisz@mail.datanet.hu

Ireland IE

IDI—Institute of Designers
in Ireland (F)
8 Merrion Square
Dublin 2
Ireland 2
T +353 1 716 78 85
F +353 1 716 87 36
idi@indigo.ie

Israel IL

GDAI—Graphic Designers Association
of Israel (F)
P.O. Box 11554
Tel Aviv
Israel 61114
T +972 3 523 49 57
F +972 3 529 00 72
abe@designcom.co.il

India IN

NID—National Institute of Design (A)
Paldi
Ahmedabad
India 380 007
T +91 79 663 96 92
F +91 79 662 11 67
info@nid.edu

Iran IR

IGDS—Iran Graphic Designers Society (F)
Post Box: 19945/664 Tehran
Tehran
Iran
T +98 21 695 20 72
F +98 21 696 95 27
info@graphiciran.com

The letter at the end of each association's
name indicates its status;
(F) full member, (A) associate member
*membership pending ratification
by Icograda General Assembly

Iceland IS

FIT—Association of Icelandic Graphic
Designers (F)
P.O. Box 8766
Reykjavik
Iceland IS-128
T +354 552 9900
fit@loremipsum.is

Italy IT

ADI—Associazione Disegno Industriale (F)
Via Bramante 29
Milano
Italy 20154
T +39 02 331 00164
F +39 02 331 00878
info@adi-design.org

AIAP—Associazione Italiana Progettazione
per la Communicazione Visiva (F)
Viale Col di Lana 12
Milano
Italy I-20136
T +390 02 5810 7207
F +390 02 5811 5016
aiap@aiap.it

Japan JP

IDCN—International Design Centre
Nagoya Inc. (A)
6 F, Design Center Building
18-1, Sakae 3-chome, Naka-Ku
Nagoya, Aichi Prefecture
Japan 460-008
T +81 52 265 2105
F +81 52 265 2107
julia@idcn.jp

JAGDA– Japan Graphic Designers
Association Inc. (F)
JAGDA Bldg., 2-27-14 Jingumae
Shibuya-ku, Tokyo
Japan 150-0001
T +81 3 3404 2557
F +81 3 3404 2554
jagda@jagda.org

JDF—Japan Design Foundation (A)
Public Relations & Research Department
3-1-800 Umeda 1, chome Kita-ku
Osaka
Japan 530-0001
T +81 6 63 46 26 11
F +81 6 63 46 26 15
info@jdf.or.jp

Korea KR

KECD—Korean Society for Experimentation
in Contemporary Design (F)
#212, Korea Design Center
Yatap 1-dong, Bundang-gu
Seongnam-si, Gyeonggi-do
South Korea 463-828
T +031 788 7215 ext. 6
kecd@kecd.org

KIDP—Korean Institute of Industrial Design
Promotion (A)
Korea Design Center Bldg
344-1 Ya'tap 1-dong, Bundang-gu
Seongnam City, Gyeonggi Province
South Korea 463-954
T +82 31 780 2151 ext. 3
F +82 31 780 2154
young@kidp.or.kr

VIDAK—Visual Information Design
Association of Korea (F)
213-1, Korea Design Centre Bldg.
Yatap 1-dong, Bundang-gu
Seongnam City, Gyeonggi-do
South Korea 463-828
T +82 502 785 4000
F +82 502 785 4001
vidak@vidak.or.kr

Lebanon LB

SPGIL—Syndicate of the Professional Graphic
Designers and Illustrators of Lebanon (F)
Moukarzel Bldg—RDC, Revue Aldabbour
(Behind Volvo Agency Musee)
Beirut
Lebanon
T +961 1 61 67 71
F +961 1 61 67 71
info@spgil.org

Lithuania LT

LGDA—Lithuanian Graphic Design
Association (F)
Maironio g. 6
Vilnius
Lithuania LT-2001
T +370 5 2780 727
F +370 5 2780 740
audrius.klimas@lgda.lt

Macau MO

MDA—Macau Designers Association (F)*
3A Residence 14 Ramal dos Mouros EDF
Chan Chu Kok, Macau
China
T +853 72 19 16
F +853 72 18 30
info@adm.org.mo

Mexico MX

Encuadre—Mexican Association of
Graphic Design Schools (A)
Calzada del Hueso 1100, edificio DG,
planta baja
Colonia Villa Quietud, Delegacion Coyoacan
Mexico
Mexico 4960
T +52 555 483 7131
F +52 555 483 7131
secretario@encuadre.org

TV—Trama Visual AC (F)
Alvaro Obregon 73 Col. Roma
Mexico City
Mexico 06700 DF
T +52 55 25 94 11
F +52 55 25 42 65
tramavis@prodigy.net.mx

Malaysia MY

WREGA—Graphic Design Association
of Malaysia (F)
Secretariat 18-3B, SunwayMas
Commercial Centre
Jalan PJU 1/3, Petaling Jaya
Selangor
Malaysia 47031
T +603 78 80 29 61
F +603 78 80 29 60
secretariat@wrega.org

Netherlands NL

BNO—Beroepsorganisatie Nederlandse
Ontwerpers (F)
(Association of Dutch Designers)
Weesperstraat 5
Amsterdam
Netherlands NL-1018 DN
T +31 20 62 44 748
F +31 20 62 78 585
bno@bno.nl

Norway NO

GRAFILL—Grafill (F)
Kongens Gate 7
Oslo
Norway N-0153
T +47 23 10 36 30
F +47 23 10 36 31
grafill@grafill.no

NDC—Norwegian Design Council (A)
Hausmanns gate 16
Oslo
Norway N-0182
T +47 23 29 25 50
F +47 23 29 25 51
jrs@norskdesign.no

New Zealand NZ

DINZ—Designers Institute of New Zealand (F)
ECC Building
P.O. Box 5521, Wellesley Street
Auckland
New Zealand
T +64 9 303 1356
F +64 9 030 1357
designer@dinz.org.nz

Poland PL

PMW—Poster Museum in Wilanow (A)*
ul. St. Kostki Potockiego 10/16
Warszawa
Poland 02-958
T +48 22 842 26 06
F +48 22 842 26 06 ext 102
plakat@mnw.art.pl

Every day, designers of all kinds are becoming responsible for a greater proportion of man's environment. Almost everything that we see and use that was not made by the Almighty has come from some designer's drawing board. This is a very heavy responsibility and every effort by designers to improve the standards, to encourage proper training, and to develop a sense of social awareness is to be welcomed.

—the Duke of Edinburgh, Zürich Icograda Congress, 1964

Russia RU

AGD—Academy of Graphic Design (F)
LiniaGrafic, Kaluzhskaya Square 1
Moscow
Russia 117049
T +7 095 211 5966
F +7 095 211 5966
serov@mega.ru

Sweden SE

FST—Foreningen Svenska Tecknare (F)
Gotgatan 48
Stockholm
Sweden S-11826
T +46 8 556 029 10
F +46 8 559 029 19
info@svenskatecknare.se

Singapore SG

DSC—Design Singapore Council (A)*
MITA Building, 140 Hill Street, #05-00
Singapore
Singapore 179369
T +65 6837 9632
F +65 6837 9686
info@designsingapore.org

Slovakia SK

SDC—Slovenske Centrum Dizajnu/
Slovak Design Centre (A)
Jakubovo Nam.12, P.O. Box 131
Bratislava
Slovakia 81499
T +421 2 5293 1800
F +421 2 5293 1838
sdc@sdc.sk

Slovenia SL

DOS—Designers Society of Slovenia (F)
Ciril Metodov trg 19, P.P. 121
Ljubljana
Slovenia 1000
T +38 61 43 05 410
F +38 61 43 05 415
d.o.s@siol.net

Turkey TR

GMK—Turkish Society of Graphic
Designers (F)
Ortaklar cad., Bahceler sok.
17/4 Mecidiyekoy
Sisli, Istanbul
Turkey 34394
T +90 212 267 27 58
F +90 212 267 27 59
info@gmk.org.tr

Taiwan TW

CPC—China Productivity Center (A)*
2nd Fl., No. 79, Sec. 1, Hsin-Tai-Wu Road
Hsichih, Taipei Hsien
Taiwan 221

GDA-Taiwan—Graphic Design Association
of Taiwan (F)
7F, No.159-2, Sih-Ta Road
Taipei
Taiwan 10092
T +886 2 23 67 85 63
F +886 2 23 65 65 21
dpgcmg@ms18.hinet.net

KCA—Kaohsiung Creators Association,
Taiwan (F)
No. 27, Min Sheng Street
Kaohsiung
Taiwan 800
T +886 7 221 22 16
F +886 7 282 78 70
adi27287@ms13.hinet.net

TaiwanDC—Taiwan Design Center (A)
Taiwan Design Center,
Design Promotion Group
3F, Bldg. G, 3-1 Park Street
Nangang, Taipei
Taiwan 115
T +886 22 655 8199
F +886 22 655 8228
tdc@tdc.org.tw

TGDA—Taiwan Graphic Design
Association (F)
No. 54, Ching-cherng Street
Taipei
Taiwan 105
T +886 2 6600 5205
F +886 2 6600 5206
moira@upcreate.com.tw

TPDA—Taiwan Poster Design Association (F)
6F-2, No. 189, Sinyi Road, Sec. 4
Taipei
Taiwan 106
T +886 2 27 03 40 96
F +886 2 27 03 45 17
taiwan.poster@msa.hinet.net

Ukraine UA

4th Block—Ukrainian Association of
Graphic Designers (F)*
Prospekt 50-letiya, VLKSM 32/186-29
Kharkov
Ukraine 61153
T +38 (057) 702 35 45
ann@4block.com

United Kingdom UK

BDC—British Design Council (A)
34 Bow Street
London
United Kingdom WC2E 7DL
T +44 20 7420 5200
F +44 20 7420 5300
info@designcouncil.org.uk

Yugoslavia YU

UPIDIV—Association of Aplied Arts Artists
and Designers of Vojvodina (F)
Ilije Ognjanovica 3
Novi Sad
Yugoslavia 21000
T +381 (0)21 524 481
F +381 (0)21 524 481
office@upidiv.org.yu

South Africa ZA

DSA—Design South Africa (F)
PO Box 84288
Greenside, Johannesburg
South Africa 2034
T +27 11 880 47 15
F +27 86 672 68 15
design.south.africa@mweb.co.za

Zimbabwe ZW

GRAZI—Graphics Association of Zimbabwe (F)
PO Box A685 Avondale
3rd floor, Redbridge North Eastgate Centre
Sam Nujoma Street
Harare
Zimbabwe
T +263 4 79 70 07
F +263 4 79 69 94
jacob@designat7.co.zw

Advisors

Mervyn Kurlansky
Copenhagen, Denmark
President, Icograda 2003–2005

Born in South Africa, Mervyn trained in London,
then practiced with Knoll International and
Crosby/Fletcher/Forbes before cofounding
Pentagram in 1972. Since 1993 Mervyn has
lived and worked in Denmark. Mervyn is a prolific
designer, consultant, author, lecturer, and juror. He
is a Fellow of the Chartered Society of Designers,
the International Society of Typographic Designers,
the Royal Society for the encouragement of Arts,
Manufacture & Commerce, and a member of Alliance
Graphique Internationale, and Dansk Designerer.
Mervyn's work has been widely published, has
won many international awards, and is in numerous
permanent collections around the world. Mervyn was
chairman of the Icograda London Design Seminar
from 1996 to 1999.

Jacques Lange
Pretoria, South Africa
President Elect, Icograda 2003–2005

Jacques qualified with a BA (FA) information design degree in
1988 from the University of Pretoria, South Africa, and spent
time in the television and advertising industries before joining
Bluprint Design, a visual communication consultancy where
he is a senior partner. Here he is responsible for strategy
consulting, as well as R&D of integrated visual communication
programs for a diverse client portfolio spanning the public and
private sectors.

Jacques has served as an Icograda board member since
2001, was chairperson of the Continental Shift 2001 Icograda
Congress in Johannesburg, and was president of Design
South Africa from 1998–2003. He is a director of the
Communication Foundation of South Africa, a member of the
Design Education Forum of Southern Africa, an editorial com-
mittee member of the academic journal *Image & Text*, and a
steering committee member of the SABS Design Institute's
Design Achievers Awards.

Jacques has received many professional awards, has served
on numerous adjudication and moderation panels, and has
authored more than 100 articles, papers, research and
consulting reports relating to visual communication. Jacques
is fluent in English and Afrikaans and has traveled to over
twenty countries on six continents.

Don Ryun Chang
Vice President, Icograda 2003–2005
Seoul, South Korea

Don Ryun Chang was born to diplomat parents and grew up on five continents—Asia, Europe, North and South America, and Africa. He was educated at the University of British Columbia in Canada, the Parsons School of Design, and received his MFA from the California Institute of the Arts. Don then worked for several organizations such as Nara Advertising, Design Focus in Korea, Steiner & Co. in Hong Kong, and was creative director for the Infinite Group.

Don founded DC&A in 1991, which later became one of the leading identity companies in Asia, with corporate identity clients such as the Shilla Hotel, the Maeil Business Group, m.net television, and brand identities such as Sunpower Battery, and Santa Fe Coffee. The company merged with Interbrand in July, 1999 and has developed acclaimed identities for 2002 FIFA World Cup, Korea Telecom, and Shinhan Bank. Don has received numerous international design awards such as the Brno and Warsaw Poster Biennale, and the Type Directors Club. Don lectures widely on branding and is currently department chair of visual communication design at Hongik University in Seoul. He has served as a vice president of the Visual Information Design Association of Korea (VIDAK) and was the executive organizing director for the 2000 Icograda Millennium Congress in Seoul.

Karen Blincoe MDD FCSD
Treasurer, Icograda 2003–2005
Copenhagen, Denmark

Karen Blincoe is director and founder of ICIS, the International Centre for Creativity, Innovation and Sustainability. She is also the chairman of the Educational Council for the Arts, Architecture, Design and Conservation for the Ministry of Culture, Denmark. Karen served as vice president of Icograda from 2001–2003, and has recently been appointed visiting professor at the University of Brighton.

Karen is Danish, and was educated in graphic design in England. She established KB Design (a graphic design consultancy) in London in 1984, and O2 UK in 1990 (environmental design). She served as Head of the Department for Visual Communication at Danmarks Designskole in Copenhagen, 1991–1998.

Karen has won many awards for her design, and received the Danish Design Vision 2002 Award for her work with ICIS. She also lectures, teaches, and writes internationally on subjects relating to visual communication, design education, corporate social responsibility, and sustainable development.

Russell Kennedy

Vice President, Icograda 2003–2005
Melbourne, Australia

Russell is a senior lecturer and course coordinator
of visual communication at Monash University
in Melbourne, Australia. He is an academic and
practitioner of both graphic design and filmmaking.
Before joining Monash in 1994, he was the principal
of Russell Kennedy Design, a corporate identity
consultancy, and codirector of Onset Productions, a
motion picture and documentary company.

Russell is a member of the Australian Graphic Design
Association (AGDA) and actively promotes a network
interface between design education and industry.
An international lecturer, Russell is often invited
to assist other educational institutions within the
Oceania/Asian region—he is currently an international
examiner/moderator for both Temasek Design
School, Singapore and Wanganui School of Design
at the University of Waikato, New Zealand. He has
been active in the development of the Icograda
Education Network and the deployment and promotion of worldwide educational exchange initiatives.

Hon Bing-wah

Vice President, Icograda 2003–2005
Hong Kong, China

Hon Bing-wah became involved in design and artistic creation
after receiving his academic qualification in design in 1972 at the
Extramural of the Chinese University of Hong Kong. His works can
be seen throughout China, Hong Kong, and Singapore, including
commercial, cultural, and environmental creations. In the past years,
he has received the Gold Award of the Hong Kong Designers
Association and numerous other awards, including the Creativity Gold
Medal Award (USA) and the China CIS Yearbook Gold Award.
His poster works have been selected at the Warsaw Poster Biennial,
Lahti Poster Biennale, the Poster Show in Toyama, Japan, and the
Korea International Poster Biennale. In 2003, the Phaidon Press,
New York, selected Hon as one of the 100 most significant graphic
designers and published his works in the book titled *Area*.

Hon has been involved in design education since 1980. He was
one of the cofounders of Hong Kong Chingying Institute of Visual
Arts, and served as its principal from 1984 to 1994. He is also a
visiting professor of the University of Shanghai. Hon's outstanding
achievements have contributed extensively to society. He received
the Ten Outstanding Young Persons Award, Hong Kong in 1985,
and the honor of Designer of the Year Award from the Hong Kong
Artists' Guild in 1992. He was invited to join the judging panel for the
Regional Flag and Emblem of the Hong Kong Special Administration
Region and was subsequently involved in the development of its final
design in 1997. He was later appointed to design the white dolphin
mascot for the reunification of Hong Kong with China.

In recent years, Hon has involved himself actively in promoting the
image of Shanghai, including the *Image of Shanghai* photographic
album and the poster design for Shanghai's World Expo 2010 bid.
He also served as one of the jurors of the emblem selection for the
World Expo 2010 Shanghai China, in 2004. Hon served as Chairman
of the Hong Kong Designers Association from 1998 to 2000 and is
now an adviser. He has served on juries for China Star 2002, Design
Biennale in Macau, and the Taiwan Design Biennale. Hon is now
the Museum Honorary Adviser of the Leisure and Cultural Services
Department in Hong Kong.

Ruth Klotzel

Vice President, Icograda 2003–2005
São Paulo, Brazil

Born to European immigrant parents in São Paulo, Ruth spent several years of her childhood in Chicago and New York, and part of her adolescence in Italy. Since graduating from Faculdade de Arquitetura e Urbanismo da Universidade de São Paulo (School of Architecture and Urbanism, São Paulo University) in 1982, she has worked as a graphic designer on projects for public and private companies, and in the education sector. Ruth is head of the design office Estudio Infinito, and is a teacher of visual communication, both at Faculdade de Arquitetura e Urbanismo da Fundação Armando Álvares Penteado (School of Architecture and Urbanism of Armando Alvares' Penteado Foundation) and at Faculdade Senac de Comunicação e Arte (Senac College of Communication and Arts). She was a cofounder in 1989 of the Associação dos Designers Gráficos in Brazil (ADG-Brazil), and has served four terms as its director.

Since 2003, she is also one of the directors of Mundaréu, a nonprofit organization aiming to create income-generation activities for people otherwise excluded from the formal job market—by training them to produce and sell handcrafted products in line with the principles of fair trade. Aside from her own design practice and teaching activities, Ruth has participated in numerous juries, events, and publications in Brazil and abroad and is active with events and committees of ADG-Brazil.

Halim Choueiry

Board Member, Icograda 2003–2005
Doha, Qatar

Originally from Lebanon, Halim Choueiry is a design educator and practitioner based in Qatar. He is currently an assistant professor at the School of the Arts, Virginia Commonwealth University in Qatar. Having obtained a bachelor and two master's degrees, he is undertaking a Ph.D. in design at Brighton University in the U.K. Halim also runs his own design studio, Cinnamon, which specializes in cultural patterning identification, visual development of bilingual corporate identities, and the simultaneous typographic representation of Latin-based languages and Arabic.

In addition to design consultancy, Halim publishes *Comma*, a quarterly pan-Arab graphic design magazine. He has won several national and international design competitions and has extensive experience in judging for student competitions and advertising awards. His involvement in international events includes conducting design conferences and chairing "creative nights," a workshop series held throughout the Arab countries. He is dedicated to bringing about changes in the approach and look of graphic design in the Middle East and the Gulf region.

Contributors

Contributers are listed alphabetically by design firm name, in country sequence, sorted by two-letter country code.

Austria AT

Lichtwitz
Büro für visuelle Kommunikation
Mariahilferstrasse 101/3/55
Vienna
Austria A-1060
T +43 1 595 48 98
F +43 1 595 272 727
mail@lichtwitz.com
www.lichtwitz.com

Australia AU

3 Deep Design
148A Barkly Street
St. Kilda, Victoria
Australia 3182
T +61 3 9593 8034
F +61 3 9534 2414
brett@3deep.com.au
www.3deep.com.au

Adstract Art P/L
593-595 Bridge Road
Richmond, Victoria
Australia 3121
T +61 3 9429 7406
F +61 3 9429 7408
paul.andrews@adstract.com.au
www.adstract.com.au

Billy Blue Creative
PO Box 728 North Sydney
North Sydney, New South Wales
Australia 2059
T +61 2 9492 3257
F +61 2 9955 9577
justin@billyblue.com.au
www.billybluecreative.com.au

Davidson Design
Level 1 Bldg 5—658 Church Street
Melbourne, Victoria
Australia 3121
T +61 3 9429 1288
F +61 3 9429 6855
grant@davidsondesign.com.au
www.davidsondesign.com.au

Designland
37B Duke Street
Windsor, Victoria
Australia 3181
T +61 3 9510 2056
F +61 3 9529 1522
info@designland.com.au
www.designland.com.au

Hemisphere Group
PO Box 1055 Rozelle
Rozelle, New South Wales
Australia 2039
T +61 2 9818 3578
F +61 2 9818 3578
clayton@hemispheregroup.net.au
www.hemispheregroup.net.au

IN full view
76 O'Farrell Street
Yarraville, Victoria
Australia 3013
T +61 3 8307 0098
design@infullview.com.au
www.infullview.com.au

Jeffrey Creative
7/95 Alma Road
St. Kilda East, Victoria
Australia 3183
T +61 3 418 363 393
F +61 3 9529 2583
paul@jeffrey-creative.com
www.jeffrey-creative.com

Jonathan Lu Design
2/4 Elizabeth Place Cronilla
Sydney, New South Wales
Australia 2230
T +61 2 404 120 449
F +61 2 9280 1499
jon@there.com.au

Linda Fu Design—Global iCom
Suite 207 City Plaza, 222 City Walk
Canberra, A.C.T.
Australia 2601
T +61 2 6248 0823
info@globalicom.com.au

Lumino Pty Ltd
16/23 James Street, Fortitude
Valley
Brisbane, Queensland
Australia 4006
T +61 7 3251 2600
F +61 7 3251 2666
design@lumino.com.au
www.lumino.com.au

Mosmondesign
122 Hopetoun Circuit Yarralumla
Canberra, A.C.T.
Australia 2600
T +61 2 6161 2302
mosmondesign@netspeed.com.au
www.home.netspeed.com.au/
mosmondesign

Natalie Woolcock Design
6 Dany Court Ferntree Gully
Melbourne, Victoria
Australia 3156
T +61 3 9758 4777
natalie@nataliewoolcockdesign.com

Octavo Design
130 Kerr Street
Fitzroy, Victoria
Australia 3065
T +61 3 9417 6022
F +61 3 9417 6255
info@octavodesign.com.au
www.octavodesign.com.au

There
Level 1–16 Foster Street Surry Hills
Sydney, New South Wales
Australia 2010
T +61 2 9280 1477
F +61 2 9280 1499
jon@there.com.au
www.there.com.au

Three's a Crowd
223 Abbotsford Street
North Melbourne, Victoria
Australia 3051
T +61 3 9326 9133
F +61 3 9326 9911
theteam@threesacrowd.com.au
www.threesacrowd.com.au

Voice
217 Gilbert Street
Adelaide, South Australia
Australia 5000
T +61 8 8410 8822
F +61 8 8410 8933
info@voicedesign.net
www.voicedesign.net

Bosnia & Herzegovina BA

ninAdesign
Sutjeska 4
Sarajevo
Bosnia & Herzegovina 71000
T +387 33 61 275 717
F +387 33 443 033
info@ninadesign.co.ba
www.ninadesign.co.ba

Belgium BE

Dorp & Dal
Begynhoflaan 85
Ghent
Belgium 9000
T +32 9 225 6236
F +32 9 233 5682
jan@dutchtype.org
www.dorpdal.com

Frank Andries Design
Volhardingstraat 53
Antwerp
Belgium 2020
T +32 3 216 1011
F +32 3 216 1032
frank.andries@skynet.be

Brazil BR

100% Design
Rua Diogo Moreira 132 cj1406
São Paulo,
Brazil 05423-010
T +55 11 3032 5100
F +55 11 3032 5100
tatiana@100porcento.net
www.100porcento.net

Book Company / Grafikz—
Andrei Polessi
Rua Pamplona, 33 casa 3
São Paulo,
Brazil 01332-000
T +55 11 3171 2153
F +55 11 3149 2461
apolessi@grafikz.com
www.grafikz.com

Claudio Novaes Design
Rua Augusta 2883 cj72
São Paulo,
Brazil 01413-100
T +55 11 3083 2770
F +55 11 3083 2770
claudio@claudionovaes.com.br

GAD' DESIGN
Rua Felipe Neri, 148 l 5º andar
Porto Alegre, RS
Brazil 90440-150
T +55 51 3378 2585
valpirio@gad.com.br
www.gad.com.br

Oz Design
Av. Eng. Luiz Carlos Berrini 1461
2nd Floor
São Paulo
Brazil 04571-903
T +55 11 5112 9200
F +55 11 5506 2007
giovanni@ozdesign.com.br
www.ozdesign.com.br

Univers Design
Rua Helena 170 cj93
São Paulo
Brazil 04552-050
T +55 11 3849 6970
F +55 11 3044 2097
marcelo@univers.com.br
www.univers.com.br

ZupiDesign
Rua Conde de Irajá 297
São Paulo
Brazil 04119-010
T +55 11 5084 9040
allan@zupidesign.com
www.zupidesign.com

Canada CA

AD Simonson Design
5753 Mayview Circle
Burnaby, British Columbia
Canada V5E 4B7
T +1 604 520 1060
F +1 604 520 6101
dale@glyph.ca
www.glyph.ca

Agence Code
4060, Boul. Saint-Laurent #209
Montreal, Quebec
Canada H2W 1Y9
T +1 514 844 0752
F +1 514 844 0935
isabel@agencecode.qc.ca
www.agencecode.qc.ca

Bounce Communication Design
302-250 McDermot Avenue
Winnipeg, Manitoba
Canada R3B 0S5
T +1 204 233 6329
F +1 204 233 3506
evan@bouncedesign.com
www.bouncedesign.com

CFX Creative
259-3495 Cambie Street
Vancouver, British Columbia
Canada V5Z 4R3
T +1 604 676 1866
F +1 877 682 2914
info@cfxcreative.com
www.cfxcreative.com

Colberg Design
305, 11027-87 Avenue
Edmonton, Alberta
Canada T6G 2P9
T +1 780 432 0130
F +1 780 432 0130
scolberg@ualberta.ca

Communications Nemesis Inc.
752 Boul. Union
Ste. Dorothee, Quebec
Canada H7X 1X6
T +1 450 969 3732
desaulniers.luc@videotron.ca
www.portfolios.com/lucdesaulniers

dossiercreative Inc.
402-611 Alexander Street
Vancouver, British Columbia
Canada V6A 1E1
T +1 604 255 2077
F +1 604 255 2097
info@dossiercreative.com
www.dossiercreative.com

Gustavo Machado Graphic Design
311-460 Eglinton Avenue E.
Toronto, Ontario
Canada M4P 1M3
T +1 416 828 4937
gustavo@gustavo-machado.com
www.gustavo-machado.com

HandyRandy Communications Inc
2219C 17 Street SW
Calgary, Alberta
Canada T2T 4M7
T +1 403 228 2525
creative@handyrandy.com
www.handyrandy.com

Ion Design Inc.
948 West 7th Avenue
Vancouver, British Columbia
Canada V5Z 1C3
T +1 604 682 6787
F +1 604 682 6769
www.iondesign.ca

Karacters Design Group
1600-777 Hornby Street
Vancouver, British Columbia
Canada V6Z 2T3
T +1 604 609 9508
F +1 604 608 4452
kerry.harrington@karacters.com
www.karacters.com

Les Éditions Vice Versa
4545 Ave. Pierre de Coubertin
Montreal, Quebec
Canada H1V 3R2
T +1 514 252 3030
F +1 514 252 3165
mjlegault@editionsviceversa.ca

MacKay | Wong
99 Blue Jays Way
Toronto, Ontario
Canada M5V 9G9
T +1 416 341 2348
F +1 416 341 2371
kmoorhead@mackaywong.com
www.mackaywong.com

MacMillan Lynch Multimedia
1657 Barrington Street
Halifax, Nova Scotia
Canada B3J 2A1
T +1 902 830 4745
F +1 902 422 1449
info@mlmedia.ca
www.mlmedia.ca

Morris Antosh
21-101 Eugenie Street
Winnipeg, Manitoba
Canada R2H 0X6
T +1 204 233 1510
mantosh@fusiongroup.mb.ca

Pagemedia
33-348 Arbuthnot Street
Winnipeg, Manitoba
Canada R3M 2R4
T +1 204 227 8026
hubert@pagemediaonline.com
www.pagemediaonline.com

Riordon Design
133 George Street
Oakville, Ontario
Canada L6J 3B9
T +1 905 339 0750
F +1 905 339 0753
alan@riordondesign.com
www.riordon.com

Ross + Doell
1407-77 Huntley Street
Toronto, Ontario
Canada M4Y 2P3
T +1 416 926 9486
alex@rossdoell.com
www.rossdoell.com

Splash Design
3-1749 Abbott Street
Kelowna, British Columbia
Canada V1Y 1B3
T +1 250 868 1059
F +1 250 868 2971
splashdesign@shaw.ca

Sub Communications
24, Mont-Royal West, #1003
Montreal, Quebec
Canada H2T 2S2
T +1 514 845 9423
info@subtitude.com
www.subcommunication.com

Subplot Design Inc.
301-318 Homer Street
Vancouver, British Columbia
Canada V6B 2V2
T +1 604 685 2990
F +1 604 685 2909
info@subplot.com
www.subplot.com

Suburbia
590 Beaver Lake Road
Victoria, British Columbia
Canada V9E 2J7
T +1 250 744 1231
F +1 250 744 1232
info@suburbiaadvertising.com
www.suburbiaadvertising.com

Supercapacity
12 Galley Avenue
Toronto, Ontario
Canada M6R 1G8
T +1 416 532 8483
F +1 416 532 0957
alison@supercapacity.com
www.supercapacity.com

Switzerland CH

CREACTIS
Rue de l'Envers 22
Tavannes
Switzerland 2710
T +41 32 481 28 04
sebastien.canepa@creactis.ch
www.creactis.ch

Mixer
Löwenplatz 5
Lucerne
Switzerland 6004
T +41 41 410 35 35
F +41 41 460 15 04
erich@mixer.ch
www.mixer.com

nothing
Effingerstrasse 4
Berne
Switzerland 3011
T +41 31 384 10 10
F +41 31 384 10 40
spot@nothing.ch
www.nothing.ch

Team hp Schneider
Alpstrasse 4
Räterschen
Switzerland 8352
T +41 52 363 25 96
F +41 52 363 22 37
hs@teamschneider.ch
www.teamschneider.ch

China CN

Armstrong International Corporate
Identity Co., Ltd.
B-2606 Lead International Business
Building
A2 Zhonghuan Nanlu
Wangjing, Beijing
P.R. China 100102
T +86 10 8427 0531
F +86 10 8427 0520
zhang-wu@vip.sina.com
www.AICI.cn

Cuba CU

Laura Llópiz
22 entre 23 y 21, El Vedado
La Habana
Cuba
T +537 831 1759
F +537 834 4554
laura@fq.uh.cu

Liber Lannes
Ayesteran, Edif. Nela, Apt. 4
La Habana
Cuba
T +537 832 1670

Luis Alonso
19 No. 1260 entre 20 y 22
El Vedado, La Habana
Cuba
T +537 41 1957
disegno@islagrande.com

Osué Rodríguez
Union #30, Santo Suárez
La Habana
Cuba
T +537 832 1670
jenny.hdz@infomed.sld.cu

Pepe Menéndez
22 entre 23 y 21, El Vedado
La Habana
Cuba
T +537 831 1759
F +537 834 4554
laura@fq.uh.cu
diseno1@casa.cult.cu

Santiago Pujol
3ra. B N° 9216, Playa
La Habana
Cuba 11600
T +537 203 3144
F +537 203 3144
spujol@cubarte.cult.cu

Czech Republic CZ

Kateřina Šachová
Cáslavská 7
Prague
Czech Republic
T +420 2 777 112623
katerina.sachova@post.cz

Studio Najbrt, s.r.o.
Fráni Šrámka 15
15 00 Praha 5
Czech Republic
T +420 251 561060
F +420 251 563515
studio@najbrt.cz
www.najbrt.cz

Germany DE

Design Zentrum Nordrhein
Westfalen
Gelsenkirchener Str. 181
Essen, NRW
Germany 45309
T +49 20 13 01 04 33
F +49 20 13 01 04 44
presse@dznrw.com
www.red-dot.de

Helmut Langer Design
P.O. Box 520713
Cologne
Germany 50943
T +49 22 13 88729
F +49 22 13 42985
helmutlanger@netcologne.de

Nina David Kommunikationsdesign
Eisenstrasse 31
Duesseldorf, NRW
Germany 40227
T +49 21 17 33 32 90
F +49 21 17 95 24 41
mail@ninadavid.de
www.ninadavid.de

sh&r
Paul-Dessau-Str. 6
Hamburg
Germany 22761
T +49 40 38 02360
bs@shr.cc
www.shr.cc

Sign.ID
Hörsterstrasse 21
Münster
Germany 48143
T +49 25 14 82 85 25
F +49 25 14 82 92 32
info@sign-id.de
www.sign-id.de

Ständige Vertretung
Oranienburger Strasse 87
Berlin
Germany 10178
T +49 30 30 87 28 18
F +49 30 28 11241
office@staendige-vertretung.com
www.staendige-vertretung.com

Denmark DK

Designbolaget
Raadmandsgade 30A
Copenhagen N
Denmark DK-2200
T +45 26 83 87 15
due@designbolaget.dk
www.designbolaget.dk

Goodmorning Technology—GMTN
Dronningens Tvaergade 8
Copenhagen
Denmark DK-1308 Cph K
T +45 33 93 95 99
F +45 33 93 95 99
www.gmtn.dk

Kontrapunkt
Refshalevej 153
Copenhagen
Denmark DK-1432
T +45 33 93 18 83
F +45 33 93 18 54
nk@kontrapunkt.com
www.kontrapunkt.com

Krogh & Co.
Klerkegade 19
Copenhagen
Denmark, DK-1308
T +45 32 64 20 30
dk@krogh.dk
www.krogh.dk

Via
112 C, Vesterbrogade
Copenhagen
Denmark DK-1620
T +45 26 27 06 74
sk@viadesign.dk
www.viadesign.dk

Spain ES

Estudio Manuel Estrada
Calle Diego de León 51, 3°D
Madrid
Spain 28006
T +34 91 559 1578
F +34 91 564 1303
info@manuelestrada.com
www.manuelestrada.com

GMI/Grupo Memelsdorff Ibérica
San Andrés 36 2° 6
Madrid
Spain 28004
T +34 91 594 3813
gabriel@webgmi.com

La Fábrica de Diseño
José Marañón, 10-1°
Madrid
Spain 28010
T +34 91 594 1214
F +34 91 594 1154
hector@lafabricadigital.com
www.lafabricadigital.com

LSD
San Andrés 36 2° 6
Madrid
Spain 28004
T +34 91 594 3813
gabriel@lsdspace.com
www.lsdspace.com

Santamarina Diseñadores
La Fesneda. C. Los Nogales 100
Siero, Asturias
Spain 33429
T +34 98 226 4190
estudio@santamarinadg.com
www.santamarinadg.com

TheDesignHouse
Pº Castellana 165
Madrid
Spain 28046
T +34 91 567 9200
F +34 91 567 9219
enrique.acosta@mccann.es
www.mccann.es

Finland FI

Kari Piippo oy
Katajamäenkatu 14
Mikkeli
Finland 50170
T +358 15 162 187
F +358 15 162 687
kari@piippo.com
www.piippo.com/kari

Hong Kong HK

Alan Chan Design Co.
1901 Harcourt House,
39 Gloucester Road
Wanchai, Hong Kong
China
T +852 2527 8228
F +852 2865 6170
acdesign@alanchandesign.com
www.alanchandesign.com

Steiner & Co.
28C Conduit Road
Hong Kong
China
T +852 2548 5548
F +852 2858 2576
hs@steiner.com.hk

Croatia HR

Branimir Lazanja
Kuhačeva 1
Zagreb
Croatia 10000
T +385 98 231 462
branimir.lazanja@zg.t-com.hr

Bruketa&Zinic
Zavrtnica 17
Zagreb
Croatia 10000
T +385 1 606 4000
F +385 1 606 4001
bruketa-zinic@bruketa-zinic.com

Cvetković & Poturica
Mrzlopolgska 12
Zagreb
Croatia 10040
T +385.1 285 9297
cip@net.hr
www.cipdizajn.com

Dubraveo Papa
Zlatarsca 16
Zagreb
Croatia 10000
T +385 91 253 0235
dubpapa@inet.hr

Elevator
Bana Berislavica 1
Split
Croatia 21000
T +385 21 332 800
F +385 21 332 801
tony@elevator.hr
www.elevator.hr

Laboratorium
Lojenov Prilaz 6
Zagreb
Croatia 10000
T +385 1 606 1512
F +385 1 606 1513
orsat@laboratorium.hr
www.laboratorium.hr

Likovni Studio
Dekanici 42, Kerestinec
Sveta Nedelja
Croatia 10431
list@list.hr
www.list.hr

Manasteriotti Design Studio
Bulićeva 3
Zagreb
Croatia 10000
T +385 98 253 466
igor@mds01.com
www.mds01.com

Parabureau
Domagojeva 16
Zagreb
Croatia 10000
T +385 91 5398 169
igor.stanislevic@zg.htnet.hr
www.parabureau.com

Studio Grafičkih Ideja
Špansko 62
Zagreb
Croatia 10000
T +385 1 387 8050
F +385 1 387 8052
sgi@sgi.hr
www.sgi.hr

Studio International
Buloujiceva 43
Zagreb
Croatia 10000
T +385 1 376 0171
F +385 1 376 0172
boris@studio-international.com
www.studio-international.com

Hungary HU

Laszlo Lelkes
Remsey krt. 2
Gödöllő
Hungary 2100
T +36 20 944 8044
F +36 28 420 436
lelkes.@euroweb.hu

Ireland IE

Design Factory
100 Capel Street
Dublin 1
Ireland
T +353 1 809 0010
F +353 1 889 8222
conor.clarke@designfactory.ie
www.designfactory.ie

Sharpshooter Design
20 Christchurch Place
Dublin 8
Ireland
T +353 1 473 3224
F +353 1 473 3224
info@sharpshooter.ie
www.sharpshooter.ie

Israel IL

Jason & Jason
Visual Communications
11 Hayetzira Street, P.O. 2432
Raanana
Israel 43663
T +972 9 744 4282
F +972 9 744 4292
tamar@jasonandjason.com
www.jasonandjason.com

Rotem Design
16 Profesor Shor Street
Tel Aviv
Israel 62961
T +972 3 602 4045
F +972 3 602 4088
info@rotemdesign.com
www.rotemdesign.com

India IN

Elephant Design Private Ltd.
13 Kumar Srushti S No. 1 Pashdan
NDA Road
Pune, Maharashtra
India 411021
T +91 20 2295 1160
F +91 20 2295 1161
vandana@elephantdesign.com
www.elephantdesign.com

mCube
2B Gitanjali, 9. N. Aamadia Road
Mumbai, Maharashtra
India 400026
T +91 22 2494 3221
F +91 22 2494 8325
mcube.design@gmail.com

National Institute of Design
N.I.D. Paldi
Ahmedabad, Gujarat
India 380007
T +91 79 2663 9692
F +91 79 2660 5240
anilsinha@nid.edu

Iran IR

Ashna Advertising
6 Entezari St., Aftab St., Vanak Ave.
Tehran
Iran 19949
T +98 21 805 4024
F +98 21 804 3176
info@ashna.org
www.ashna.org

Did Graphics Inc.
10 Palizi Avenue
Tehran
Iran 15579-74611
T +98 21 875 0217
F +98 21 875 0282
art-director@didgraphics.com
www.didgraphics.com

Eshareh Advertising Agency
No. 13, Golazin Alley, Ashkani St.,
32nd St., Vozara Ave.
Tehran
Iran 15119-46811
T +98 21 888 0063
F +98 21 877 0674
mostafazadeh@eshareh.com
www.eshareh.com

Meshki Studio
No. 16, 55th St.
Asadabadi Avenue
Tehran
Iran 14349-54975
T +98 21 760 7472
F +98 21 764 6255
saed@saedmeshki.com
www.saedmeshki.com

Iceland IS

Ó!
Klapparstíg 16
Reykjavík
Iceland 101
T +354 562 3300
einar@oid.is
www.oid.is

Italy IT

Cacao Design
Corso San Gottardo, 18
Milan
Italy 20136
T +39 02 8942 2896
F +39 02 5810 6789
mauro@cacaodesign.it
www.cacaodesign.it

Iliprandi Associati
Via Vallazze, 63
Milan
Italy 20131
T +39 02 7060 0843
F +39 02 7060 0843
info@ili-asso.com
www.ili-asso.com

Jekyll & Hyde
Via Bertani, 2
Milan
Italy 20154
T +39 02 3310 4498
info@jeh.it
www.jeh.it

Luca Egidio Galessi
Via Rollo, 14
Villa Di Serio, Bergamo
Italy 24020
T +39 03 566 4250
F +39 340 353 5040
gildino@inwind.it

Martina De Rui Graphic Design
Via Bellotti, 7
Milan
Italy 20129
T +39 02 7639 4417
F +39 02 7634 0841
derui@planet.it
www.martinaderui.com

no.parking
Contrà S. Barbara, 19
Vicenza, VI
Italy 36100
T +39 04 4432 7861
F +39 04 4432 7861
inbox@noparking.it
www.noparking.it

Publicis Design
Via Tata Giovanni, 8
Rome
Italy 00154
T +39 06 570 201
massimiliano.sagrati@publicis.it

Studio Amato
Via Zandonai, 95
Rome
Italy 00194
T +39 06 329 3816
silvana.amato@tiscali.it

studiocharlie
via Beato Angelico, 27
Milan
Italy 20133
T +39 02 7012 0030
mail@studiocharlie.org
www.studiocharlie.org

Studio Laura Moretti
Via Trieste, 2/B
Montevarchi, Arezzo
Italy 52025
T +39 055 983045
F +39 055 983045
studio@lauramoretti.com
www.lauramoretti.com

Univisual
Via Lepanto, 1
Milan
Italy 20125
T +39 02 668 4268
F +39 02 6073 0588
gaetano.grizzanti@univisual.it
www.univisual.it

Korea KR

Ahn Sang-Soo
Ahn Graphics Ltd.
260-88 Songbuk 2-Dong
Songbuk, GU
Seoul
Korea 136-823
T +82 2 743 8065
F +82 2 743 3352
ssahn@chol.com
www.ag.co.kr

Interbrand Korea
4F Shinsa Building 630-2
Shinsa-Dong, Kangnam-Gu
Seoul
Korea 135-895
T +82 2 515 9150
F +82 2 515 9152
ywshin@interbrand.co.kr
www.interbrand.co.kr

Lebanon LB

Jimmy Ghazal
Mar Roukoz
Dekwanew, Beirut
Lebanon 90-017
T +961 3 89 58 41
F +961 1 68 54 05

Mayda Freije Makdessi
PO Box 165249
Beirut
Lebanon 2063-6223
T +961 1 20 38 84
F +961 1 44 49 54
pyenno@inco.com.lb